RFID Security and Privacy

Synthesis Lectures on Information Security, Privacy, & Trust

Editors
Elisa Bertino, *Purdue University*
Ravi Sandhu, *University of Texas, San Antonio*

The Synthesis Lectures Series on Information Security, Privacy, and Trust publishes 50- to 100-page publications on topics pertaining to all aspects of the theory and practice of Information Security, Privacy, and Trust. The scope largely follows the purview of premier computer security research journals such as ACM Transactions on Information and System Security, IEEE Transactions on Dependable and Secure Computing and Journal of Cryptology, and premier research conferences, such as ACM CCS, ACM SACMAT, ACM AsiaCCS, ACM CODASPY, IEEE Security and Privacy, IEEE Computer Security Foundations, ACSAC, ESORICS, Crypto, EuroCrypt and AsiaCrypt. In addition to the research topics typically covered in such journals and conferences, the series also solicits lectures on legal, policy, social, business, and economic issues addressed to a technical audience of scientists and engineers. Lectures on significant industry developments by leading practitioners are also solicited.

RFID Security and Privacy
Yingjiu Li, Robert H. Deng, and Elisa Bertino
2013

Hardware Malware
Christian Krieg, Adrian Dabrowski, Heidelinde Hobel, Katharina Krombholz, and Edgar Weippl
2013

Private Information Retrieval
Xun Yi, Russell Paulet, and Elisa Bertino
2013

Privacy for Location-based Services
Gabriel Ghinita
2013

Enhancing Information Security and Privacy by Combining Biometrics with Cryptography
Sanjay G. Kanade, Dijana Petrovska-Delacrétaz, and Bernadette Dorizzi
2012

Analysis Techniques for Information Security
Anupam Datta, Somesh Jha, Ninghui Li, David Melski, and Thomas Reps
2010

Operating System Security
Trent Jaeger
2008

RFID Security and Privacy

Yingjiu Li, Robert H. Deng, and Elisa Bertino

ISBN: 978-3-031-01212-9 paperback
ISBN: 978-3-031-02340-8 ebook

DOI 10.1007/978-3-031-02340-8

A Publication in the Springer series
SYNTHESIS LECTURES ON INFORMATION SECURITY, PRIVACY, & TRUST

Lecture #7
Series Editors: Elisa Bertino, *Purdue University*
　　　　　　　　Ravi Sandhu, *University of Texas, San Antonio*
Series ISSN
Synthesis Lectures on Information Security, Privacy, & Trust
Print 1945-9742　Electronic 1945-9750

RFID Security and Privacy

Yingjiu Li
Singapore Management University

Robert H. Deng
Singapore Management University

Elisa Bertino
Purdue University

SYNTHESIS LECTURES ON INFORMATION SECURITY, PRIVACY, & TRUST #7

ABSTRACT

As a fast-evolving new area, RFID security and privacy has quickly grown from a hungry infant to an energetic teenager during recent years. Much of the exciting development in this area is summarized in this book with rigorous analyses and insightful comments. In particular, a systematic overview on RFID security and privacy is provided at both the physical and network level. At the physical level, RFID security means that RFID devices should be identified with assurance in the presence of attacks, while RFID privacy requires that RFID devices should be identified without disclosure of any valuable information about the devices. At the network level, RFID security means that RFID information should be shared with authorized parties only, while RFID privacy further requires that RFID information should be shared without disclosure of valuable RFID information to any honest-but-curious server which coordinates information sharing. Not only does this book summarize the past, but it also provides new research results, especially at the network level. Several future directions are envisioned to be promising for advancing the research in this area.

KEYWORDS

RFID technology, RFID system, RFID security, RFID privacy, authentication, access control, EPCglobal Network

Contents

Preface

The purpose of this book is to provide a systematic overview on RFID security and privacy which has been rigorously researched over the past decade. A unique feature of this book is that it organizes all material in two dimensions: (i) RFID security and privacy at (ii) physical and network levels. Consequently, the following chapters are covered in this book.

- **Chapter 1: Introduction.** This chapter provides background knowledge about RFID technology as well as the two dimensions by which we organize this book. In one dimension, RFID technology at the physical level is used to identify physical objects with RFID devices, and RFID technology at the network level is used to share RFID information among networked parties. In another dimension, security means that authorized entities can operate correctly in the presence of attacks, and privacy implies that an adversary cannot obtain any unauthorized information from its attacks.

- **Chapter 2: RFID Security at the Physical Level.** The major concern in this chapter is how to identify RFID devices correctly in the presence of attacks. This concern is addressed in RFID tag/reader/mutual authentication, key distribution, path authentication, and clone tag detection. RFID tag/reader/mutual authentication requires that only valid tags or/and valid readers are accepted under certain adversary models. Since most RFID authentication solutions rely on secret keys which are shared between tags and readers, the key distribution problem should be addressed which deals with how to distribute necessary keys to readers in a secure and timely manner. Another security issue at the physical level is path authentication, which accepts only those valid tags that have passed through valid paths. Finally, clone tag detection is used to identify possible clone tags which bear the same IDs as genuine tags in an RFID system.

- **Chapter 3: RFID Privacy at the Physical Level.** RFID privacy at the physical level requires that RFID devices should be identified without disclosure of any valuable information about the devices. While fixed pseudonyms may be used to prevent an adversary from knowing real tag IDs, it is more challenging to ensure that an adversary cannot trace the movement of any target tag from RFID communications. Various privacy notions are defined, analyzed, and compared in a single-reader system, including indistinguishability based privacy (an adversary cannot distinguish between two uncorrupted tags), unpredictability based privacy (an adversary cannot distinguish protocol messages from random numbers), zero knowledge-based privacy (whatever information an adversary can obtain from interacting with a target tag can be derived by any simulator without interacting with the target tag), Vaudenay's privacy framework with eight types of adversaries, and universal composibility-based privacy framework. In addition, various privacy notions are investigated in a multi-reader system, including tag unlinkability, step unlinkability, and path privacy in path authentication, as well as old owner's privacy and new owner's privacy in ownership transfer.

- **Chapter 4: RFID Security at the Network Level.** RFID security at the network level requires that RFID information should be shared with authorized parties only. In EPCglobal Network, which is a standard architecture for sharing RFID information, a new type of access control (namely List-Chain-BAC) policies is defined for each EPCIS to specify who can access its event data in EPCIS and who can query its event indexing data in EPCDS. A unique feature of such access control policies is that they are defined based on partner relationship with respect to certain RFID tags. This chapter also presents efficient new algorithms for (i) EPCDS to enforce all policies defined by participating EPCISes and (ii) EPCIS to enforce its policy when its event data are queried by users.

- **Chapter 5: RFID Privacy at the Network Level.** At the network level, RFID privacy requires that RFID information should be shared without disclosure of valuable information to any honest-but-curious server which coordinates information sharing. In EPCglobal Network, it is crucial to protect the information registered by each EPCIS at EPCDS if EPCDS is not fully trusted. This chapter discusses how to achieve anonymity of tag ID and anti-tracing of tag ID in EPCDS.

- **Chapter 6: Summary and Future Directions.** After summarizing the major content of this book, this chapter provides a list of promising directions for advancing the research in RFID security and privacy.

FOCUS AND AUDIENCE OF THIS BOOK

In this book, we focus on providing a big picture with easy-to-understand descriptions and necessary technical details, while leaving out some formal proofs which can be found in the references. This book does not intend to be historical, as the material presented is out of historical order. It is not encyclopedic either, in a sense that some sub-areas are omitted. For example, we do not cover the whole sub-area of hardware design of crypto-tags.

This book is suitable for both academic researchers and RFID practitioners to explore the fast-growing world of RFID security and privacy. Academic researchers may find it useful in identifying interesting research problems, understanding the challenges of solving such problems, and inspiring new ideas from existing solutions. RFID practitioners can find available solutions to address security and privacy challenges in RFID applications, understand the tradeoffs to be made in choosing among various available solutions, and recognize the state of the art in RFID security and privacy research.

The authors welcome any comments and discussions on this book. Since the development in some of the research areas in RFID security and privacy is still in an early stage, more interesting material would be added in possible future editions of this book.

Yingjiu Li, Robert H. Deng, and Elisa Bertino
December 2013

Acknowledgments

The authors would like to thank their collaborators, postdocs, and students, especially Dr. Tieyan Li, Professor Yunlei Zhao, Professor Changshe Ma, Dr. Eng Wah Lee, Wei He, Dr. Guilin Wang, Dr. Junzhuo Lai, Dr. Kuo-Hui Yeh, Dr. Kevin Chiew, Dr. Chunhua Su, Dr. Jie Shi, Dr. Qiang Yan, Dr. Zhongyang Zhang, Hongbing Wang, Shaoying Cai, Su Mon Kywe, Bing Liang, and Ge Fu for their valuable contributions in research on RFID security and privacy.

The authors are also grateful to Diane D. Cerra and her colleagues at Morgan & Claypool Publishers for their help and support in preparing this book for publication.

Yingjiu Li, Robert H. Deng, and Elisa Bertino
December 2013

CHAPTER 1

Introduction

1.1 RFID TECHNOLOGY

Radio-Frequency IDentification (RFID) is a technology for an automated identification of objects using radio waves. RFID technology is widely envisioned to replace barcode technology in the near future. Currently, RFID technology has been increasingly diffused in many applications and industries, including supply chain management, manufacturing, logistics, supermarket, pharmaceutical, hospital, library, airport, transportation, passport, bank notes, smartphone, payment, asset management, and many more. In an emerging world of *Internet of Things (IoT)*, RFID technology enables almost everything in the real world to be connected to a virtual cyber world so that people can interact with the things remotely and conveniently. In this sense, RFID technology would revolutionize network and IT technology, improve productivity, and change human life significantly.

RFID technology can be investigated and applied at both the physical and network levels. *RFID technology at a physical level* is mainly used to identify physical objects with RFID devices, while *RFID technology at a network level* is mainly used to share the RFID related information among networked parties.

1.2 RFID TECHNOLOGY AT THE PHYSICAL LEVEL

At the physical level, RFID technology is used to identify physical objects with RFID devices. A particular universal identifier for physical objects is *electronic product code (EPC)*. EPC Tag Data Standard [1] includes various coding schemes such as General Identifier (GID), a serialized version of the GS1 Global Trade Item Number (GTIN), GS1 Serial Shipping Container Code (SSCC), GS1 Global Location Number (GLN), GS1 Global Returnable Asset Identifier (GRAI), GS1, Global Individual Asset Identifier (GIAI), DOD Construct, Global Service Relation Number (GSRN), and Global Document Type Identifier (GDTI). In particular, an EPC consists of a header (8 bits), an EPC manager (28 bits), an object class (24 bits), and a serial number (36 bits), which is illustrated in Fig. 1.1. To be specific, we introduce EPC as a typical case of physical object identifiers in this book, though any other physical object identifiers can be used in practice.

Physical objects can be identified using unique IDs such as EPC numbers in an *RFID system*. An RFID system typically consists of a set of RFID tags and RFID readers, as well as a back-end server. RFID tags, usually attached to or embedded in physical objects, are small RFID devices, which can be used to store physical object IDs (e.g., EPC numbers) and related

Header 8 bits	EPC Manager 28 bits	Object Class 24 bits	Serial Number 36 bits

Figure 1.1: EPC code structure.

information. RFID readers are more powerful RFID devices which interact with nearby RFID tags via a wireless radio wave channel, and interact with a back-end server via the traditional network connections (e.g., bluetooth, LAN, or internet). An *RFID communication protocol* is executed by an RFID reader, its nearby tags, and a back-end server so as to identify the IDs associated with the tags and to obtain more information about corresponding physical objects.

RFID technology is different from a traditional barcode technology in the following aspects. First, an RFID reader can interact with multiple RFID tags automatically and speedily (certain RFID tags can be read at a speed of 1000 tags per second), while a barcode reader must scan barcodes one by one manually. Second, an RFID reader can interact with RFID tags at a distance (which may range from several centimeters to over 100 meters) without a line of sight, while a barcode must be scanned with a line of sight in close proximity. Third, compared to a barcode, an RFID tag can store much more information regarding physical objects such as ID and access password. Lastly, the information stored in an RFID tag can be updated easily while the information contained in a barcode is static. With all these differences, RFID technology has triggered tremendous interests in replacing a barcode technology and developing numerous innovative applications.

RFID tags can be active, passive, or battery-assisted passive. An active tag has a battery on board and it can transmit electronic signals periodically. A passive tag has no battery, which harvests power from the electronic signals of nearby RFID readers. A battery-assisted passive tag has a small battery on board but it is activated only when receiving signals of nearby RFID readers.

The electronic signals between RFID readers and tags may operate in different frequency bands, such as standard near field communication (NFC) band 13.56 MHz (HF), and standard EPC Gen 2 band 860-960 MHz (UHF). Usually, the higher the frequency, the longer the operating distance between RFID reader and RFID tag, and the higher the data transmission rate. NFC may operate in a range of centimeters, while EPC Gen 2 in a range of meters.

The nominal distances specified in RFID standards represent the maximal distances at which a normal reader can reliably interact with a tag. An adversary equipped with sensitive readers may interact with a tag from a distance longer than the nominal distance. In addition, an adversary may eavesdrop on existing tag-to-reader communications and reader-to-tag communications at increasingly longer distances.

A major concern in RFID applications is the cost of RFID tags, especially in a large-scale deployment. Passive tags may cost a few U.S. cents each, while battery-assisted tags and active tags are more expensive, at a cost of a few U.S. dollars or even higher. With the Moore's Law, the cost of RFID tags drops fast. A wide adoption of RFID technology is unstoppable when the cost is low enough as compared to the various benefits it brings in.

Several organizations, including EPCglobal and ISO, have set up standards for RFID technology. In particular, EPCglobal, a joint venture between GS1 and GS1 US, leads the development of industry wide global standards for the use of mostly passive RFID tags and EPC in today's global trading networks. It defines a UHF Class 1 Generation 2 (EPC Gen 2) air interface for communication between RFID reader and EPC Gen 2 tags [2]. EPC Gen 2 tags are widely adopted low-cost passive tags with a memory structure illustrated in Fig. 1.2. An EPC Gen 2 tag consists four memory banks, including 96 bit EPC number, 32-64 bit tag identifier (TID) indicating the manufacturer of the tag, 64 bit reserved bank consisting of 32 bit kill password and 32 bit access password, and a user memory bank which may vary from 0–2048 bits or even more depending on the manufacturer. EPC Gen 2 tags can be read at a speed of 1000 tags per second and written at 7 tags per second given correct access passwords. EPC Gen 2 tags support on-chip Cyclic Redundancy Code (CRC) computation, 16-bit Pseudo-Random Number Generator (PRNG), and other lightweight operations such as XOR, MOD, and string concatenation.

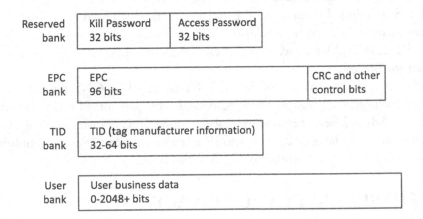

Figure 1.2: EPC Gen2 tag memory structure.

1.3   RFID TECHNOLOGY AT THE NETWORK LEVEL

At the network level, RFID technology is used to share RFID information among networked parties. EPCglobal Network is a standard architecture of computer networks created by EPCglobal for sharing RFID information. Fig. 1.3 illustrates the architecture of EPCglobal Network [3], which consists of the following components: EPC Information Services (EPCIS), EPC Discovery Services (EPCDS), and Object Naming Services (ONS).

EPCIS is essentially a database management system which is used by a networked party to manage its own RFID-related information in a repository and share with other parties via a

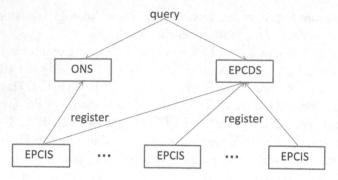

Figure 1.3: EPCglobal network architecture.

query interface. The RFID-related information is called RFID events in EPCglobal Network, which consist of EPC numbers and application information such as time, location, and business step for processing the physical objects indexed by the EPC numbers.

EPCDS is designed to discover all EPCIS systems which hold events about certain EPC. It can be compared to a search engine in the Internet which returns a series of URL links given a keyword. EPCDS enables networked parties to discover physical objects and to share RFID events about the objects.

ONS is a simplified version of EPCDS. Given an EPC, ONS returns the address of a single party which originally assigns the EPC code. In comparison, EPCDS returns the pointers to all parties which hold event information about an EPC. ONS can be compared to DNS in the Internet which translates URL names to IP addresses. Since ONS is a simplified version of EPCDS, we focus on EPCDS instead of ONS in this book.

1.4   RFID SECURITY AND PRIVACY

We address the security and privacy issues in RFID technology at both the physical and network levels. Roughly speaking, security means authorized entities can operate correctly in the presence of attacks, while privacy implies that an adversary cannot obtain any un-authorized information from its attacks. At the physical level, an authorized entity, which could be RFID reader, RFID tag, or backend server, operates according to an RFID communication protocol for the purpose of identifying physical objects. At the network level, an authorized entity, which could be any networked party, makes queries to EPCDS and EPCISes for the purpose of sharing RFID information.

Considering that RFID technology may be used in a hostile and competitive environment, the security and privacy issues in RFID technology should be addressed appropriately in the presence of attacks such as industry espionage and hacking. Various *adversary models* can be used to model an adversary's capability of launching attacks. An adversary may control the communication channel at different locations: eavesdropping, modifying, blocking, replaying, injecting, and initiating communication messages. An adversary may compromise or masquerade as an authorized entity in its attacks. An adversary model should be realistic in modeling the attacks in practical environment. If a weak adversary model is sufficient, one should not choose any stronger one as it may lead to over-secure solutions. One may remember what Ravi Sandhu said, "things should be made as secure as possible, but not securer" in a spirit of Albert Einstein's saying "things should be made as simple as possible, but not simpler." [10]

Given an adversary model, one of the major challenges in designing RFID security and privacy solutions is to reduce the cost of RFID tags. According to the cost of tags, RFID security and privacy solutions can be roughly classified into two categories: (i) *lightweight solutions*, which are suitable for low-cost tags such as those equipped with very limited memory storage and most basic bitwise and arithmetic operations; and (ii) *crypto-tag solutions*, which require tags to perform standard crypto operations such as hash, AES, cryptographic pseudo-random function (PRF), and digital signature.

CHAPTER 2

RFID Security at the Physical Level

At the physical level, physical objects are identified through interactions among RFID tags, RFID readers, backend servers, and involving parties. RFID security at the physical level requires that the identification process be performed appropriately in the presence of attacks under certain adversary model.

A common adversary model allows an adversary to control the communication channel between tags and readers via standard RFID air interfaces in a sense that the adversary may eavesdrop, modify, block, replay, inject, and initiate communication messages between tags and readers, and the adversary may masquerade as readers or tags according to the information obtained in the attacks. The model also allows an adversary to corrupt a tag in a sense that all secret information stored in the tag at the moment when it is corrupted is known to the adversary. We exclude the case where an adversary launches side channel attacks [16] to uncorrupted tags, permanently blocks tags' interactions with valid readers, or physically manipulates or damages uncorrupted tags by any means.

The following topics of RFID security will be covered in this chapter.

- Tag/Reader/Mutual Authentication: Tag authentication means that only valid tags are accepted by valid readers, while reader authentication requires that only valid readers are accepted by valid tags. Mutual authentication implies both tag authentication and reader authentication.

- Key Distribution: Most RFID authentication solutions rely on secret keys which are shared between tags and readers. In the case that a large number of tags are processed by multiple parties, the key distribution problem should be addressed which deals with how to distribute all necessary keys to each party in a secure and timely manner.

- Path Authentication: Path authentication is to accept only those valid tags that have passed through valid paths, where valid paths are legitimate sequences of steps which valid tags should follow.

- Clone Tag Detection: Clone tags bear the same IDs as genuine tags. Clone tag detection identifies possible clone tags when both genuine tags and clone tags are processed in an RFID system.

2.1 TAG/READER/MUTUAL AUTHENTICATION

RFID tag/reader authentication means that only valid tags/readers are accepted by valid readers/tags. Tag/reader authentication is usually performed based on certain secret keys stored in each valid tag/reader and this fact is verified by a valid reader/tag in authentication process. Tag/reader authentication being secure means that without corrupting a target tag/reader, it is computationally infeasible for an adversary to impersonate the tag/reader.

More formally, the security property of RFID authentication can be defined in terms of completeness and soundness [98, 110, 116]. Intuitively, completeness means that after any attacks made by an adversary, authentication processes are still complete (i.e., uncorrupted tags and readers can resume authentication processes whenever attacks stop). Soundness means that an uncorrupted tag/reader is authenticated only if the corresponding protocol conversations complete correctly. A formal description of these concepts will be given in Chapter 3.

In general, authentication may be performed with or without identification. Since identification is a major purpose of using RFID technology, we consider identification as a necessary step in authentication.

2.1.1 PUBLIC KEY SOLUTIONS

Let us start with a simple public key solution for RFID tag authentication. Assuming that a private signature key k_i and a public key certificate $cert_i$ are stored in each valid tag T_i, the tag can authenticate itself to a valid reader in the following steps:

1. the reader generates a random bit string r and sends it to the tag;

2. the tag digitally signs r with its privacy key k_i and transmits generated signature sig_i and its certificate $cert_i$ to the reader; and

3. the reader verifies $cert_i$ and sig_i,

where the certificate $cert_i$ is issued to tag T_i's ID and it is signed by a certification authority trusted by the reader. In this solution, the random string r should be long enough to thwart replay attacks.

A simple public key solution can also be used for reader authentication as shown in [9], where a public key-enabled tag attended by a person can verify a reader's public key certificate with efficient revocation checking. Hein et al. proved that it is feasible to implement ECC on RFID chips [13].

2.1.2 SYMMETRIC KEY SOLUTIONS

Public key-enabled tags can be used for high-value items such as shipping containers. Under the pressure of reducing tag cost, however, it is more demanding to investigate on symmetric key-based solutions.

Let k_i be a secret key stored in a valid tag T_i and the key is shared with a valid reader, which stores k_i with the tag's ID value ID_i. Let F_k be a keyed one-way function (e.g., encryption function or keyed hash function) with key k. A simple tag authentication solution is given below.

1. The reader generates a random bit string r and sends it to the tag.

2. The tag computes $h = F_{k_i}(r)$ and transmits h and its ID value ID_i to the reader.

3. The reader authenticates the tag by verifying that $h = F_{k_i}(r)$ according to k_i indexed by ID_i.

Provided that r is long enough and the keyed one-way function F_{k_i} is appropriately constructed and deployed, it is computationally infeasible for an adversary to simulate any valid tag without corrupting it. This protocol can be easily revised to achieve mutual authentication.

1. The reader generates a random bit string r_1 and sends it to the tag.

2. The tag generates another random bit string r_2, computes $h_1 = F_{k_i}(r_1)$ and transmits h_1, r_2 and its ID value ID_i to the reader.

3. The reader authenticates the tag by verifying that $h_1 = F_{k_i}(r_1)$. If the tag is authenticated, the reader computes $h_2 = F_{k_i}(r_2, ID_i)$ and transmits it to the tag; else it aborts the protocol.

4. The tag authenticates the reader by verifying that $h_2 = F_{k_i}(r_2, ID_i)$.

Plenty of work has demonstrated efficient hardware implementations of standard symmetric key primitives on RFID tags, including AES [11], the stream ciphers Grain and Trivium [12], SHA-1 [14], and the PRESENT block cipher [15]. According to Moore's law, the cost of implementing such primitives on RFID tags would drop dramatically in the future.

2.1.3   HASH-BASED SOLUTIONS

A number of RFID authentication protocols have been developed based on cryptographic hash functions [17]. We summarize typical hash-based RFID authentication protocols and compare them in terms of security and performance. Note that besides tag/reader authentication, some of the protocols are designed to have additional privacy-related properties such as tag anonymity, anti-tracing, and forward privacy, which we will elaborate in the next chapter. We focus on tag/reader authentication and relevant security attacks in this chapter.

OSK Internal Hash Chain   In [44], Ohkubo, Suzuki and Kinoshita (OSK) proposed a scheme which can be used for tag authentication. Under the scheme, each tag T_i has a initial secret key k_i^1 in its storage, which is different from other tags. The tag is equipped with two different one-way hash functions H and G, where H is used to update the tag secret and G is used to compute a tag pseudonym. A backend server maintains a list of pairs (ID_i, k_i^1).

Each time tag T_i is queried by a reader, the tag will compute a pseudonym $G(k_i^j)$ from its current secret key k_i^j, transmit the pseudonym to the reader, and update its secret key to $k_i^{j+1} = H(k_i^j)$. To authenticate the tag, the backend server would perform an exhaustive search to compute $G(H^\ell(k_i^1))$ for all keys stored in its database, incrementally iterating through each value of ℓ (starting from zero) until a match with the received pseudonym is found.

This scheme provides tag authentication against passive attacks only. An active adversary can simply query a valid tag and then replay its response to a valid reader, which would verify the response and assume that it is from a valid tag [47].

Due to the need to compute hash chains and to perform exhaustive search during tag authentication, a large amount of computational overhead is incurred at the backend server. Avoine and Oechslin described a way to improve the efficiency of key search in OSK scheme based on time-memory trade-off [46]; however, the security vulnerability of OSK scheme still exists.

YA-TRAP In [48], Tsudik proposed Yet Another Trivial RFID Authentication Protocol (YA-TRAP). The protocol uses a time-based challenge issued by a reader to authenticate a tag. Each tag T_i stores a secret key k_i shared with a valid reader (or backend server) and records a timestamp t_{last} which could be updated by a reader during the last protocol session. During the next protocol session, the tag receives a timestamp t_{curr} from the reader and checks whether $t_{curr} > t_{last}$ and $t_{curr} \leq t_{max}$. If the conditions are satisfied, the tag replies with the response

$$h = H_{k_i}(t_{curr}),$$

where H_{k_i} is a keyed hash function computed with the secret key k_i. The tag then updates $t_{last} \leftarrow t_{curr}$. On the other hand, if any of the conditions is violated, the tag would simply respond with a random number. To authenticate the tag, a valid reader (or backend server) searches for appropriate k_i in its record which can be used to verify $h = H_{k_i}(t_{curr})$. To improve the efficiency of tag authentication, the reader can pre-compute a table of h for all k_i and all possible t_{curr} in a time interval; tag authentication can be performed by looking up in the table.

YA-TRAP can be used to authenticate tags in the presence of passive attacks. An active adversary who monitors the communication between various valid tags and readers can predict a legitimate value for t_{curr}, use it to query a valid tag, and obtain a valid response. Moreover, the adversary can repeatedly query the tag and use the obtained responses to impersonate it at different time.

This scheme is also vulnerable to a denial of service attack, in which an adversary may send $t_{curr} = t_{max}$ to a target tag. In this case, a legitimate reader would no longer obtain any valid responses from the target tag.

YA-TRAP+ and O-TRAP In [49], Chatmon et al. proposed YA-TRAP+ and the Optimistic Trivial RFID Authentication Protocol (O-TRAP) to mitigate the drawbacks in YA-TRAP. Both protocols provide tag authentication, while YA-TRAP+ can perform reader authentication as well.

In YA-TRAP+, each tag T_i stores k_i and t_{last} and receives t_{curr} as a challenge from a reader as in YA-TRAP. In addition, the tag also receives a random challenge r_1 from the reader. The tag's response h_1 is computed as follows:

$$h_1 \;\; = \;\; \begin{cases} H_{k_i}(0,\, t_{curr},\, r_1) & \text{if } t_{curr} > t_{last} \\ H_{k_i}(1,\, r_2,\, r_1) & \text{otherwise} \end{cases} ,$$

where r_2 is a random number generated by the tag. Both r_2 and h_1 are sent to the reader. Under YA-TRAP+, a valid reader would authenticate the tag by searching for appropriate k_i which can be used to verify h_1. Note that this authentication can be performed no matter whether the tag's copy of t_{last} is valid or not.

A valid reader can check out whether a tag has been desynchronized (i.e., $t_{curr} \le t_{last}$) based on the value of h_1. If the tag is desynchronized, YA-TRAP+ provides an optional pass to allow the reader to resynchronize itself with the tag by sending a message h_2 as follows:

$$h_2 \;\; = \;\; H_{k_i}(2,\, r_2,\, t_{curr}).$$

The tag can then verify h_2 and update $t_{last} \leftarrow t_{curr}$ accordingly. While this step can be used to verify the authenticity of the timestamp t_{curr}, it can also be used to authenticate the reader.

YA-TRAP+ is essentially a challenge response protocol with an additional capability of detecting whether a tag has been desynchronized. To authenticate a tag, YA-TRAP+ requires a valid reader (or backend server) to perform an exhaustive search of tag keys for verifying h_1.

The authors of YA-TRAP+ also proposed another tag authentication scheme, O-TRAP. In O-TRAP, a reader uses a random challenge instead of a timestamp to authenticate a tag. Each tag T_i uses a pseudonym n_i^j to identify itself. The pseudonym has to be kept secret until it is revealed by the tag when queried by a reader. Thereafter, the pseudonym is updated with

$$n_i^{j+1} \leftarrow H_{k_i}(n_i^j),$$

where k_i is a secret key stored in tag T_i and in the reader's database, and H_{k_i} is a keyed hash function. In O-TRAP, tag T_i generates a response h when queried by a reader with a random challenge r, where

$$h \;\; = \;\; H_{k_i}(r, n_i^j).$$

Both n_i^j and h are sent to the reader. The reader uses tag pseudonym n_i^j to locate tag secret key k_i (provided that the tag has not been desynchronized from the reader) and verify h. If h is verified successfully, the reader updates $n_i^{j+1} \leftarrow H_{k_i}(n_i^j)$ in its database so that the pseudonym is synchronized between tag and reader.

A valid tag would be desynchronized if an adversary induces the tag to update its pseudonym. A valid reader would have to perform an exhaustive search on k_i so as to find the right match for h.

LRP-PTCA In [47], Dimitriou proposed a Lightweight RFID Protocol to Protect against Traceability and Cloning Attacks (LRP-PTCA). Under this protocol, each tag T_i has a unique secret value k_i^j in its storage; a valid reader (or backend server) has a record $(H(k_i^j), k_i^j, ID_i)$ in its database, where H is cryptographic hash function. Let H_k be a keyed hash function and G be a one-way function. LRP-PTCA mutual authentication scheme works as follows between tag T_i and a valid reader.

1. The reader generates a random number r_1 and sends it to the tag.

2. The tag generates a random number r_2, computes, and transmits $H(k_i^j), r_2, H_{k_i^j}(r_2, r_1)$ to the reader.

3. The reader retrieves k_i^j from its database using $H(k_i^j)$ as an index and verifies $H_{k_i^j}(r_2, r_1)$; if successful, the reader accepts the tag, updates $k_i^{j+1} = G(k_i^j)$ in its database, computes, and transmits $H_{k_i^{j+1}}(r_2, r_1)$ to the tag; otherwise, the reader rejects the tag and aborts this protocol.

4. The tag verifies $H_{G(k_i^j)}(r_2, r_1)$; if successful, the tag accepts the reader and updates its key $k_i^{j+1} = G(k_i^j)$; otherwise, the tag rejects the reader.

In this protocol, a tag key is updated only after the tag authenticates the reader; therefore, an adversary cannot induce a tag to update its key as in desynchronization attacks. It is possible that an adversary blocks or alters the last message sent from reader to tag so that the tag does not update its key while the reader has already updated it. To mitigate this attack, the reader can maintain two records for each tag T_i, the updated one $(H(k_i^{j+1}), k_i^{j+1}, ID_i)$ and the old one $(H(k_i^j), k_i^j, ID_i)$. Tag authentication can be performed efficiently without exhaustive search.

TBPA In [51], Molnar and Wagner proposed a Tree-Based Private Authentication (TBPA) scheme. Let F_k be a cryptographic pseudo-random function (PRF); let ID and k be a tag's ID and secret key, respectively. At the server side, a balanced binary tree of secrets is used to index all tags, where each leaf note points to a pair of (ID, k). In a tag's memory, the following are stored: a pair of (ID, k), and a sequence of secrets k_1 (root), $k_2, \ldots, k_d$ (leaf) corresponding to the notes along a path in the binary tree with the leaf note pointing to the tag's (ID, k). The scheme works as follows between reader and tag.

- [*Round 1 challenge*:] The reader generates a random number r_1 and sends it to the tag.

- [*Round 1 response*:] The tag generates a random number r_1', computes $\sigma_1 = F_{k_1}(0, r_1, r_1')$, and transmits r_1', σ_1 to the reader.

- [*Round 2 challenge*:] The reader finds k_1 in its tree (root) that satisfies σ_1, generates a random number r_2, computes $\tau_1 = F_{k_1}(1, r_1, r_1')$, and sends r_2, τ_1 to the tag.

- [*Round 2 response*:] The tag verifies τ_1, generates a random number r_2', computes $\sigma_2 = F_{k_2}(0, r_2, r_2')$, and transmits r_2', σ_2 to the reader.

- ...

- [*Round d challenge*:] The reader finds k_{d-1} in its tree that satisfies σ_{d-1}, generates a random number r_d, computes $\tau_{d-1} = F_{k_{d-1}}(1, r_{d-1}, r_{d-1}')$, and sends r_d, τ_{d-1} to the tag.

- [*Round d response*:] The tag verifies τ_{d-1}, generates a random number r_d', computes $\sigma_d = F_{k_d}(0, r_d, r_d')$, and transmits r_d', σ_d to the reader.

- [*Last round challenge*:] The reader finds k_d in its tree (leaf) that satisfies σ_d, retrieves (ID, k), computes $\tau_d = F_{k_d}(1, r_d, r_d')$, generates a random number r, and sends τ_d, r to the tag.

- [*Last round response*:] The tag verifies τ_d, generates a random number r', computes $\sigma = ID \oplus F_k(0, r, r')$, and transmits r', σ to the reader.

- [*Tag authentication*:] The reader authenticates the tag by verifying $ID = \sigma \oplus F_k(0, r, r')$; if successful, the reader computes $\tau = ID \oplus F_k(1, r, r')$ and sends τ to the tag.

- [*Reader authentication*:] The tag authenticates the reader by verifying $ID = \tau \oplus F_k(1, r, r')$.

In this protocol, whenever the verification of σ_i, τ_i, for $1 \leq i \leq d$, or ID fails, the protocol aborts. The computation overhead incurred for tag authentication is $O(\log n)$, which is more efficient as compared to $O(n)$ if an exhaustive search of tag key is performed in tag authentication, where n is the total number of tags in the system. The tradeoffs of this efficiency improvement are high communication overhead ($O(\log n)$ rounds of communications), high storage requirement on tag ($O(\log n)$ secrets in each tag), and high computation overhead on tag ($O(\log n)$ random number generations and $O(\log n)$ PRF evaluations).

A vulnerability of this protocol is that if one tag is corrupted, other tags which share some secrets with the corrupted tag will be affected (which may lead to privacy breach as discussed in the next chapter). It is also costly to update tag secrets since some keys are shared across different tags. For example, if the root secret k_1 is updated, all tags in the system should update their secrets.

SPA   Dimitriou [50] investigated how to reduce the communication overhead in RFID authentication using a tree structure similar to TBPA scheme. Based on Dimitriou's method, Lu *et al.* [52] further investigated on how to update tag secrets in their Strong and Lightweight RFID Private Authentication (SPA) protocol. Slightly different from TBPA scheme, SPA assumes that each leaf note in the tree structure points to a tag's *ID*. It also assumes that each tag stores a sequence of secrets k_1 (root), $k_2, \ldots, k_d$ (leaf) which are the notes lying along a path of the index tree. Let H be a cryptographic hash function. SPA works as follows between a reader and a tag.

1. The reader generates a random number r and sends it to the tag.

2. The tag generates a random number r', computes hash values $H(k_1, r), H(k_2, r), \ldots, H(k_d, r)$, transmits the random number and the hash values to the reader.

3. The reader uses the hash values to locate k_d in the tree structure and identify the tag with ID. Let $sync$ be the set of indexes of the keys $k_1, \ldots, k_d$ which need to be updated (e.g., $sync = (2, 3)$ means k_2 and k_3 to be updated); the reader computes a hash value $H(k_d, r, r')$, and sends the hash value and $sync$ to the tag.

4. The tag authenticates the reader by verifying $H(k_d, r, r')$; then the tag updates its keys according to $sync$.

The update of any key k_i is performed by hashing the key: $k_i \leftarrow H(k_i)$. Since the reader's last message in the above protocol (step 3) may not go through, the reader or backend server needs to keep both updated keys and their previous versions in its tree structure for tag authentication.

This protocol is subject to desynchronization attacks since there is no integrity protection on the $sync$ component in the reader's last message (step 3 in the protocol). An active adversary can make changes to $sync$ so that the tag is led to perform wrong updates to some of its keys. The tag would then become desynchronized from the backend server. This attack can be mitigated by a simple revision on the hash value in step 3: the reader sends $H(k_d, r, r', sync)$ instead of $H(k_d, r, r')$ to the tag, which verifies this hash value in step 4.

Compared to TBPA Scheme, SPA reduces the number of rounds significantly from $O(\log n)$ to $O(1)$; however, the communication overhead, the computation overhead on tag, and the storage requirement on tag are still high ($O(\log n)$).

Since some keys are shared across different tags, SPA shares the same vulnerability as TBPA Scheme [51] and Dimitriou's scheme [50] in a sense that if one tag is corrupted, other tags which share some keys with the corrupted tag will be affected (which may lead to privacy breach as discussed in the next chapter). It is also costly to implement key updating.

RIPP-FS   In [53], Conti, et al. proposed the RFID Identification and Privacy Preserving Protocol with Forward Secrecy (RIPP-FS). Under the protocol, a valid reader stores a hash chain computed from a cryptographic hash function and uses a hash value from the chain to authenticate itself to a tag over time. Let k be a random secret chosen by a valid reader and H be a secure hash function. The reader stores a hash chain $H(k), H^2(k) = H(H(k)), \ldots, H^{max}(k)$ computed from k so as to authenticate itself to a tag.

Suppose the initial time at the reader is t_0 and the time is discrete such that $t_n = t_{n-1} + 1$ for all $n > 0$. Each valid tag T_i shares a secret key k_i with the valid reader, and the tag stores the time t_{stored} of the last valid protocol session carried out with the reader, and a corresponding hash value h_{stored} received from the reader in the last valid protocol session. In the beginning, $t_{stored} = t_0$ and $h_{stored} = H^{max}(k)$. The reader stores (ID, k_i, t_{stored}) for each tag T_i.

RIPP-FS authenticates the reader first. During time t_n, the reader broadcasts t_n and a Lamport hash value $h = H^{max-n}(k)$ to all tags in its read range. A tag T_i in the range first checks

$t = t_n - t_{stored} > 0$ and then, verifies $h_{stored} = H^t(h)$ to authenticate the reader. If the authentication fails, the tag sends a random number to the reader and aborts the protocol; otherwise, the tag updates $k_i \leftarrow H^t(k_i)$, $t_{stored} \leftarrow t_n$, and $h_{stored} \leftarrow h$, computes and transmits an HMAC value $H(k_i, t_n)$ to the reader.

The reader then authenticates the tag by verifying the HMAC value $H(k_i, t_n)$. Given time t_n, the reader/server can compute all (updated) tag keys k_i and verify the HMAC value with an exhaustive search. Alternatively, as it is suggested in [53], the server can pre-compute a key lookup table containing tuples $(ID, k_i, H(k_i, t_n))$ for all possible t_n in some interval; then, the tag verification can be performed by simply search in the table. The table can be updated periodically.

RIPP-FS achieves tag authentication; however, reader authenticity cannot be guaranteed because of a replay attack that can take place. Suppose there are two mutually exclusive sets of tags S_A and S_B, and all the tags in both sets last took part in a valid protocol session under RIPP-FS before time t_n, i.e., the value of t_{stored} in all those tags are less than t_n. Then, at time t_n, an authorized reader communicates with all the tags in S_A but not those tags in S_B by transmitting (t_n, h). An adversary who eavesdrops over the session can then replay (t_n, h) to any of the tags in S_B and impersonate as an authorized reader.

Triggered Hash Chain and Variants   In [54], Henrici and Muller proposed the Triggered Hash Chain scheme. The scheme uses three different secure hash functions F, G, and H. The first hash function is used by a valid tag to authenticate itself to a reader, the second hash function is used by a valid reader to authenticate itself to a tag and to trigger an update of the tag's key, and the third hash function is used by both reader and tag to update the tag's key. Let k be a tag's key and let (k, ID) be a tuple stored in the backend server connected by a valid reader. The protocol works as follows between a reader and a tag.

1. The reader sends an authentication request to the tag.

2. The tag computes and transmits $F(k)$ to the reader.

3. The reader authenticates the tag by verifying $F(k)$ in the server's database (which can be implemented by searching in a pre-computed table of $(k, ID, F(k))$; if it fails, the protocol aborts; otherwise, the reader sends $G(k)$ to the tag, and updates the tag key $k \leftarrow H(k)$.

4. The tag authenticates the reader by verifying $G(k)$; if it fails, the protocol aborts; otherwise, the tag updates its key $k \leftarrow H(k)$.

Since the reader's last message in the above protocol (i.e., $G(k)$ in step 3) may not go through (e.g., due to desynchronization attacks or electronic noise), the backend server needs to keep a copy of each tag's previous key in its database. The backend server will use the previous tag key to authenticate a tag if the current tag key fails.

While this solution provides resilience to desynchronization attacks, it gives rise to a major problem. When a tag is in a desynchronization status, an active adversary who has eavesdropped the previous protocol running can impersonate the tag by replaying $F(k)$, or impersonate a valid reader by replaying $G(k)$.

In order to thwart the attack of replaying $F(k)$, two variants of the Triggered Hash Chain scheme were proposed by Lim et al. [55]. The first variant (Challenge-Response Triggered Hash or CRTH scheme) uses a challenge-response mechanism to enhance the original scheme: (i) the reader sends a random number r in step 1, (ii) the tag replies with $F(k, r)$ in step 2, and (iii) this reply $F(k, r)$ is verified by the reader in step 3 with an exhaustive search on k. Note that it is not possible to pre-compute a table of $F(k, r)$ for all k and r due to the use of a fresh random number in each protocol session.

The second variant (Forward-Rolling Triggered Hash or FRTH scheme) adopts a similar mechanism used in the RIPP-FS protocol: (i) the reader sends the current time t_n and a Lamport hash value h to the tag in step 1, (ii) the tag replies with $F(k, t_n)$ in step 2 provided that the reader is authenticated by verifying t_n and h as in the RIPP-FS protocol, and (iii) the tag's reply $F(k, t_n)$ is verified by the reader in step 3. By enumerating all possible t_n, the reader can maintain a table of pre-computed $(k, t_n, F(k, t_n))$ for tag authentication in step 3.

In order to thwart the attack of replaying $G(k)$, the tag can generate a random number r' and append r' to its reply message in step 2. Then, the reader sends $G(k, r')$ to the tag in step 3, and the tag updates its key k after verifying $G(k, r')$ in step 4.

RCSC In [18], Li and Ding proposed a protocol for RFID Communications in Supply Chains (RCSC). In this protocol, each tag T_i shares a secret key k_i with a backend server connected to valid readers. Let ID_i be the ID of tag T_i. The tag stores a pseudonym $\alpha = ID_i \oplus k_i$ in its memory. A backend server maintains a database of (ID_i, k_i). Let H be a cryptographic hash function. The protocol works as follows between a reader and a tag.

1. The reader sends a random number r to the tag.

2. The tag computes and transmits $h = H(r \oplus \alpha)$ to the reader.

3. The reader authenticates the tag by searching in its database for a single record (ID_i, k_i) such that $h = H(r \oplus ID_i \oplus k_i)$; if the verification fails, the protocol aborts; otherwise, the reader updates k_i to a random k_i' and transmits $a = k_i \oplus k_i'$ and $b = H(a \oplus ID_i \oplus k_i)$ to the tag.

4. The tag authenticates the reader by verifying $b = H(a \oplus \alpha)$. If it fails, the protocol aborts; otherwise, the tag updates its pseudonym α to be $\alpha \oplus a$.

To improve the efficiency of tag authentication, it is assumed that a fresh random number r can be used for authenticating a batch of multiple tags, instead of a single tag. Before the arrival of a batch of tags, the reader can generate a random number r and pre-compute a table (ID_i, k_i, h) for all unmarked tags in its database. Therefore, the authentication of each batch of tags can be performed by searching in the pre-computed table.

Since the reader's last message in the above protocol (i.e., (a, b) in step 3) may not go through, the reader needs to keep a copy of each tag's previous key in its database. The reader will use the previous tag key to authenticate a tag if the current tag key cannot be verified.

Similar to Triggered Hash Chain and its varints, this protocol is subject to an attack of replaying a, b in step 3 if the tag's pseudonym is not updated in the last valid protocol session. Moreover, an active adversary can query a valid tag with any random number r in step 1 and get its reply h in step 2; then, the adversary can send (r, h) instead of (a, b) to the tag in step 3 and update the tag's pseudonym α in step 4. This desynchronization attack would render the tag unrecognizable in the future.

In order to address the above attacks, the tag can generate a random number r' and send h, r' in step 2. Then, the reader sends $a = k_i \oplus k_i'$ and $b = H(r' \oplus a \oplus ID_i \oplus k_i)$ to the tag in step 3, and the tag updates its pseudonym α after verifying $b = H(r' \oplus a \oplus \alpha)$ in step 4.

A Brief Summary on Hash-Based Solutions   Among the hash-based solutions reviewed above, we highlight that OSK Internal Hash, YA-TRAP, and Triggered Hash Chain provide no guarantee on tag authentication; OSK Internal Hash, YA-TRAP, YA-TRAP+, and O-TRAP are not designed to provide reader authentication; and RIPP-FS and Triggered Hash Chain are weak in reader authentication.

In terms of computation on the reader/server side, the hash based solutions can be classified into three categories: (i) exhaustive search, (ii) tree-based search, and (iii) table look-up. OSK Internal Hash, YA-TRAP+, O-TRAP (for desynchronized tags), and CRTH belong to the first category. Given an RFID system of n tags, the complexity of authenticating a tag is $O(n)$ in this category. In the second category, TBPA and SPA use a tree structure to reduce the complexity to $O(\log n)$. The last category includes LRP-PTCA, YA-TRAP, O-TRAP (for synchronized tags), RIPP-FS, Triggered Hash Chain, FRTH, and RCSC. The complexity of a table look-up is negligible (often considered as $O(1)$) as compared to an exhaustive search or tree-based search.

In terms of computation on the tag side, most schemes require $O(1)$ hash or PRF computations except that the tree-based schemes, including TBPA and SPA, require $O(\log n)$ hash or PRF computations.

All schemes require $O(n)$ storage on the server side for storing tag IDs, keys, and other information for all n tags. In terms of tag memory, the tree-based schemes (TBPA and SPA) require $O(\log n)$ storage while other schemes require $O(1)$ storage.

The communication cost can be measured by both the number of rounds and the communication overhead in each round. Except for TBPA scheme, which requires $O(\log n)$ rounds, other schemes requires two or three rounds of communication. The communication overhead of each round is $O(1)$ for all schemes except that it is $O(\log n)$ for the tag-to-reader communication in SPA.

2.1.4   LIGHTWEIGHT SOLUTIONS

Symmetric key-based and hash-based RFID authentication protocols are still too costly for low-cost RFID tags. Low-cost tags, such as EPC Gen 2 tags, are equipped with a couple of thousand gates in hardware implementations, which are mainly devoted to basic operations [19]. Only a few hundred gates can be used for security operations [20]. In comparison, the smallest known AES 128-bit implementation requires 3400 gate equivalents [11] on RFID tag design. As for on-tag hash functions, the most compact hash function requires about 4000 gate equivalents [21] constructed based on the block cipher PRESENT [15] with 128-bit output; a SHA-1 implementation on RFID tags requires about 5500 gate equivalents [14].

Lightweight (or ultra-lightweight) RFID authentication protocols are designed for low-cost tags to perform only the most basic bitwise and arithmetic operations. Unfortunately, most lightweight RFID authentication protocols have security flaws. Several examples are given below.

Peris-Lopez *et al.* proposed two lightweight RFID mutual authentication protocols, LMAP [22] and M^2AP [23]. These two protocols use only simple bitwise operations, including bitwise XOR, bitwise OR, bitwise AND, and modular addition, which require only about 300 gate equivalents in tag design. Li and Wang discovered that these protocols suffer from a denial of service attack (an adversary who eavesdrops one protocol run can desynchronize a tag and make it unrecognizable) and full disclosure attack (an adversary who interacts with a reader and a tag can derive all secret information about the tag) [24]. Li and Wang also proposed countermeasures to improve the security of LMAP and M^2AP. Unfortunately, Chien and Huang discovered that the improved scheme is still subject to a full disclosure attack [25].

Another example is "SASI: an new ultra-lightweight RFID authentication protocol providing strong authentication and strong integrity" proposed by Chien [26]. A passive attack can be used to reveal the secret information of tag by eavesdropping a number of protocol sessions [28]. In addition, two desynchronization attacks are discovered by Sun *et al.* to break this protocol [27].

For EPC Gen 2 tags, no authentication mechanism is given in EPC class 1 generation 2 standards (or ISO 18000-6C standards). Each EPC Gen 2 tag is in its open state by factory default; that is, access password is all zeros and all memory banks can be read or written by any EPC Gen 2 reader. If a non-zero access password is assigned to a tag, the tag is moved to its secured state. After that, an EPC Gen 2 reader can send the right access password to the tag and choose to lock any of its memory bank or change the lock state (only reserved bank, including kill password and access password, can be both read and write locked; other banks can be read locked only). The kill password can be used by an EPC Gen 2 reader to disable the tag permanently.

Since the access password sent by a reader to a tag is not protected, an adversary can eavesdrop it and access the tag later. To address such vulnerability, Konidala et al. proposed a lightweight RFID mutual authentication protocol [29], where a simple pad generation (PadGen) function is used to generate cover-coding pads to mask a tag's access password before it is transmitted between reader and tag. The pads are generated based on the tag's access password, kill password, and random numbers which are known to both reader and tag in interaction for mutual authentication.

Peris-Lopez *et al.* discovered some security flaws in this protocol such that an adversary can recover both access password and kill password with a high probability [30]. To address the weaknesses of Konidala-Kim-Kim protocol, different PadGen functions are proposed by Huang *et al.* [31, 32]; unfortunately, the revised solutions are still vulnerable since an adversary can recover a tag's access password with a high probability [33].

There exist many other lightweight RFID authentication protocols such as [70, 71, 72]. Most of these protocols are weak in terms of security or they need more assessment. It is still challenging to design lightweight RFID authentication protocols that are provably secure under a strong adversary model. A promising direction to address this challenge is given below.

HB Protocol and Variants   HB is a lightweight tag authentication protocol due to Hopper and Blum [56]. Let k be an ℓ-bit secret key shared between a tag and a reader. Let ϵ be a random noise bit generated by a tag which takes value 1 with probability $\eta < 0.5$. HB protocol works as follows between a reader and a tag.

- A single round:

    1. The reader generates a ℓ-bit random number r and sends it as challenge to the tag.

    2. The tag generates a random noise bit ϵ with parameter η, computes $a = (r \circ k) \oplus \epsilon$ (where $\circ$ means binary inner product), and transmits a as response to the reader.

    3. The reader checks whether the tag's response a is correct (i.e., $a \overset{?}{=} r \circ k$).

- Repeat ρ rounds.

- Accept if fewer than $\eta\rho$ of tag responses are incorrect.

HB protocol is lightweight since it requires a tag to perform bitwise AND and XOR operations only; also, a single noise bit ϵ can be cheaply generated in each round. HB protocol is proven secure against passive adversary. If the noise bit ϵ is not used in HB, a passive adversary capturing enough challenge-response pairs can easily derive k by solving a linear equation system. However, with the noise bit ϵ involved, the problem of deriving k from multiple challenge-response pairs is NP-Hard. This problem is often referred to as the Learning Parity in the Presence of Noise (LPN) problem.

HB protocol is vulnerable to active adversary. For example, an active adversary can send a challenge $r = (1, 0, 0, \ldots, 0)$ to a tag. The tag will reply with $k_1 \oplus \epsilon$ where k_1 is the first bit of k. Observing multiple rounds, the adversary can get the true value of k_1 from the majority of tag responses. Similarly, the adversary can derive $k_2, \ldots k_\ell$.

To address the vulnerability of HB against active adversary, Juels and Weis proposed HB+ [57], where tag and reader share two keys k, k' of length ℓ. The protocol works as follows between a reader and a tag.

- A single round:

    1. The tag generates an ℓ-bit random number r' and sends it as blinding factor to the reader.

    2. The reader generates an ℓ-bit random number r and sends it as challenge to the tag.

    3. The tag generates a random noise bit ϵ with parameter η, computes $a = (r \circ k) \oplus (r' \circ k') \oplus \epsilon$, and transmits a as response to the reader.

    4. The reader checks whether the tag's response a is correct (i.e., $a \stackrel{?}{=} (r \circ k) \oplus (r' \circ k')$);

- Repeat ρ rounds.

- Accept if fewer than $\eta\rho$ of tag responses are incorrect.

HB+ protocol is proven secure in a detection-based model where an adversary can only initiate or observe successful authentication sessions in its learning phase—if an authentication session fails, the adversary is considered to have been unsuccessful. A more desirable model is prevention based, in which an adversary can learn from both successful sessions and unsuccessful sessions (e.g., by monitoring a valid reader's output). The prevention-based model can be used to ensure against tag cloning regardless of whether or not an adversary is detected in its learning process.

Under the prevention-based model, HB+ is vulnerable to an active man-in-the-middle attack [58]. In this attack, an adversary modifies all reader challenges r to $r \oplus (1, 0, 0, \ldots 0)$, which lead to tag responses

$$
\begin{aligned}
a &= ((r \oplus (1, 0, 0, \ldots 0)) \circ k) \oplus (r' \circ k') \oplus \epsilon \\
&= (r \circ k) \oplus ((1, 0, 0, \ldots 0) \circ k) \oplus (r' \circ k') \oplus \epsilon \\
&= (r \circ k) \oplus k_1 \oplus (r' \circ k') \oplus \epsilon.
\end{aligned}
$$

Therefore, all tag responses are affected by k_1 – either all are flipped ($k_1 = 1$) or they remain to their original values. The adversary observes the reader's reaction: if the reader accepts the tag, then $k_1 = 0$; otherwise, $k_1 = 1$. Similarly, the adversary can obtain $k_2, \ldots k_\ell$.

Besides the attack, it should be noted that HB+ may not be suitable for efficient implementation on low-cost tags because: (i) a multi-bit random number must be generated by tag in each round and (ii) there is no good set of parameters so far for choosing ℓ, ρ, and η in HB+ due to contradictory upper bounds and lower bounds of these parameters. The upper bounds of these parameters should be determined according to tag memory constraint (on ℓ), time and bandwidth constraint (on ρ), false acceptance rate, and false reject rate requirements (on η). On the other hand, the lower bounds of these parameters should be determined such that a computationally bounded adversary cannot succeed in impersonating a tag with a probability noticeably higher than 1/2.

Besides HB+, many other HB variants exist, including HB++ [59], HB-MP [60], HB* [61], HB-MP+ [62], Trusted-HB [63], and HB# [64]. However, all of these protocols are proven insecure against certain man-in-the-middle attacks. Some recent results (e.g., HB^N [65]) requires a two-dimensional matrix as tag key, which may not fit into the memory of low-cost RFID tags such as EPC Gen 2 tags. Clearly, more research effort should be made on designing lightweight RFID authentication protocols that are suitable for low-cost RFID tags.

2.1.5 RADIO FREQUENCY DISTANCE BOUNDING

In many RFID applications such as access control and payment, it is required that an RFID reader and an RFID tag in interaction must be within certain distance, which is usually the nominal read range specified in RFID standards. It is considered as attacks if the distance between tag and reader is longer than certain threshold (even if both tag and reader are valid). For instance, an adversary may relay RFID communications such that, from a distance much longer than nominal read range, an NFC card can be used to open a door or an RFID enabled credit card can be used to make a payment. Typical attacks include distance fraud and mafia fraud. In *distance fraud*, the adversary is the prover trying to shorten the distance measured by the verifier. In *mafia fraud*, the adversary is an external attacker making the verifier believe that the protocol is executed successfully with a shortened distance measurement.

Radio frequency distance bounding can be used to address such attacks [69]. Radio frequency distance bounding denotes a class of RFID communication protocols in which a verifier (reader or tag) measures an upper bound on its distance to a prover (tag or reader) in communications. The distance is measured in a challenge response protocol in which the verifier sends a challenge message to the prover; when the prover receives the challenge, it generates a response message and sends it back to the verifier, who can verify the validity of the response. In this process, it is required that a prover cannot generate a valid response before it receives and processes the verifier's challenge. Let t be the time moment when the verifier sends out its challenge message to the prover, and t' be the time moment when the verifier receives a response to the challenge from the prover. Let δ be the time duration taken by the prover for processing the verifier' challenge and generating a response depending on the challenge. Let c be the speed of electro-magnetic waves traveling near the speed of light (i.e., 299,792,458 meters per second). Then, the distance d between the verifier and the prover can be calculated as

$$ d = \frac{\Delta t - \delta}{2} \cdot c, $$

where $\Delta t = t' - t$. The distance measurement is sensitive to the prover's processing time δ. If it is overestimated, then the prover is able to pretend to be closer to the verifier. On the other hand, if δ is underestimated, the distance measured could be too large to be useful. In order to obtain a good enough upper bound on distance measurement, the verifier needs to estimate an accurate lower bound on δ. Notice that even one nanosecond difference in δ would result in a distance error of about 15 cm. A major challenge in distance bounding protocol design is to reduce the prover's processing time as much as possible.

Rasmussen and Čapkun [66] proposed using a specially implemented concatenation function as the prover's processing function such that the prover's processing time is below one nanosecond. This means that a malicious prover can pretend to be about 15 cm closer to a verifier in the worst case. Previous distance bounding protocols using XOR [67] or comparison [68] as processing function require radio signals carrying the verifier's challenge to be demodulated, which results in additional processing time typically greater than 50 ns [66].

The distance bounding protocol proposed by Rasmussen and Čapkun [66] is summarized below.

1. The prover generates a random number (fresh nonce) r_P of sufficient length and sends a commitment to the nonce (e.g., a signed hash of the nonce) to the verifier; the prover activates its distance bounding hardware waiting for the verifier's challenge.

2. Upon receiving the commitment, the verifier generates a random number (fresh nonce) r_V of sufficient length, starts a high precision clock, and begins transmitting r_V as challenge to the prover.

3. Upon receiving the challenge, the prover generates and transmits a response by concatenating r_P and r_V in a specific way such that its processing time δ is no greater than one nanosecond.

4. The verifier records Δt once receiving the response from the prover. After this, the verifier recovers the prover's nonce from the response.

5. The prover sends a signed message containing its identity, its nonce r_P and the verifier's nonce r_V to the verifier.

6. The verifier verifies the prover's signature and the prover's nonce (against the corresponding commitment). If all the checks pass, the verifier can calculate an upper bound of its distance to the prover according to Δt and δ with maximum error of 15 cm.

This distance bounding protocol is shown to be secure against distance fraud and mafia fraud (in a sense that an adversary cannot shorten the measured distance by more than 15 cm as compared to the real distance) if the random numbers used in the protocol are sufficiently long and the underlying commitment scheme and signature scheme are secure. This protocol, however, may not be suitable for low-cost tags due to the use of commitment and signature schemes.

2.2   KEY DISTRIBUTION

In many RFID applications, such as supply chain management, a large volume of tags are processed by multiple readers which are owned by different parties. If such applications require solutions such as tag authentication which rely on secret keys to be shared between tags and readers, it is indispensable to address the key distribution problem which concerns on how to deliver all necessary tag keys to each party in a secure and efficient manner before the tags are processed by the party.

2.2.1 SECRET SHARING ACROSS SPACE AND TIME

It may not be practical to assume that there always exist secure channels between parties for delivering individual tag keys. Even if such secure channels exist, it may not be scalable to deliver a large number of tag keys among all parties. To address these challenges, Juels et al. proposed two key distribution solutions, *secret sharing across space* and *secret sharing across time*, which are suitable for EPC Gen 2 tags [73].

Consider two parties, A and B, communicating via a unidirectional channel, where party A is the sender, and party B is the receiver for delivering a particular set of tagged items packaged in a case. It is assumed that the two parties do not have pre-existing relationship, but they share a channel with limited adversary access, where limited adversary access means that an adversary cannot access a large number of tags in physically secure areas (e.g., within supply chain), but can access smaller number of tags in other areas (e.g., in retail store or in customers' hands). The key distribution problem is addressed by transporting secret keys in RFID tags without using any additional channel.

Secret Sharing Across Space   Sender A shares a secret key y with receiver B across a set of tags $T_1, \ldots T_n$ in a case (or pallet). A transforms y into n shares $S_1, \ldots, S_n$ and stores each share S_i in tag T_i such that y can only be recovered from at least k (where $k < n$) shares. In this case, the limited adversary access assumption means that an adversary cannot access any k or more than k tags in a case of n tags.

In a perfect secret sharing scheme, the length of each share S_i is the same as that of key y (e.g., 128 bits). Of course, for RFID applications, the shorter the length of each share, the better. A generic robust secret sharing scheme with tiny shares, which is named as tiny secret sharing (TSS) scheme, is proposed in [73] to reduce the length of each share to 16 bits or less with proper parameters.

The fact of B being able to recover a secret key y in a secure environment means that most of the tags (at least k out of n tags) in the case are present and thus authenticated. This means that party B can authentication a group of tags in a case with no necessity of authenticating individual tags.

In order to protect the secrecy of tag data (e.g., EPC code) m_i associated with each tag T_i, one may encrypt m_i with y and store the ciphertext $E_y(m_i)$ together with the share S_i in T_i. Only the legitimate receiver who can read at least k shares from a case of n tags can recover the key y and thus have access to the content m_i of each tag.

Secret Sharing Across Time   In the case that an adversary has the capability of scanning all tags in some whole cases, it is vulnerable to use "secret sharing across space" since the adversary can recover the secret key with enough shares in attacks. A "secret sharing across time" solution, which is named sliding-window information secret sharing (SWISS), is proposed to address this vulnerability. The assumption is that an adversary cannot get access to more than $k-1$ cases in any contiguous sequence of n cases.

In SWISS, a secret key y_i is assigned for each case i. A share S_j of y_i is generated by the sender A and written to case j (the share can be distributed across tags or written on a case-specific tag). The sender A sends a sequence of cases to the receiver B. Within any contiguous sequence of n cases, only the legitimate receiver who receives at least k shares is able to recover all assigned keys for the received cases. The construction of SWISS ensures that the size of each share is a small constant independent of n and k [73].

2.2.2 RESILIENT SECRET SHARING

The above key distribution solutions (including TSS and SWISS) proposed by Juels, Pappu, and Parno [73], JPP for short, are particularly efficient for delivering tagged items in RFID-enabled supply chains since they eliminate the need for distributing a database of tag keys among supply chain parties. However, they pose a threat due to the use of weak adversary model: an adversary who can scan at least k shares can recover a secret. Even without recovering the secret, any adversary who can read a tag is able to clone the tag as the tag's content is not protected. Even if a tag's content is protected by an access password which is not known to an adversary, it is still subject to tag cloning attacks in a strong adversary model where tags can be corrupted.

To address these threats, Li et al. target on two adjacent parties in any supply chain and a third party who transfers goods for these two parties [74]. In common practice in supply chain management (usually referred to as third party logistics, or 3PL), it is reasonable to assume that these parties know each other via some trust relationships such as a signed contract for their business transactions. It is required that the third party delivering a batch of tagged goods should be able to verify that most tags in a batch or case are presented. If necessary, the third party can authenticate any individual tag as well. However, the third party is restrained from accessing to any tag's content or cloning any tags even in a strong adversary model where tags can be corrupted.

Batch Goods Delivery Scenario   Three different roles in a batch goods delivery scenario: Alice, Bob and Carol. Alice, denoted by **A**, is the sender of a batch of goods (e.g., a manufacturer); Bob, denoted by **B**, is the receiver of the batch (e.g., a distributor who receives the goods from **A**); and Carol, denoted by **C**, is the Third Party Logistics (3PL) partner (e.g., a transporter or carrier of the goods from **A** to **B**).

Suppose **A** and **B** (and **C**) signed contracts for the purchase and delivery of some goods beforehand. Now, the goods must be delivered from **A** to **B** by **C** to fulfill the contracts. If each item of the goods is attached with an RFID tag, a supply chain party can process the goods in an efficient way (by scanning all items once in a whole). It is also desirable to provide necessary security features such as anti-cloning without incurring much additional cost.

As an example, Fig. 2.1 illustrates the scenario where a batch of 50 tags are packed into 3 cases, including a 5×5 case, a 4×4 case and a 3×3 case. These cases are delivered from **A** to **B**

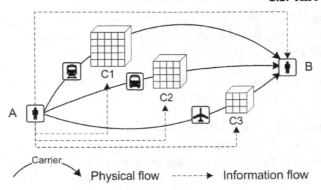

Figure 2.1: Batch goods delivery from **A** to **B**, by **C** [74].

via different physical flows by **C** (including C1, C2, C3, respectively). Some shared information prepared by **A** can be sent to **B** and **C** separately via the information flow. Facilitated with RFID technology, **C** can scan all RFID tags periodically during delivery, until all of them arrive at **B**. The scanning can be used to check the existence of most tags in the batch. If any adversary exists in the delivery path, however, s/he may clone some tags and thus replace authentic goods with counterfeited goods even though the adversary may not be able to know the secret keys for decrypting the tags' contents as in the secret sharing schemes proposed in [73]. To address this concern, it is proposed that the RFID tag authentication problem should be tackled such that nobody (even **C**) except **A** and **B** can access the tags' content while **C** is enabled to check the existence of most of the tags in a batch conveniently.

Two kinds of flows are identified during the process of goods delivery. One is the physical flow in which the goods are transported by **C** through containers on ships or trucks. The other is the information flow between **A**, **B**, and **C**. The information collected from both flows is used for the purpose of achieving certain desired security properties.

Desired Security Properties   The following security properties are identified for guaranteeing secure goods delivery in the batch goods delivery scenario.

- **Authentication of tags in cases. C** wants to authenticate RFID tags case by case periodically. Other than authentication purpose, **C** has no more advantage to access or even clone any tags. Both group authentication (case based), and individual tag authentication are necessary for **C** to operate efficiently and accurately.

- **Authentication of tags in batch. B** wants to authenticate RFID tags in batches as the final verification. Being the new owner of the tags, **B** shall grasp all (secret) information about individual tags and have the capability to update the tags.

- **Accessibility of individual tags.** Besides $\mathcal{A}$, only **B** can access individual tags. **C** or any adversaries cannot access nor clone any tags.

• **Secrecy of tag IDs.** In the sense of protecting tag identifier, all tags' IDs are encrypted by a secret key, which can only be recovered by **B**. Without necessary authorization, **C** cannot even access the encrypted IDs.

To address the "key distribution" problem, Li et al. designed a resilient secret sharing (RSS) scheme which has the desired properties [74].

Resilient Secret Sharing Scheme: Preliminaries.   In order to achieve all the security properties, a resilient secret sharing (RSS) scheme is designed. The proposed scheme inherits the merits of JPP solutions in terms of tiny shares and secret sharing based on error-correcting code. It also enhances JPP solutions with stronger security due to collecting shares from two different sources, including physical flow and information flow.

As defined in [73]: an n-party secret-sharing scheme is a pair of algorithms $\Pi = $ (Share, Recover) operating over a message space $\mathbb{X}$, where

◇ Share is a deterministic algorithm which takes an input $x \in \mathbb{X}$ and outputs an n-vector $S \leftarrow_R$ Share(x), where $S_i \in \{0, 1\}^*$. On invalid input $\hat{x} \notin \mathbb{X}$, Share outputs an n-vector of special ("undefined") symbol $\perp$.

◇ Recover is a deterministic algorithm which takes input $S \in (\{0, 1\}^* \bigcup \Diamond)^n$, where $\Diamond$ represents a share being erased (or otherwise unavailable). The output is Recover$(S) \in \mathbb{X} \bigcup \perp$, where $\perp$ is a distinguished value indicating a recovery failure.

Utilizing Error Correcting Code (ECC), a generalization of the secret sharing scheme is defined as $\Pi^{ECC} = $ (Share^{ECC}, Recover^{ECC}). An $(n, k, d)_Q$-ECC operates over an alphabet Σ of size $|\Sigma| = Q$. Share^{ECC} maps $\Sigma^k \to \Sigma^n$ such that the minimum Hamming distance in symbols between (valid) output vectors is d. For such share function (Share^{ECC}), there is a corresponding recover function (Recover^{ECC}) that recovers a message successfully with up to $(d - 1)/2$ errors or $d - 1$ erasures.

An adversary model for RSS is adapted from [73], which in turn is obtained by extending the model given in [75]. Two security requirements are defined under the adversary model: *privacy* and *robustness*. Given a limited number of shares, an attack against privacy aims to recover a secret x shared among n parties. A robustness attacker tries to tamper a number of shares such that a legal user cannot recover the correct secret x. Formal definitions on the two security requirements are given below.

An ordinary adversary can actively attack the communication links. The privacy requirement means that an underinformed adversary, who has access to limited number of shares, should not be able to recover the secret unless he can get access to at least k correct shares. In particular, we consider *gradated*, rather than *perfect* or *computational* secret sharing schemes. In gradated secret sharing schemes, an adversary with limited number of shares may be able to get *partial* information about the secret, though it cannot completely recover the secret itself. Moreover, the more the shares the adversary obtains, the more information it reveals. In the following formal definition of privacy, oracle corrupt(S, i) is defined as a function of (S, i), i.e., when the adversary submits i it will get S_i, the i-th share of a secret x.

Definition 2.1   Privacy   A (k, n)-RSS scheme $(\mathbf{\Pi}, \mathbb{X})$ satisfies $(q_p, t_p, \varepsilon_p)$-privacy w.r.t. under-informed attackers, if for any adversary $\mathcal{A}$ who can make q_p corrupt queries to acquire q_p shares (S_p denotes the set of these q_p shares) corresponding to a shared secret x and can run within the time of t_p, $\mathcal{A}$'s advantage to win the following experiment $\mathbf{Exp}_{\mathcal{A}}^{Pri}$, i.e., $\mathbf{Exp}_{\mathcal{A}}^{Pri}$ outputs 1, is not greater than ε_p:

$$\mathrm{Adv}_{\mathcal{A}}^{Pri}[\mathbf{\Pi}, \mathbb{X}] \triangleq \Pr[\mathbf{Exp}_{\mathcal{A}}^{Pri} = 1] \leq \varepsilon_p. \tag{1}$$

Experiment $\mathbf{Exp}_{\mathcal{A}}^{Pri}$

1) $x \leftarrow_R \mathbb{X}$
2) $S = (S_1, \cdots, S_i, \cdots, S_n) \leftarrow \mathsf{Share}(x)$
3) $x' \leftarrow \mathcal{A}^{\mathsf{corrupt}(S, \cdot)}(S_p : S_p \subset S \wedge |S_p| = q_p)$
4) Return '1' if $x = x'$, else '0'.

Privacy Experiment

Informally, the robustness requirement means that the original secret can be recovered even if the adversary has tampered some of the shares corresponding to the shared secret.

Definition 2.2   Robustness   A (k,n) RSS scheme $(\mathbf{\Pi}, \mathbb{X})$ is $(q_r, t_r, \varepsilon_r)$-robust, if for any adversary $\mathcal{A}$ who can make q_r corrupt queries to get and tamper q_r shares (those original and tampered q_r shares form sets S'_r and S''_r, respectively) of a shared secret x, which is selected by $\mathcal{A}$ itself, and has running time within t_r, $\mathcal{A}$'s advantage to win the following experiment $\mathbf{Exp}_{\mathcal{A}}^{Rob}$, i.e., $\mathbf{Exp}_{\mathcal{A}}^{Rob}$ outputs 1, is not greater than ε_r:

$$\mathrm{Adv}_{\mathcal{A}}^{Rob}[\mathbf{\Pi}, \mathbb{X}] \triangleq \Pr[\mathbf{Exp}_{\mathcal{A}}^{Rob} = 1] \leq \varepsilon_r. \tag{2}$$

Definition and Security of RSS   Recall McEliece's secret sharing scheme based on Reed-Solomon (RS) codes [76]. Let $B = (b_1, b_2, \ldots, b_k)$ be the secret, where b_i is an m-bit symbol in $\mathbf{GF}(2^m)$. There exists a unique codeword D in the (k, n)-RS code ($n < 2^m$) with $D = (d_1, d_2, \ldots, d_n)$, where $d_i = b_i$ for $1 \leq i \leq k$. Only the rest $n - k$ symbols $\{d_i | (k + 1 \leq i \leq n)\}$ are available for distribution to those sharing the secret. Of all shares, at least k shares are required to recover the secret.

Experiment $\mathbf{Exp}_{\mathcal{A}}^{Rob}$
1) $x \leftarrow \mathcal{A}$, where $x \in \mathbb{X}$
2) $S = (S_1, \cdots, S_i, \cdots, S_n) \leftarrow$ Share(x)
3) $S_r'' \leftarrow \mathcal{A}^{\text{corrupt}(S, \cdot)}$, where $|S_r''| = q_r$
4) $x' \leftarrow$ Recover$\{S_r'' \cup (S - S_r')\}$
5) Return '1' if $x \neq x'$, else '0'.

Robustness Experiment

At a high level, RSS scheme aims at achieving resiliency by combining shares from both physical flow and information flow. Suppose there is only one case containing r tags in the physical flow, and a database as the source of an information flow. One portion of the shares (typically one share for each tag) is assigned to the tags, while the other portion of the shares is stored in the database. For a (k, n)-RS code, one may assign r shares to r tags and $n - k - r$ shares to the database (assuming $r < n - k$). It is required that any single flow can not contribute enough shares on recovering the secret (so, $r < k$ and $n - k - r < k$). In other words, the secret is recovered with shares contributed from both flows as illustrated in Fig. 2.2.

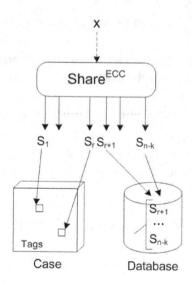

Figure 2.2: RSS Scheme [74]. A secret x is shared into $n - k$ available shares, in which r shares are distributed into r tags respectively and the other $n - k - r$ shares are stored in a database.

Ideally, all r tags in a case can be scanned for sorting out all r shares. However, 100% reading is typically not guaranteed in practice as there always be some (e.g., $2 - 3\%$) reading failures in realistic RFID deployments. Suppose all but δ tags are correctly scanned, up to $r - \delta$ shares can be obtained from the readings. Tolerating the reading errors, RSS scheme allows more shares contributed from the information flow so as to compensate the missing shares in the physical flow. To ensure this resiliency, δ more shares are required to be stored in the database.

In ECC-based secret sharing scheme, a share is a symbol in a codeword (e.g., in RS code), which is much shorter than the original secret. An adversary could launch a guessing attack to try all the possibilities of a missing share. For instance, for a RS-code on $\mathbf{GF}(2^m)$, such guessing attack needs 2^m brute-force trials. To defend against the guessing attack launched by an adversary who can scan all tags, RSS scheme requires at least t shares contributed by the server in any recovery operation. Thus, a brute-force guessing attack may take $2^{t \times m}$ trials to recover the secret. This means, given system security parameter 128 bits, and $m = 16$, one may choose $t = 8$.

According to the above requirements, RSS scheme allocates a minimum t shares and a maximum $t + \delta$ shares to be stored in the database. On the other hand, the server should not be able to calculate the secret alone with its own shares, or even in a brute force attack; therefore, it is required that $k \geq 2t + \delta$. The assumption on server is that it either collects all tags in a case and reads $r \sim r - \delta$ tags, or collects no tag/case at all. Since any combination of $r + t$ shares is enough to recover the original secret, the threshold is set to $k = r + t$. Also, $k \geq 2t + \delta$ implies $r \geq t + \delta$; otherwise, the server is able to guess up to $t - 1$ shares.

A formal definition on RSS and a theorem on its security are given below [74].

Definition 2.3 RSS Scheme   A $(k, n)_{m,t,r,\delta}$-RSS scheme is a tuple $(\boldsymbol{\Pi}^{\mathbf{ECC}}, \mathbb{X})$, satisfying $t \times m \geq \tau$ (τ is the security parameter of the system), $k = r + t, r \geq t + \delta$, and $n = 2r + 2t + \delta$; $\boldsymbol{\Pi}^{\mathbf{ECC}}$ distributes $n - k$ shares of a secret $x \in \mathbb{X}$, to the tags (totally r shares) and to the database (totally $t + \delta$ shares). Collecting $r - \delta \sim r$ shares from tags, and correspondingly, $t + \delta \sim t$ shares from the database, suffices to recover x.

Theorem 2.4 Security of RSS   (a) For $(k, n)_{m,t,r,\delta}$-RSS scheme $(\boldsymbol{\Pi}^{\mathbf{ECC}}, \mathbb{X})$, any underinformed adversary $\mathcal{A}$'s advantage is bounded by ε_p:

$$\mathrm{Adv}_{\mathcal{A}}^{Pri}[\boldsymbol{\Pi}^{ECC}, \mathbb{X}] \leq \varepsilon_p \leq 1/2^{m(k-q_p)}, \tag{3}$$

where $q_p \leq k = r + t$.

(b) For $(k, n)_{m,t,r,\delta}$-RSS scheme $(\boldsymbol{\Pi}^{\mathbf{ECC}}, \mathbb{X})$, any adversary $\mathcal{A}$ with unbounded running time making up to $q_r \leq d/2$ (or $q_r \leq \lfloor(d - 1)/2\rfloor$) corruptions has advantage zero to win the experiment $\mathbf{Exp}_{\mathcal{A}}^{Rob}$:

$$\mathrm{Adv}_{\mathcal{A}}^{Rob}[\boldsymbol{\Pi}^{ECC}, \mathbb{X}] = \varepsilon_r = 0. \tag{4}$$

Secret Generation and Sharing   Consider an example where there are totally R tags attached on goods as a batch to be transferred from **A** to **B**, via **C**. The tags in the batch are allocated equally into l cases, each having r tags ($R = l \times r$). It is assumed the batch has a suitable size such that r or R is not too big to be contained; otherwise, the batch can be considered as a number of blocks with suitable sizes, which are processed as one unit.

Before the delivery of goods, **A** generates a secret x for each case and y for the whole batch such that $x, y \in \mathbb{X}$ and $|x| = |y| = \tau$, where τ is the security parameter of the system.

At case level, **A** employs a $(k, n)_{m,t,r,\delta}$-RSS scheme according to the definition of RSS and distributes the case secret x. For all r tags in a case, **A** assigns one share to each tag. **A** also assigns $t + \delta$ shares to **C** to facilitate the verification by **C** on such case during delivery.

At batch level, **A** employs a $(K, N)_{m,t,R,\Delta}$-RSS scheme to distribute the batch secret y. For all R tags in a batch, **A** assigns one share to each tag. **A** then assigns $t + \Delta$ shares to **B** to facilitate the verification by **B** on the whole batch.

In this setting, a tag is assigned with two shares: one for the case and one for the batch. Collecting the shares from the tags, **C** and **B** can recover the case secret and batch secret, respectively, together with their contributed shares given by **A**. The schematic of RSS construction is illustrated in Fig. 2.3.

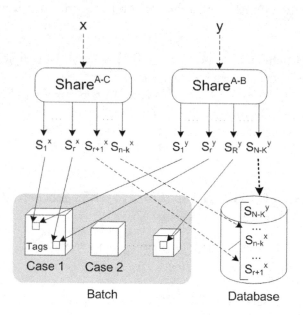

Figure 2.3: Schematic of RSS Construction [74]. The case secret x is shared for Case 1, in which r shares are distributed into tags and the rest $n - k - r$ shares are stored in the database (to be assigned to **C**); the batch secret y is shared, in which R shares are distributed into all tags in the batch and the rest $N - K - R$ shares are stored in the database (to be assigned to **B**). Thus, an encoded tag carries 2 shares.

Tag Encoding Two shares are assigned to each tag T_i, including a case share $S_i^x \leftarrow \mathsf{Share}^{\mathbf{A}-\mathbf{C}}(x)$ $(1 \leq i \leq r)$ and a batch share $S_j^y \leftarrow \mathsf{Share}^{\mathbf{A}-\mathbf{B}}(y)$ $(1 \leq j \leq R)$. The size of each share could be $m = 16$ bits, which is tiny (e.g., 32 bits in total for carrying 2 shares) and suitable to be embedded into an EPC Gen 2 tag. In practice, another 16 bits (or less) are used for making the shares in an ordered sequence. Thus, for an EPC Gen 2 tag, 48 lower significant bits (LSBs) of the EPC memory bank can be used for storing the sequence number and the shares; the other 48 bits can be left untouched for classification purpose, or filled with arbitrary random value for privacy purpose. The overall value in the EPC memory is then named as pseudo-ID (or *PID*) for a tag.

The original 96-bit EPC code, denoted as *ID*, is moved from the "EPC Memory" Bank to the "User Memory" Bank. To provide secrecy protection to the EPC code, it is stored in an encrypted form, so that no one can decrypt it and obtain the original code without a proper key. As **B** will be the next owner of the tags, **B** should possess the proper secret to decrypt the real *ID*s of received tags. Since y is the only secret shared between **A** and **B**, the encryption key e is derived from y such that $e = H(y)$, where $H(.)$ is a cryptographic hash function. Then the encryption key e is used to encrypt the EPC code (in any authenticated encryption mode): $\widetilde{ID} = Enc\_Auth(e, ID)$, where $Enc\_Auth(.)$ is any authenticated encryption algorithm.

To achieve authentication purpose, a tag's Access and Kill passwords (or PINs), denoted as *APIN* and *KPIN*, serve as authenticators by **C** or **B** on performing password-based authentication as in [77]. Slightly different from the protocol [77] on using a full (32-bit) Access password or Kill password for authentication purpose, two halves of Access and Kill passwords of a tag are used for the same purpose, such that **C** is refrained from either access or kill a tag with its own knowledge on the halves of passwords. Party **B** can still authenticate and access a tag individually, by deriving the full Access and Kill passwords.

A specific construction is to generate a half APIN and a half KPIN with **C**'s secret x, and the other halves with **B**'s secret y. Let $\kappa_{\mathbf{C}} = H(x||PID)$ and $\kappa_{\mathbf{B}} = H(y||PID)$ for a tag with EPC *PID*. The 16 lowest significant bits (LSBs) of $\kappa_{\mathbf{C}}$ are used as the 16 LSBs of *APIN*; the other 16 most significant bits (MSBs) of $\kappa_{\mathbf{C}}$ are used as the 16 LSBs of *KPIN*. Also, the 16 LSBs of $\kappa_{\mathbf{B}}$ are used as the 16 MSBs of *APIN*; the other 16 MSBs of $\kappa_{\mathbf{B}}$ are used as the 16 MSBs of *KPIN*. Thus,

$$APIN = [APIN]_{31:16}||[APIN]_{15:0} = [\kappa_{\mathbf{B}}]_{15:0}||[\kappa_{\mathbf{C}}]_{15:0}$$
$$KPIN = [KPIN]_{31:16}||[KPIN]_{15:0} = [\kappa_{\mathbf{B}}]_{31:16}||[\kappa_{\mathbf{C}}]_{31:16}$$

Note that for **C** to conduct the password-based authentication, a positive or negative result is expected from the tag indicating whether the correct halves of Access and Kill passwords are presented to it. Although this is not fully conforming with current EPC Gen 2 specifications, it is argued that achieving the above half-password-based authentication on a tag is rather simple with a re-designed circuit on the password logic.

To summarize, a tag is encoded by writing (i) the secret shares in the EPC memory, (ii) the encrypted EPC code in the user memory, and (iii) the access and kill passwords in the reserved memory.

Secret Recovery and Verification   During delivery, **C** would verify the tags in a case from time to time. Let p be the total number of collected shares in a case. If $r - \delta \leq p \leq r$, **C** can recover the secret x by contributing up to $t + r - p$ shares; otherwise, there is no enough shares for **C** to recover the secret. Based on the secret value, **C** can generate the halves of Access and Kill passwords for each tag. **C** can then authenticate each tag by performing the half-password-based authentication protocol described above.

When all goods are delivered to **B**, **B** would verify the tags in a batch. Let P denote the number of shares that **B** collects from all the cases in the batch. If $R - \Delta \leq P \leq R$, **B** can recover the secret y by contributing up to $t + R - P$ shares; otherwise, there is no enough shares for **B** to recover the secret. Based on the secret value, **B** can generate the other halves of Access and Kill passwords for each tag in the batch. **B** can obtain from **C** the complementary halves of Access and Kill passwords of each tag, or generate by itself the half passwords by collecting all shares from **C**.

Whatsoever, **B** can access all the tags and even kill all the tags as the new owner. Suppose **B** accesses a tag and reads its encrypted ID ($\widetilde{ID}$), **B** can decrypt and authenticate it with e derived from y and obtain the original EPC code of the tag.

Summary of Security Properties   We summarize the desired security properties in secure goods delivery and show how they are achieved using the RSS scheme.

► **Key distribution.** RSS scheme ensures that only **B** and **C** can derive the secrets they share with **A**. Without additional shares from **B** and **C**, no adversary can derive any secret by solely collecting shares from tags. **A** securely distributes the secrets to **B** and **C** via both physical and information flows.

► **Authentication.** **C** can verify that most tags in a batch or case are presented by recovering a secret. In addition, every single tag can be authenticated by **C** via half-password-based authentication. Similarly, **B** can verify the whole batch together and authenticate individual tags one by one.

► **Accessibility and Anti-cloning.** Only **B** except **A** can derive full Access and Kill passwords for all tags in a batch, and thus access these tags with proper passwords. No adversary, including **C**, can derive full passwords for accessing or cloning the tags.

► **Secrecy of tag ID.** Only **B** except **A** can obtain the original tag ID. The secrecy of the tag's ID is protected against **C** or any adversary.

Compared to the JPP mechanisms [73], the RSS scheme improves the security with additional shares contributed from information flow. Other than key distribution, RSS construction provides more desired security properties such as anti-cloning.

Parameterization   In real-world implementations, the "Philips UCODE" Gen 2 tag can be employed. The tag has 512 bits of on-chip memory, containing a 96-bit EPC memory, a 32-bit TID memory, a 128-bit programmable user memory and a 64-bit reserved memory for storing Access and Kill passwords. As required by the scheme, the original EPC code is replaced with the shares in EPC memory, and the encrypted (and authenticated) EPC code is stored into the user memory.

As an example, consider totally 100 tags in a batch which are packed equally into 5 cases each having 20 tags exactly. At the case level, a $(28, 60)$-RSS scheme is employed so that given a case, at least 28 shares are required to recover the case secret. The RSS scheme works over the field $GF(2^{16})$, so a share (codeword) should have 16 bits. At the beginning, **A** generates uniformly at random a 448-bit secret x for **C**. The secret is then encoded into 60 16-bit symbols with a $(28, 60)$-RS code. From which, 32 parity symbols are ready to be shared. Exactly one share is assigned to each tag and 12 shares are sent to **C** by **A**. Without the shares from **C**, one can maximally collect 20 shares from the tags so that s/he is not able to recover the secret (even by brute force attacks). Given additional shares for recovering the secret, **C** can tolerate up to 4 or 20% reading errors on scanning the tags in the case.

Similarly, at the batch level, **A** and **B** employ a $(108, 236)$-RSS scheme so that one needs to collect at least 108 shares to recover the batch secret. **A** generates uniformly at random a 1728-bit long secret y for **B**. In the working field $GF(2^{16})$, the secret is extended into 236 16-bit symbols with a $(108, 236)$-RS code, of which 128 symbols are ready to be shared. Thus, 28 shares are assigned to **B** and 100 share to the tags. With this setting, no one, except **B**, can collect more than 108 shares to successfully recover the secret. Given additional shares for recovering the secret, **B** can tolerate up to 20 or 20% errors on scanning all the tags in the batch.

As an ECC algorithm requires that the codewords be in an ordered sequence, the sequence numbers of codewords should be assigned to tags explicitly. For this reason, additional 16 bits in the EPC memory bank are used for the purpose of storing a sequence number. This allows a quite long sequence containing enough number (up to 65536) of tags in a whole batch. To this end, 48 LSBs of the EPC memory are used (to store shares and sequence number) and the other 48 MSBs are left untouched. Depending on applications, one may either retain these 48 MSBs serving as an EPC header for rough classification purpose, or fill this field with random values for privacy protection.

The next step is to encrypt the EPC code which is now set as 48 bits discarding the header. The secret y is hashed with SHA-256 and the lowest significant 128 bits of the output are taken as the encryption key. Then a block cipher (AES-128) in an authenticated encryption mode (e.g., OCB mode [78]) is applied on the EPC code with padding bits. The 128-bit encrypted and authenticated message is then stored in the user memory.

Note that both EPC memory and user memory have similar physical and deployment characteristics (regarding the *password-based lock, unlock, permalock,* and *password-based write* operations on these memory banks) according to EPCglobal Gen 2 standard [2]. To allow **B** update the tags while passing the goods to some downstream parties, the EPC memory and user memory should be rewritable. Such *(re)write* operation is typically allowed in a **secured** state, which is transitioned from an **open** state by providing the correct Access password. Only the sender **A** and the receiver **B** can derive 32-bit Access password and Kill password, while the deliverer **C** can only derive the lower halves of the passwords. Note that it is not practical for **C** to access or kill a tag with the knowledge of the halves of its passwords, since guessing the other half of the Access password needs 2^{16} trials on the tag, which could be efficiently prevented by tag manufacture's disabling the tag when multiple false passwords are tried (to thwart denial of service attack by anyone but **C**, a false password is counted only if the lower half of the password is correct).

The following parameters should be known in practice: the total number of tags in a batch, the number of tags r in a case, and the threshold values k and K on recovering the secrets. In the example given above, the tags are formatted with $(28, 60)$-RSS scheme for a case and $(108, 236)$-RSS scheme for a batch. The thresholds k and K can be set small (e.g., $k = 28$, $K = 108$) but a bit greater than the total number of tags in a case or batch so that the recovery of secrets must involve additional shares from **C** or **B**, instead of solely depends on reading all the tags in a case or batch. On the other hand, n or N should be chosen properly to maximally tolerate reading errors (20% for example) in a case or batch.

Recall that it is required $r \geq t + \delta$ in the definition of RSS scheme. If the number r of tags in a case is relatively small, one can adjust some parameters in RSS scheme. Without loss of security, one may put multiple shares on a tag or enlarge the size of a single share to minimize the value of t. For instance, if there are only 2 tags in a case, one can use $(8, 16)_{32,4,2,0}$-RSS scheme with 2 shares on a tag or $(4, 8)_{64,2,2,0}$-RSS scheme with one big share on a tag. In an extreme case where there is only one tag per case, a $(2, 4)_{96,1,1,0}$-RSS scheme can be used for filling tag EPC memory with a single share so as to achieve a maximum 96-bit security.

A Note on Group Authentication and Grouping Proof   Group authentication means that only certain groups of valid tags are accepted as a whole (instead of individually) by a valid reader. Group authentication is particularly useful in some application scenarios such as third party logistics (3PL), where a third party delivering tagged items should be able to authenticate a group (case or batch) of tags without the capability of identifying or cloning individual tags. The secret sharing schemes presented in this section, including TSS, SWISS, and RSS, can be used for group authentication of EPC Gen 2 tags which tolerate certain error readings as common in practice.

Group authentication is slightly different from grouping proof [79, 81, 82, 83, 84] where a reader aims to prove to a verifier that a group of tags coexist or are processed together. In grouping proof, the reader is not trusted in a sense that it cannot generate a grouping proof without reading the corresponding tags; it is the verifier who authenticates the group of tags by verifying the grouping proof submitted by the reader. In comparison, group authentication enables a reader to authenticate a group of tags directly without involving a verifier. In 3PL applications, a reader in group authentication is not fully trusted in a sense that it cannot identify or clone individual tags.

The RSS scheme is designed for group authentication of low-cost tags such as EPC Gen 2 tags. For crypto tags, Cai et al. proposed two other group authentication schemes in 3PL supply chain scenario [80], one based on aggregate MAC, and the other based on aggregate signature. These two schemes, however, are not resilient to any error readings.

2.3   PATH AUTHENTICATION

RFID path authentication means that a valid reader accepts only those tags that have passed through valid paths, where a valid path is a legitimate sequence of steps/readers which a valid tag could pass. Path authentication is different from tag authentication since the latter does not verify the path through which a tag passes.

An RFID system with multiple valid readers (which may have different identities or are owned by different parties) and one or more valid paths are often referred to as an RFID-enabled supply chain. Path authentication in RFID-enabled supply chains can help thwart clone tags, faked products and counterfeit products, which are serious concerns in supply chain management. According to 2011 report of International Chamber of Commerce, it is estimated that the counterfeit products account for 5-7% of world trade, or about 600 billion U.S. dollars per year [85].

A straightforward way of verifying a tag's path is to ask each reader who has processed the tag to report to a central server, e.g., EPCDS, about the tag's ID, the reader's ID, and possibly the time the tag is processed. Assuming that the central server knows all possible valid paths for all tags, it can verify whether any tag passes a valid path or not.

However, this straightforward solution requires that the central server be online and that each reader report to the server in time about every tag being processed. It may not be practical to meet such requirements, especially when a large number of tags need to be processed and verified. To relax this requirement, various path authentication solutions have been proposed, which leverage on RFID tags to store path information.

In this section, we introduce a few typical RFID path authentication solutions which are suitable for processing low-cost tags such as EPC Gen 2 tags. We focus on path authentication without any privacy features in this section and leave the complete versions of these solutions with additional privacy features to Section 3.5.

2.3.1   TRACKER

Blass et al. proposed a path authentication solution, named TRACKER, which is suitable for EPC Gen 2 tags [86]. TRACKER does not rely on a centralized server to collect and store path information from readers; instead, it relies on each tag to store its path information, which is updated by each reader along its path, and finally verified by a manager against a set of valid paths. After an initialization stage, all readers and the manager can work offline.

TRACKER System   In TRACKER, an RFID-enabled supply chain is defined as a digraph $G = (V, E)$ with vertices V and edges E. Each vertex $v_i \in V$ represents a step in supply chain, which is uniquely associated with a reader R_i. Each edge $e = \overrightarrow{v_i v_j} \in E$ indicates that step v_j is a possible next step to step v_i in the supply chain. Whenever a tagged product proceeds from v_i to v_j, the reader R_j interacts with the tag attached to the product.

A tag T_i is an EPC Gen 2 tag with re-writable memory representing the tag's current state, denoted $s_{T_i}^j$. Let $\mathcal{S}$ denote all possible states (e.g., $|\mathcal{S}| > 2^{160}$). When a reader R_k interacts with tag T_i, R_k reads out T_i's current stage $s_{T_i}^j$ and writes an updated state $s_{T_i}^{j+1}$ into T_i. The updated state is generated by R_k with a function $f_{R_k}: s_{T_i}^{j+1} = f_{R_k}(s_{T_i}^j)$.

A path is a sequence of steps $\mathcal{P} = \{v_0, \ldots v_\ell\}$ such that for each $0 \le i < \ell$, $\overrightarrow{v_i v_{i+1}} \in E$ (note that v_{i+1} can be the same as v_i in TRACKER), where ℓ is the length of $\mathcal{P}$. A valid path $\mathcal{P}_{valid_i}$ is a path representing a particular legitimate sequence of steps in the supply chain against which a tag is checked in path authentication. There are total v different valid paths, denoted as $\mathcal{S}_{valid} = \{\mathcal{P}_{valid_1}, \ldots, \mathcal{P}_{valid_v}\}$ in the supply chain.

There are an issuer I and a manager M in TRACKER, where the issuer I is responsible for initializing TRACKER and preparing all tags for deployment (I is represented as the only vertex in G with indegree zero), while the manager M is responsible for path authentication when a tag arrives at a specific step in supply chain, called a checkpoint. There could be multiple checkpoints in a supply chain.

Polynomial Path Encoding In TRACKER, a path $\mathcal{P} = \{v_0, \ldots v_\ell\}$ is represented as a polynomial in Galois Field $\mathbf{F}_q$, where q is a large prime. The polynomial corresponding to path $\mathcal{P}$ is given below:

$$Q_{\mathcal{P}}(x) = a_0 x^\ell + \sum_{i=1}^{\ell} a_i x^{\ell-i} \tag{2.1}$$

where all coefficients and operations are in $\mathbf{F}_q$. Given a path $\mathcal{P}$, a path mark $\phi(\mathcal{P})$ is defined as the evaluation of $Q_{\mathcal{P}}(x)$ at x_0, where x_0 is a generator of $\mathbf{F}_q^*$. The probability that two different paths result in the same path mark is $1/q$ [92].

TRACKER Initialization Issuer I selects a generator x_0 of the finite field $\mathbf{F}_q$, and selects randomly a value $a_0 \in \mathbf{F}_q$, where q is a large prime with length $|q| = 160$ bits. I also generates a random bit string k_0 with length $|k_0| = 160$ bits. The initial step v_0, which represents the issuer, is associated with (x_0, a_0, k_0).

Let $\eta = |V|$ be the number of steps/readers in the supply chain. For each reader R_i, $1 \le i \le \eta$, issuer I generates a random number $a_i \in \mathbf{F}_q$ and a random bit string k_i of 160 bits. I sends to each R_i, which represents step v_i, the tuple (x_0, a_i, k_i) using a secure channel.

Also using a secure channel, Issuer I sends to manager M the following information: x_0 and (i, a_i, k_i) for $0 \le i \le \eta$. It is assumed that M knows all valid paths in $\mathcal{S}_{valid}$; then M computes path marks $\phi(\mathcal{P}_{valid})$ and records pairs $(\mathcal{P}_{valid}, \phi(\mathcal{P}_{valid}))$ for all valid paths $\mathcal{P}_{valid} \in \mathcal{S}_{valid}$. M also initiates a database DB_{clone} to be empty for clone tag detection.

For each new tag T entering the supply chain, issuer I writes into the tag an initial state $s_T^0 = (ID, \phi^0, \sigma^0)$, where ID is the tag's ID value, $\phi^0 = a_0$ is the path mark for step v_0, and $\sigma^0 = HMAC_{k_0}(ID)$ is an HMAC signature combining ID and step v_0.

Tag and Reader Interaction   Assume that tag T arrives at step v_i after taking path $\mathcal{P} = \overrightarrow{v_0 v_1 \cdots v_{i-1}}$. At step v_i, reader R_i reads out the tag's current state $s_T^{i-1} = (ID, \phi^{i-1}, \sigma^{i-1})$. With (x_0, a_i, k_i), reader R_i computes a new state $s_T^i = (ID, \phi^i, \sigma^i)$ and writes it into T, where

$$
\begin{aligned}
\phi^i &= \phi^{i-1} x_0 + a_i \\
\sigma^i &= HMAC_{k_i}(\sigma^{i-1}).
\end{aligned}
$$

With $|q| = 160$ bits and HMAC of output size of 160 bits, the storage requirement on each tag is $3 \cdot 160 = 480$ bits, which is suitable for EPC Gen 2 tags.

Path Verification   When tag T arrives at a checkpoint in supply chain, manager M reads out the tag's state $s_T^\ell = (ID, \phi^\ell, \sigma^\ell)$. First, M checks whether ID is in DB_{clone}. If $ID \in DB_{clone}$, then M outputs and rejects T. In such a case, T is considered as a clone tag since it has been accepted by the manager before and thus it appears in DB_{clone}.

Otherwise, M checks whether ϕ^ℓ is a valid path mark in its list of pairs $(\mathcal{P}_{valid}, \phi(\mathcal{P}_{valid}))$ for all $\mathcal{P}_{valid} \in \mathcal{S}_{valid}$. If there is no match, M outputs and rejects T.

If there is a match $\phi^\ell = \phi(\mathcal{P}_{valid_i})$, M checks whether T's signature σ^ℓ satisfies the following equation assuming $\mathcal{P}_{valid_i} = \overrightarrow{v_0 v_1 \cdots v_\ell}$:

$$
\sigma^\ell = HMAC_{k_\ell}(HMAC_{k_{\ell-1}}(\cdots HMAC_{k_0}(ID))).
$$

If the above equation holds, M outputs $\mathcal{P}_{valid_i}$ and adds ID into DB_{clone}; otherwise, M outputs and rejects T.

Security Claims and Comments   The security of TRACKER can be evaluated with respect to soundness and completeness in the presence of attacks. Soundness means that if a valid path $\mathcal{P}_{valid}$ of tag T is returned by manager M, then T must have gone through path $\mathcal{P}_{valid}$ exactly in the supply chain. Completeness means that if T has gone through a valid path $\mathcal{P}_{valid}$ when it arrives at a checkpoint, manager M must return $\mathcal{P}_{valid}$.

An adversary in TRACKER is modeled to have full control over the network and know about the validity of tags' states. In a learning stage, the adversary can move forward all tags in supply chain, select tags, read and re-write tags, and query for tag states. The adversary is not assumed to know any secret information from issuer, manager or any readers. In a challenge stage, the adversary may choose any tag, read and re-write with any state information; alternatively, the adversary may create a new tag and write some state in it.

TRACKER is said to be secure in terms of soundness if an adversary is not able to generate a state corresponding to a valid path with a probability higher than simply guessing, where the probability of simple guessing is $|\mathcal{S}_{valid}|/|\mathcal{S}|$. The completeness of TRACKER cannot be guaranteed since any adversary can simply write arbitrary information into a tag and thus spoil its path

detection. The completeness of TRACKER could be assumed if all valid tags are write-protected with access passwords; nonetheless, the distribution of access passwords must be addressed appropriately.

2.3.2   OTHER PATH AUTHENTICATION SOLUTIONS

The major advantage of TRACKER is that it does not need the steps (readers or parties) in a supply chain to have any connections except at the initialization stage, and it does not require any readers to be online for updating any tags' path information. The major restrictions of TRACKER include: (i) the path authentication can be carried out by a trusted third party (manager M) only; (ii) it requires the manager to possess secrets of all involving steps; and (iii) it assumes that the manager knows all valid paths before path authentication. These constraints imply that it is difficult to enable on-site path verification, especially in dynamic supply chains. Other path authentication solutions are proposed to relax the constraints.

Checker   In [88], Elkhiyaoui et al. proposed CHECKER, to enable each reader in supply chain to perform path authentication instead of global path authentication performed by a trusted third party at checkpoints. In CHECKER, it is assumed that each reader R_k knows a set $S_k = \{\mathcal{P}_k^1, \ldots \mathcal{P}_k^{\nu_k}\}$ of ν_k valid paths leading to it. For each valid path $\mathcal{P}_k^j$ with path mark $\phi(\mathcal{P}_k^j)$, issuer I generates a verification key $K_k^j = h^{\phi(\mathcal{P}_k^j)}$ and sends it to reader R_k via a secure channel, where h is a generator of a subgroup of $\mathcal{E}$ of a large prime order q, and $\mathcal{E}$ is an elliptic curve over a finite field F_p (e.g., $|p| = |q| = 160$ bits).

In CHECKER, each tag T is stored with a state $s_T^j = (ID, \sigma_{\mathcal{P}}(ID))$, where $\sigma_{\mathcal{P}}(ID) = H(ID)^{\phi(\mathcal{P})}$ is a signature on the tag's ID. The signing key of this signature is the path mark $\phi(\mathcal{P})$ of the path $\mathcal{P}$ which the tag goes through.

Assume that the tag T with state s_T^j arrives at reader R_k. To verify whether the tag has gone through a valid path or not, reader R_k checks whether there is a verification key $K_k^i = h^{\phi(\mathcal{P}_k^i)}$ in its record satisfying

$$e(\sigma_{\mathcal{P}}(ID), h) = e(H(ID), K_k^i) = e(H(ID), h^{\phi(\mathcal{P}_k^i)}),$$

where $e : \mathbf{G}_1 \times \mathbf{G}_2 \to \mathbf{G}_T$ is a bilinear pairing given subgroups $\mathbf{G}_1, \mathbf{G}_2$, and $\mathbf{G}_T$ of $\mathcal{E}$ of prime order q. If there is a match, then tag T has gone through a valid path $\mathcal{P} = \mathcal{P}_k^i$ leading to R_k; otherwise, the tag is rejected.

If the tag's state $s_T^j = (ID, \sigma_{\mathcal{P}}(ID))$ is valid, the signature $\sigma_{\mathcal{P}}(ID)$ is updated by reader R_k as: $\sigma_{\mathcal{P}}(ID)^{x_0} H(ID)^{a_k} = H(ID)^{x_0 \phi(\mathcal{P}) + a_k}$.

Compared to TRACKER, CHECKER treats each reader as a manager so that it can verify tag paths according to a set of verification keys corresponding to valid paths known to the reader. Instead of storing a path mark and an HMAC signature on a tag, CHECKER stores a single path signature on the tag. While the manager in TRACKER uses a path mark as an index in verifying a tag's state, each reader in CHECKER searches among all verification keys (or all valid paths

leading to the reader) in verifying a tag's state. It is clear that a tradeoff can be made between tag storage and the efficiency in verifying a tag's state.

PRF-Based Path Authentication   Cai et al. proposed a path authentication solution without using a polynomial to represent a path [91]. Instead, it uses a pseudorandom function (PRF) to generate a path signature, in a way similar to the HMAC signature used in TRACKER.

In the initialization stage, issuer I generates a random secret key k_j for each reader R_j and sends it to R_j via a secure channel. Issuer I generates a random key k_0 for itself, which is the starting point of all valid paths. For each tag T_i, issuer I writes an initial state $(ID_i, PRF_{k_0}(ID_i))$ to the tag, where ID_i is the tag ID, and PRF_{k_0} is a PRF function with parameter k_0.

It is assumed that each tag T_i goes through a valid path $\mathcal{P}_i = (R_{i_0}, R_{i_1}, \dots R_{i_\ell})$ from issuer I to manager M. Knowing this fact, issuer I computes $v_i = PRF_{k_{i_\ell}}(PRF_{k_{i_{\ell-1}}}(\cdots PRF_{k_0}(ID_i)))$ and stores a copy of (ID_i, v_i) in manager M's database.

When tag T_i reaches reader R_j, reader R_j reads out the tag's current state (ID_i, v_i), and updates v_i with $PRF_{k_j}(v_i)$ in the tag. When the tag arrives at a checkpoint, manager M reads out the tag's state (ID_i, v_i) and checks whether there is a same tuple in M's database for path authentication.

It is not difficult to extend this solution to a more general case in which each tag may go though multiple valid paths. It is also easy to extend this solution to a case where each reader can perform path authentication provided that each reader knows all valid paths leading to it.

Distributed Path Authentication   Cai et al. proposed a distributed path authentication scheme which can be used in dynamic supply chains [89]. Similar to CHECKER [88], this solution allows each reader to perform path authentication. The difference is that it is not assumed that each reader knows all valid paths leading to it as well as corresponding path verification keys; instead, it involves a trusted server to store and update all valid paths as well as corresponding path verification keys. Similar to TRACKER [86], each tag's state consists of a tag ID, a path mark, and a path signature on tag ID. While the tag ID and the path mark are the same as used in TRACKER, the path signature is formed using an ordered multisignature scheme (OMS) proposed by Boldyreva et al. [93]. The path signature can be verified by any reader using appropriate path verification keys, which can be obtained by querying the trusted server with corresponding path mark. After the path signature is verified, the current reader may update the path mark and the path signature using its own secret keys. Finally, the current reader queries the trusted server again: if the updated path mark is new in the server's record, then the current reader updates the server with a new valid path and corresponding verification key for future path authentication.

To reduce the reliance on the trusted server in path authentication, each reader may cache path marks and path verification keys so that it does not need to query the trusted server in path authentication unless the path mark is not in its cache.

Compared to CHECKER [88], all valid paths and verification keys are maintained by a trusted server rather than by each reader. This solution is more suitable to be used in a dynamic supply chain where readers may leave or join the supply chain freely and where existing valid paths may be updated at any time. Another difference is that CHECKER involves exhaustive search on verification keys due to no use of path mark in tag state, while in this distributed path authentication scheme, path mark is used to index path verification key in the trusted server.

Compared to TRACKER [86] and PRF-based path authentication [91], which require that all tags start from the issuer and that the manager knows all valid paths and all secret information of all readers, the distributed path authentication scheme assumes that all readers are independent: each reader does not share its secret with any other readers or trusted server; each reader is able to initialize tags, perform path authentication, and update valid paths.

Two-Level Path Authentication   Wang et al. proposed a two-level path authentication protocol in EPCglobal Network structure [90]. In this protocol, a tag's path can be generated dynamically without a centralized control where each reader in a tag's path can verify the tag's path using the reader's own private key. This protocol can be performed at two levels, within EPCIS and among EPCIS. Within EPCIS, all tag paths are constructed as a tree structure in which a parent node/reader generates a private key for each of its son nodes/readers. Among EPCIS, a tag's state is signed by the current EPCIS and encrypted using the next EPCIS' public key. This protocol may not be practical as a reader's private key is generated by its parent reader; a parent reader may impersonate its son nodes in path authentication.

2.4   CLONE TAG DETECTION

Clone tag detection aims to detect faked products and counterfeit products, which are major concerns in global supply chains. While clone tags may be prevented with tag authentication, group authentication, or path authentication, all such prevention based solutions require secret keys and security primitives to be used, which lead to either high cost or low efficiency in practice. Another issue of such solutions is that once an adversary compromises the secret keys which are used, the adversary is able to clone tags.

In principle, clone tag detection can be performed via continuous monitoring of tags which are processed by multiple readers or parties. However, real world applications of RFID technology such as supply chain management often contain blind zones where tag readings are unavailable or not reported [94]. A practical approach to clone tag detection should be robust against blind zones and reader errors and should be suitable for detecting standard low-cost tags such as EPC Gen 2 tags.

Zanetti et al. proposed such an approach named *tailing* [94]. Tailing requires a non-interactive centralized detector to detect clone tags with no modification of existing supply chain data flow. The visibility of the detector is limited to a subset of readers which participate in clone detection and may be affected by blind zones and reader errors in practice. The detector is assumed to have no pre-defined information about supply chain structure or product flow; therefore, tailing can be used in dynamic supply chains where supply chain partners may join or leave continuously and where product flow may change unpredictably (e.g., due to recalls and misdeliveries).

Adversary Model   The adversary model used in tailing is strong in a sense that an adversary controls a subset of readers and it may corrupt some readers participating in clone detection. At a corrupted reader, an adversary may simulate the presence of an RFID tag, block the scanning of selected nearby tags, and modify the data contents except for tag IDs of passing tags. Note that the IDs of valid tags are assumed to be read-only, which cannot be modified by an adversary.

At any point in a supply chain, an adversary may insert a clone tag, which carries a valid tag ID appearing in the supply chain. It is assumed that the clone tag must appear after the corresponding genuine tag enters the supply chain (in a verifiable event called into-the-chain) and before it leaves the chain (in a verifiable event called out-of-the-chain); otherwise, it can be easily detected in a whitelist-based detection.

An adversary is assumed to know all the paths of valid tags (or genuine products) and clone tags (or counterfeit products). However, the adversary is not capable of modifying the paths of valid tags, or the timing of valid tags spending in different steps of supply chain.

Tailing   In tailing, each tag stores a *tag tail* and a *tail pointer* for clone detection besides the tag's normal data content (e.g., EPC and access password). A tag tail consists of a sequence of random bits[1]. When a tag goes through a series of readers participating in clone detection, the n-th reader writes a random bit in the (n mod t)-th position in the tag's tail, where t is the size of the tag tail in bits. Without requiring that each reader know its position in writing, a tail pointer is used to record the most recently tail position which is written in each tag.

More precisely, when a tag passes a reader, the reader (i) reads out the tag's ID, tail, and tail pointer, (ii) increments the tail pointer by 1 mod t and stores it in the tag's memory, (iii) generates a random bit and writes to the tag's tail indexed by the tail pointer, and (iv) creates a tag event with attributes (ID, T, L, S, TT, TP, TF) in its local database, where ID is the tag's ID, T is the timestamp for processing this tag, L is the location in which the tag is processed, S indicates the type of event process (e.g., receiving, stocking, or shipping), TT is the tag tail, TP is the tag's pointer, and TF is a tailing flag which is used to indicate whether the reader participates in the clone detection for this tag.

Upon requested by a supply chain partner for clone detection on a particular tag, the centralized detector collects all of the events about this tag from participating readers. The collected events form the tag's trace. For each pair of time-consecutive events e_i and e_{i+1} in the trace, the following rules are verified:

$$TT_{i+1}[n] = TT_i[n], \text{ for all } n \neq TP_{i+1}$$
$$TP_{i+1} - TP_i = 1 \text{ (mod } t)$$

---

[1]In general, a tag tail consists of a sequence of random symbols; it is shown that the use of 1-bit symbols is better than multi-bit symbols in terms of the probability in clone detection [94].

where TT_i and TP_i are tag tail and tail pointer in event e_i, respectively, and TT_{i+1} and TP_{i+1} are tag tail and tail pointer in event e_{i+1}, respectively. If any pair fails the rule verification, it shows an evidence of cloning.

Evaluation of Tailing   Clone detection may fail due to two reasons: false event consistency and weak visibility. False event consistency means suppression or loss of clone evidence due to attacks. This can certainly happen in the extreme case in which an adversary controls all the readers through which a clone tag passes. In other cases, the probability of detection failure (i.e., false negative) should be measured on how difficult an adversary can make a clone tag tail and tail pointer consistent with corresponding genuine tag in different settings.

Another reason for clone detection to fail is weak visibility, which is a result of blind zones and reader errors in practice. Weak visibility is modelled by the existence of misevents, misreads, and miswrites in processing tags by participating readers. A misevent happens when an event relevant to clone detection is not reported to the detector, while the involving tag's tail and tail pointer are correctly updated. The lost event may lead to a false positive in clone detection since two reported time-consecutive events, the event right before the lost event and the event right after, are not consistent.

A misread occurs when a tag is not read by a reader which participates in clone detection; consequently, no tail update or event creation is performed. A misread may lead to false negative since a cloned tag may pass unnoticed due to misread.

Finally, a miswrite means that a tag write operation fails after performing a read operation correctly. In this situation, a reader should flag the tailing flag of created event so as to make the event unusable by the detector. A miswrite happens when a reader (i) receives a write failure message, or receives no reply when writing a tag. In this latter case, the tag's memory is either (ii) not modified, or (iii) correctly modified, or (iv) incorrectly modified. The above cases (i) and (ii) are similar to a misread, case (iii) is comparable to a misevent, and case (iv) creates inconsistencies which may raise a false positive in clone detection.

The false negative rate, or an adversary's success probability of avoiding clone detection, can be measured analytically. The false negative rate is limited in tailing even if an adversary corrupts a majority of readers in a clone path. For example, blocking 2, 3, 4 out of 5 readers randomly gives false negative rate of 0.81, 3.6, and 12.5%, respectively. If the adversary chooses the optimal strategy in attacks, corrupting 2, 3, 4 out of 5 readers leads to false negative rate of 15, 52, and 90%, respectively. The false negative rate due to misreads can be analyzed similarly as random blocking of readers.

Formally, let $E = (\epsilon_0, \ldots \epsilon_n)$ denote a sequence of clone evidences (a clone evidence is a pair of time-consecutive events involving a clone event and a genuine event) observed by the detector. The probability P_{pass} that all clone evidences pass rule verification is

$$P_{pass}(E) = (\frac{1}{2^{t-1+\log t}})^{a_0} \cdot \sum_{i=1}^{n} (\frac{1}{2^{t-1}})^{a_i} b_i,$$

where $\log t$ is the entropy of tail pointer, $a_i = 0$ when an adversary cancels out evidence ϵ_i (otherwise, $a_i = 1$), $b_i = 0$ when the number of events (no matter clone or genuine events) between evidence ϵ_{i-1} and ϵ_i is not a multiple of t (otherwise, $b_i = 1$). The overall adversary's success probability can be written as

$$P_{succ} = \sum_E Prob(E) \cdot P_{pass}(E),$$

where $Prob(E)$ is the probability of clone evidence sequence E appearing among all possible clone evidence sequences which could be observed by the detector. Note that the above analysis depends on an adversary's capability which affects the values of $Prob(E)$, a_i, and b_i. A hierarchy of adversaries with increasing capability is modeled in [94], including the following.

- An adversary inserts clone tags at selected points without corrupting readers.

- An adversary can corrupt a set of readers chosen randomly on a clone path. However, the adversary has no knowledge of genuine paths.

- An adversary can eavesdrop on a genuine path so as to inject clones with correct memory content.

- An adversary knows relative event timestamps and genuine paths. After injecting a clone with correct memory content, it can corrupt any reader in its path to cancel out clone evidence in certain attack strategy.

The higher the adversary's capability, the higher the percentage of clone evidence sequences leading to $P_{pass} = 1$. On the other hand, it is shown in tailing that the negative impacts (i.e., false positives) due to misevents and miswrites can be mitigated without increasing the false negative rate significantly. Misevents can be mitigated by tolerating a particular type of tail and pointer inconsistencies between two reported time-consecutive events assuming that there could be some misevents in between. Miswrites are mitigated by recording write failures if a reader does not receive a correct write response from a tag. If an event is marked as write-failure, then the inconsistencies between this event and succeeding event are ignored in clone detection.

Recent Development on Batch Clone Detection   A major challenge in supply chain management is to efficiently handle a increasing number of RFID products. The tailing approach suffers from performance bottlenecks because a centralized detector records and analyzes traces of individual products. A practical solution should work efficiently in real-world RFID systems, where products are moved and processed in batches. The authors of this book are currently working on a batch clone detection scheme which can solve the above challenges. It requires a few bits of storage in RFID tags and it is suitable for standard EPC Gen 2 tags. Clone detection is performed on batch level, which significantly reduces the storage and computational overheads.

CHAPTER 3

RFID Privacy at the Physical Level

In the previous chapter, we focus on RFID security at the physical level, which requires that RFID identification process should be performed correctly in the presence of attacks. In this chapter, we shift our focus on RFID privacy at the physical level, which *further* requires that an adversary cannot obtain any un-authorized information in its attacks to RFID identification process. Note that it is meaningless to achieve RFID privacy without first achieving RFID security at the physical level.

One type of un-authorized information which should be protected for RFID privacy at the physical level is RFID tag identity. To protect tag ID, a unique pseudonym, instead of true tag ID, could be stored in each RFID tag and used in RFID identification process. An authorized reader can identify a tag according to its pseudonym given access to a mapping from tag pseudonym to tag ID. An adversary cannot obtain a tag ID from RFID identification process without compromising an RFID reader or getting access to the mapping.

Another type of un-authorized information which should be protected for RFID privacy at the physical level is tag traceability. If a fixed pseudonym is sent by a tag whenever it is read, an adversary, who is able to read RFID tags everywhere, can trace the movement of any particular tag. Even without knowing the true ID of any tag, such adversary may infer much valuable information in RFID applications. For example, in RFID-enabled supply chain management, an adversary who can trace RFID tags may infer valuable information about its competitors, such as inventory levels, trading partners, trading volumes, and trading strategies. In the case where an individual person carries a set of RFID tags (e.g., in the person's wallet and clothes), a combination of the tags in fixed pseudonyms can be used to identify and trace the person.

A typical solution to achieve anti-tracing in RFID protocol design is to ensure that each time a tag is queried, it replies with a different "pseudonym." Recall the tag authentication protocol between a reader and a tag based on symmetric key in Section 2.1.2:

1. the reader generates a random bit string r and sends it to the tag;

2. the tag computes $h = F_{k_i}(r)$ and transmits h and its ID value ID_i to the reader; and

3. the reader authenticates the tag by verifying that $h = F_{k_i}(r)$ according to k_i indexed by ID_i,

where k_i is a secret key stored in tag T_i, and F_k is a keyed one-way function with key k. Clearly, this protocol is subject to tag identity attack since a tag's ID is given in the tag's reply. This protocol can be easily modified to protect tag identity as follows:

1. the reader generates a random bit string r and sends it to the tag;

2. the tag computes $h = F_{k_i}(r)$ and transmits h to the reader; and

3. the reader authenticates the tag by verifying that $h = F_{k_i}(r)$ for an existing pair (k_i, ID_i) in its database.

However, this revised protocol is subject to tag traceability attack since an adversary can use the same r to query all tags at different locations all the time so that a target tag can be traced with the same "pseudonym" h. To address this issue, the protocol can be further revised as:

1. the reader generates a random bit string r_1 and sends it to the tag;

2. the tag generates another random bit string r_2, computes $h = F_{k_i}(r_1, r_2)$ and transmits r_2, h to the reader; and

3. the reader authenticates the tag by verifying that $h = F_{k_i}(r_1, r_2)$ for an existing pair (k_i, ID_i) in its database.

In this protocol, a tag's reply to any query (even if the same query is repetitively sent by an adversary) is randomized due to the use of tag random r_2. Such technique can be used to achieve RFID privacy in RFID protocol design.

The notion of RFID privacy in terms of anti-tracing can be extended from uncorrupted tags to corrupted ones, leading to the notions of forward privacy and backward privacy. Intuitively, forward privacy means that an adversary cannot trace a tag according to the tag's past communication messages before the tag is corrupted by the adversary. Backward privacy means that an adversary cannot trace a tag even after the tag is corrupted by the adversary. A tag being corrupted means that all information stored in the tag at the moment of tag corruption is available to an adversary.

Note that in Section 2.1.3, many authentication protocols are designed to have additional privacy features such as anti-tracing and forward privacy. The anti-tracing property is usually achieved by randomizing a tag's reply, while forward privacy can be achieved by updating a tag's secret during authentication process. In the former case, it is possible to reduce the complexity of identifying a tag from exhaustive search to tree-based search or table look-up. In the latter case, desynchronization threats should be addressed so as to make the updated secret consistent on the reader side and on the tag side.

In this chapter, we focus on various RFID privacy notions which define what anti-tracing means in an RFID system where an adversary exists. The adversary's goal is to trace a target tag, which could be modeled as wining a privacy game with a probability higher than a random guess or distinguishing between an adversary's world and a simulator's world.

We first consider the privacy notions in a single-reader system, including indistinguishability based privacy, unpredictability based privacy, zero-knowledge based privacy, Vaudenay's privacy framework, and universal composibility based privacy. We analyze and compare these RFID privacy notions. We also discuss RFID privacy notions in a multi-reader system, including path privacy and ownership transfer. In this chapter, we clarify that all privacy notions are investigated at protocol level instead of at lower levels such as tracing based on fingerprints of radio frequency signals or based on physical appearance of products/tags.

3.1 INDISTINGUISHABILITY-BASED PRIVACY AND UNPREDICTABILITY-BASED PRIVACY

Intuitively, indistinguishability-based privacy means that an adversary cannot distinguish between two uncorrupted tags, and unpredictability-based privacy means that an adversary cannot distinguish the protocol message between a reader and an uncorrupted tag from a dummy message generated randomly. Both privacy notions imply that an adversary cannot trace an uncorrupted tag in an RFID system.

3.1.1 PRELIMINARIES

To provide formal definitions on the privacy notions, we need to provide a formal treatment of underlying math notation, pseudorandom functions, RFID system model, adversary model, completeness, and soundness of RFID systems [95, 97].

Mathematical Notation If $A(\cdot, \cdot, ...)$ is a randomized algorithm, then $y \leftarrow A(x_1, x_2, ...; cn)$ means that y is assigned with the unique output of algorithm A on inputs $x_1, x_2, ...$ and coins cn, while $y \leftarrow A(x_1, x_2, ...)$ is a shorthand for first picking cn at random and then setting $y \leftarrow A(x_1, x_2, ...; cn)$. Let $y \leftarrow A^{O_1, ..., O_n}(x_1, x_2, ...)$ denote that y is assigned with the output of algorithm A which takes $x_1, x_2, ...$ as inputs and has oracle accesses to $O_1, ..., O_n$. If S is a set, then $s \in_R S$ indicates that s is chosen uniformly at random from S. If $x_1, x_2, ...$ are strings, then $x_1 || x_2 || \cdots$ denotes the concatenation of them. If x is a string, then $|x|$ denotes its bit length in binary code. If S is a set, then $|S|$ denotes its cardinality (i.e., the number of elements of S). Let $\Pr[E]$ denote the probability that an event E occurs, $\mathbb{N}$ denote the set of all nonnegative integers, and $\mathbb{R}$ denote the set of all real numbers.

Definition 3.1 Negligible Function A function $f : \mathbb{N} \to \mathbb{R}$ is said to be *negligible* if for every $c > 0$ there exits a number $m \in \mathbb{N}$ such that $f(n) < \frac{1}{n^c}$ holds for all $n > m$.

Pseudorandom Functions Let $F : \mathcal{K} \times \mathcal{D} \to \mathcal{R}$ be a family of functions, where $\mathcal{K}$ is the set of keys (or indexes) of F, $\mathcal{D}$ is the domain of F, and $\mathcal{R}$ is the range of F. Let $|\mathcal{K}| = \gamma$, $|\mathcal{D}| = m$, and $|\mathcal{R}| = n$. Let $\mathsf{Rand}^{\mathcal{D} \to \mathcal{R}}$ be the family of all functions with domain $\mathcal{D}$ and range $\mathcal{R}$. A *polynomial time predictable test* (*PTPT*) for F is an experiment, where a probabilistic polynomial

$$\text{Exp}_T^{ptpt}(F, \gamma, m, n)$$

1. $b \in_R \{0, 1\}$
2. if $b = 1$ then $k \in_R \mathcal{K}$ and set $f = F_k$,
   otherwise $f \in_R \text{Rand}^{\mathcal{D} \to \mathcal{R}}$
3. $b' \leftarrow T^{O_f}$

Figure 3.1: Polynomial time predictable test.

time algorithm T, given γ, m, n as input and with access to an oracle O_f for a function $f \in_R$ F or $f \in_R \text{Rand}^{\mathcal{D} \to \mathcal{R}}$, outputs either 0 or 1. Figure 3.1 shows a PTPT for F.

Definition 3.2   An algorithm T passes *PTPT* for function family F if it correctly guesses the random bit which is selected by the *PTPT* experiment, i.e., $b' = b$. The advantage of algorithm T is defined as

$$\text{Adv}_T(\gamma, m, n) = |\Pr[b' = b] - \frac{1}{2}|, \tag{3.1}$$

where the probability is taken over the choice of f in F and the coin tosses of algorithm T.

Definition 3.3   Pseudorandom Function Family   A function family $F : \mathcal{K} \times \mathcal{D} \to \mathcal{R}$ is said to be a pseudorandom function family if it has the following properties:

Indexing Each function in F has a unique γ-bit key (index) associated with it. It is easy to select a function $f \in F$ randomly if γ random bits are available.

Polynomial Time Evaluation There exists a polynomial time algorithm such that, given input of a key (index) $k \in \mathcal{K}$ and an argument $x \in \mathcal{D}$, it outputs $F(k, x)$.

Pseudorandomness No probabilistic polynomial time algorithm T can pass the *PTPT* for F with non-negligible advantage.

For convenience, $F_k(x)$ and $F(k, x)$ are used interchangeably for a PRF family F.

Model of RFID System   An RFID system comprises of a single legitimate reader R and a set of ℓ tags $\mathcal{T}_1, ..., \mathcal{T}_\ell$. Note that the single reader may represent multiple readers without distinguishing their identities; also, an adversary can use its own readers to interact with tags. The reader and the tags are probabilistic polynomial time interactive Turing machines. Typically, each tag is a passive transponder identified by a unique ID and has only limited memory which can be used to store only several keys and/or some state information. The reader is composed of one or more transceivers and a backend processing subsystem. It is assumed that the reader is secure,

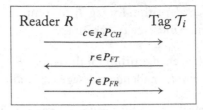

Figure 3.2: Canonical RFID protocol.

which means that an adversary cannot obtain any information about the RFID system from the legitimate reader except the information obtained from RFID communications and from tags (in other words, the legitimate reader is a "black-box" to an adversary).

Every tag exchanges messages with the reader through a protocol π. In the following, a *canonical protocol* is used to describe a generic privacy-preserving challenge-response RFID authentication protocol as shown in Figure 3.2. The protocol π is invoked by the reader R sending a challenge message c to the tag $\mathcal{T}_i$, which upon receiving the challenge message c responds with a message r, where r is computed according to the tag's key $k_{\mathcal{T}_i}$, the challenge message c, its coin toss $cn_{\mathcal{T}_i}$, and its internal state $s_{\mathcal{T}_i}$. The response r can be written as $r = F_{\mathcal{T}_i}(k_{\mathcal{T}_i}, cn_{\mathcal{T}_i}, s_{\mathcal{T}_i}, c)$, where $F_{\mathcal{T}_i}$ is a function computed by the tag. This protocol can be executed in two or three rounds. In the third round, if exists, the reader sends the tag the final message f, which is computed according to the reader's internal state s_R, it's coin toss cn_R, the challenge message c, and the tag's response r. The final message can be written as $f = F_R(k_R, cn_R, s_R, c, r)$, where F_R is a function computed by the reader based on a key k_R, which may or may not be the same as $k_{\mathcal{T}_i}$. Let $P_{CH}, P_{FT}, P_{FR}, P_K, P_{CN}, P_S$ denote the challenge message space, the range of function $F_{\mathcal{T}}$, the final message space, the key space of the tag, the coin space of the tag, and the state information space of the tag, respectively. This canonical form of RFID protocols will be used in defining indistinguishability based privacy notion and unpredictability based privacy notion.

Definition 3.4   RFID System   An RFID system RS is defined to be a tuple $(R, \mathcal{T}, \mathsf{ReaderSetup},$ $\mathsf{TagSetup}, \mathsf{ReaderStart}, \mathsf{TagCompute}, \mathsf{ReaderCompute}, \pi)$, where

$\mathsf{ReaderSetup}(\kappa)$ It is a setup procedure which generates the system parameter σ and key k_R (if needed) for the reader R according to the security parameter κ. It also setups a database for the reader R to store necessary information for tag identification.

$\mathsf{TagSetup}(\mathcal{T}_i, \kappa)$ It is a setup procedure which generates key $k_{\mathcal{T}_i}$ for a tag $\mathcal{T}_i$ and sets the tag's initial internal state st_0. It also associates the tag $\mathcal{T}_i$ with its unique ID as well as other necessary information such as tag key and/or tag state information as a record in the database of reader R.

$\mathsf{ReaderStart}$ It is an algorithm for reader R to generate a session identifier *sid* of a new session and a challenge message c_{sid} of the session.

TagCompute($\mathcal{T}_i$, sid, c_{sid}) It is an algorithm for tag $\mathcal{T}_i$ to compute its response r_{sid}, taking a session identifier sid and challenge message c_{sid} as input.

ReaderCompute(sid, c_{sid}, r_{sid}) It is an algorithm for the reader R to compute the final message f_{sid}, taking a session identifier sid, challenge message c_{sid} and response message r_{sid} as input.

Protocol $\pi(R, \mathcal{T}_i)$ It is a canonical interactive protocol between the reader R and the tag $\mathcal{T}_i$. Each session of protocol π is associated with a unique session identifier sid. As an abusing of the notation, let

$$(c_{sid}, r_{sid}, f_{sid}) \leftarrow \pi(R, \mathcal{T}_i, sid)$$

denote the running of protocol π between R and $\mathcal{T}_i$ with challenge message c_{sid} and session identifier sid. The external output of the protocol $\pi(R, \mathcal{T}_i)$ is the tuple $(c_{sid}, r_{sid}, f_{sid})$. A tuple (c, r, f) is said to be a valid set of protocol messages of $\pi(R, \mathcal{T}_i)$ if there exists a session identifier sid such that

$$\pi(R, \mathcal{T}_i, sid) = (c, r, f).$$

A tag $\mathcal{T}_i$ is said to be *accepted* if its corresponding record is identified by the reader R in its database upon performing protocol $\pi(R, \mathcal{T}_i)$.

Note that, ReaderStart, TagCompute, and ReaderCompute algorithms can be obtained from the protocol π. For convenience, let $RS = (R, \mathcal{T}, \mathsf{ReaderSetup}, \mathsf{TagSetup}, \pi)$ denote an RFID system.

Adversary Model   In a nutshell, an adversary $\mathcal{A}$ is a probabilistic polynomial time interactive Turing machine that is allowed to perform oracle queries during attacks. In particular, the following oracles can be accessed by adversary $\mathcal{A}$ in queries.

InitReader It invokes the reader R to start a session of protocol π and generate a session identifier sid and challenge message $c_{sid} \in_R P_{CH}$. The reader returns the session identifier sid and the challenge message c_{sid}.

InitTag($\mathcal{T}_i$, sid, c_{sid}) It invokes tag $\mathcal{T}_i$ to start a session of protocol π with session identifier sid and challenge message $c_{sid} \in P_{CH}$. The tag $\mathcal{T}_i$ responds with the session identifier sid and a message $r_{sid} \in P_{FT}$.

SetTag($\mathcal{T}_i$) It updates the key and state information to tag $\mathcal{T}_i$ and returns the tag's current key and internal state information.

SendRes(sid, c, r) It takes the challenge and response messages c, r with session identifier sid as input and (in three-round protocol) returns the reader's final message f_{sid}.

Let O_1, O_2, O_3, and O_4 denote InitReader, InitTag, SetTag and SendRes oracles, respectively.

The four kinds of queries defined above can be used to model most, if not all, of the attacks to RFID communications or tags, including eavesdropping, alteration of communication messages, replay attacks, corruption of tags, and physical or side-channel attacks to tags. For example, eavesdropping can be modeled as follows: first call InitReader() to get (sid, c_{sid}), then call InitTag(sid, c_{sid}) to get (sid, r_{sid}), and finally call SendRes(sid, c_{sid}, r_{sid}) to get f_{sid}. For another example, any tag key compromise due to tag corruption or physical or side-channel attacks can be modeled by sending the SetTag query to the tag.

Completeness and Soundness of RFID System   The completeness and soundness of RFID systems are defined by Damgård and Pedersen [98]. Informally, completeness means that a legitimate tag will always be accepted by the legitimate reader, and the soundness means that only a legitimate tag will be accepted by the legitimate reader.

Definition 3.5   Completeness   Assume that at the end of every session with sid, the output of session is tuple $(c_{sid}, r_{sid}, f_{sid})$, where r_{sid} is correctly generated by a legitimate tag. Completeness means that the reader outputs "accept" with probability 1 for any such session.

Experiment $\mathbf{Exp}_{\mathcal{A}}^{sound}[\kappa, \ell, q, s, v]$
1. setup the reader R and a set of tags $\mathcal{T}$ with $|\mathcal{T}| = \ell$;
2. $\{(c_{sid^*}, r_{sid^*}, f_{sid^*}), \mathcal{T}_j\} \leftarrow \mathcal{A}^{O_1, O_2, O_4}(R, \mathcal{T})$.

Figure 3.3: Soundness experiment.

Next, consider the soundness experiment $\mathbf{Exp}_{\mathcal{A}}^{sound}[\kappa, \ell, q, s, v]$ as shown in Figure 3.3, where ℓ, q, s, v are experiment parameters. The adversary $\mathcal{A}$ is given an RFID system RS as input and is allowed to launch O_1, O_2, and O_4 oracle queries without exceeding q, s, and v overall calls, respectively. At the end of the experiment, $\mathcal{A}$ outputs a tuple $(c_{sid^*}, r_{sid^*}, f_{sid^*})$ and a tag $\mathcal{T}_j \in \mathcal{T}$. Let E denote the event that r_{sid^*} is not sent by tag $\mathcal{T}_j$ in session sid^* while the reader R accepts the tag $\mathcal{T}_j$ in session sid^* with protocol message tuple $(c_{sid^*}, r_{sid^*}, f_{sid^*})$.

Definition 3.6   An adversary $\mathcal{A}$ (ϵ, t, q, s, v)-breaks the soundness of the RFID system RS if the probability that event E occurs is at least ϵ and the running time of $\mathcal{A}$ is at most t.

Definition 3.7   Soundness   The RFID system RS provides (ϵ, t, q, s, v)-soundness if there exists no adversary $\mathcal{A}$ which can (ϵ, t, q, s, v)-break the soundness of RS.

Note that the above definition of soundness is compatible with the weak soundness introduced in [98], in which strong soundness has also been defined (strong soundness allows an adversary to launch SetTag oracle, or O_3, queries to corrupt any tags except tag $\mathcal{T}_j$).

Experiment $\mathbf{Exp}_{\mathcal{A}}^{ind}[\kappa, \ell, q, s, u, v]$
1. setup the reader R and a set of tags $\mathcal{T}$ with $|\mathcal{T}| = \ell$;
2. $\{\mathcal{T}_i, \mathcal{T}_j, st\} \leftarrow \mathcal{A}_1^{O_1, O_2, O_3, O_4}(R, \mathcal{T})$; //*learning stage*
3. set $\mathcal{T}' = \mathcal{T} - \{\mathcal{T}_i, \mathcal{T}_j\}$;
4. $b \in_R \{0, 1\}$;
5. if $b = 0$ then $\mathcal{T}_c = \mathcal{T}_i$, else $\mathcal{T}_c = \mathcal{T}_j$;
6. $b' \leftarrow \mathcal{A}_2^{O_1, O_2, O_3, O_4}(R, \mathcal{T}', st, \mathcal{T}_c)$; //*guess stage*
7. the experiment outputs 1 if $b' = b$, 0 otherwise.

Figure 3.4: Ind-privacy experiment.

3.1.2   INDISTINGUISHABILITY-BASED PRIVACY

Juels and Weis [99] presented an indistinguishability-based RFID privacy model (ind-privacy for short) which is reminiscent of the classic indistinguishability under chosen-plaintext attack (IND-CPA) and under chosen-ciphertext attack (IND-CCA) in cryptosystem security.

Figure 3.4 illustrates the ind-privacy experiment $\mathbf{Exp}_{\mathcal{A}}^{ind}[\kappa, \ell, q, s, u, v]$ ($\mathbf{Exp}_{\mathcal{A}}^{ind}$, for simplicity), in which an adversary $\mathcal{A}$ is comprised of a pair of algorithms $(\mathcal{A}_1, \mathcal{A}_2)$ and runs in two stages. Throughout the experiment, the adversary $\mathcal{A}$ is allowed to launch O_1, O_2, O_3, and O_4 oracle queries without exceeding q, s, u, and v overall calls, respectively. The experiment proceeds as follows. At first, the experiment initializes the RFID system by producing a reader R and a set of tags $\mathcal{T} = \{\mathcal{T}_1, ..., \mathcal{T}_\ell\}$ according to the security parameter κ. Then, in the *learning stage*, algorithm $\mathcal{A}_1$ outputs state information st and a pair of tags $\{\mathcal{T}_i, \mathcal{T}_j\}$ to which it has not sent SetTag queries. Next, the experiment selects a random bit b and sets a challenge tag $\mathcal{T}_c = \mathcal{T}_i$ if $b = 0$, and $\mathcal{T}_c = \mathcal{T}_j$ otherwise. Finally, in the *guess stage*, algorithm $\mathcal{A}_2$ is asked to guess the random bit b by outputting a bit b'. During this stage, algorithm $\mathcal{A}_2$ is allowed to launch $O_1, O_2, O_3 teps$: and O_4 oracle queries to $\mathcal{T}_c$ and any tag in set $\mathcal{T}' = \mathcal{T} - \{\mathcal{T}_i, \mathcal{T}_j\}$ with the restriction that it cannot query SetTag($\mathcal{T}_c$).

Definition 3.8   The advantage of adversary $\mathcal{A}$ in experiment $\mathbf{Exp}_{\mathcal{A}}^{ind}[\kappa, \ell, q, s, u, v]$ is defined as:

$$\mathrm{Adv}_{\mathcal{A}}^{ind}(\kappa, \ell, q, s, u, v) = |\Pr[\mathbf{Exp}_{\mathcal{A}}^{ind}[\kappa, \ell, q, s, u, v] = 1] - \frac{1}{2}|,$$

where the probability is taken over the choice of tag set $\mathcal{T}$ and the coin tosses of adversary $\mathcal{A}$.

Definition 3.9   An adversary $\mathcal{A}$ $(\epsilon, t, q, s, u, v)$-breaks the ind-privacy of RFID system RS if the advantage $\mathrm{Adv}_{\mathcal{A}}^{ind}(k, \ell, q, s, u, v)$ of $\mathcal{A}$ in experiment $\mathbf{Exp}_{\mathcal{A}}^{ind}$ is at least ϵ and the running time of $\mathcal{A}$ is at most t.

Definition 3.10 Ind-Privacy An RFID system RS is said to be $(\epsilon, t, q, s, u, v)$-ind-private if there exists no adversary who can $(\epsilon, t, q, s, u, v)$-break the ind-privacy of RS.

The ind-privacy implies that an adversary cannot distinguish between any two tags in the tag set $\mathcal{T}$ which the adversary has not corrupted. This definition can be easily extended to the case where an adversary cannot distinguish between any ι tags in the tag set $\mathcal{T}$ that have not been corrupted. This latter case may be considered as an incarnation of the notion of ι-privacy (or ι-anonymity) [100] in the RFID system.

3.1.3 UNPREDICTABILITY-BASED PRIVACY

The goal of an adversary in the above ind-privacy game is to distinguish two different tags within its computational power. The idea is intuitively appealing; however, the ind-privacy model is difficult to apply *directly* in proving that a given protocol is ind-private. To our knowledge, no mutual authentication RFID protocol has been proven *directly* to be ind-private. To address this concern, Ha et al. [101] proposed a different privacy model based on the unpredictability of tag outputs, denoted as unp-privacy.

Experiment $\mathbf{Exp}_{\mathcal{A}}^{unp}[\kappa, \ell, q, s, u, v]$
1. setup the reader R and a set of tags $\mathcal{T}$ with $|\mathcal{T}| = \ell$;
2. $\{\mathcal{T}_c, st\} \leftarrow \mathcal{A}_1^{O_1, O_2, O_3, O_4}(R, \mathcal{T});$ // *learning stage*
3. $b \in_R \{0, 1\};$
4. if $b = 0$ then $r^* \in_R P_{RS}$,
     else r^* is taken from $(c^*, r^*, f^*) \leftarrow \pi(R, \mathcal{T}_c, sid);$
5. $b' \leftarrow \mathcal{A}_2(r^*, st);$ // *guess stage*
6. the experiment outputs 1 if $b' = b$, 0 otherwise.

Figure 3.5: Unp-privacy experiment.

Figure 3.5 illustrates the unp-privacy experiment $\mathbf{Exp}_{\mathcal{A}}^{unp}[\kappa, \ell, q, s, u, v]$ ($\mathbf{Exp}_{\mathcal{A}}^{unp}$, for simplicity), in which an adversary is also comprised of a pair of algorithms $(\mathcal{A}_1, \mathcal{A}_2)$ and runs in two stages. In the *learning stage*, algorithm $\mathcal{A}_1$ is required to select only one challenge tag $\mathcal{T}_c$. It also outputs state information st which will be transmitted to algorithm $\mathcal{A}_2$. Throughout the experiment, adversary $\mathcal{A}$ is allowed to launch O_1, O_2, O_3, and O_4 oracle queries without exceeding q, s, u and v overall calls respectively under the condition that $\mathcal{A}_1$ cannot query $\mathsf{SetTag}(\mathcal{T}_c)$. Next, the experiment selects a random bit b and sets a challenge message r^* to be random if $b = 0$, and taken from the output of $\pi(R, \mathcal{T}_c)$ if $b = 1$. Then in the *guess stage*, algorithm $\mathcal{A}_2$ is required to infer whether the challenge message r^* is chosen from the output of running the protocol $\pi(R, \mathcal{T}_c)$. Note that, $\mathcal{A}_2$ is not allowed to query any oracle.

Definition 3.11   The advantage of adversary $\mathcal{A}$ in experiment $\mathbf{Exp}_{\mathcal{A}}^{unp}$ is defined as:

$$\mathrm{Adv}_{\mathcal{A}}^{unp}(\kappa, \ell, q, s, u, v) = |\Pr[\mathbf{Exp}_{\mathcal{A}}^{unp}[\kappa, \ell, q, s, u, v] = 1] - \frac{1}{2}|,$$

where the probability is taken over the choice of tag set $\mathcal{T}$ and the coin tosses of adversary $\mathcal{A}$.

Definition 3.12   An adversary $\mathcal{A}$ $(\epsilon, t, q, s, u, v)$-breaks the unp-privacy of RFID system RS if the advantage $\mathrm{Adv}_{\mathcal{A}}^{unp}(\kappa, \ell, q, s, u, v)$ of $\mathcal{A}$ in experiment $\mathbf{Exp}_{\mathcal{A}}^{unp}$ is at least ϵ and the running time of $\mathcal{A}$ is at most t.

Definition 3.13   Unp-Privacy   An RFID system RS is said to be $(\epsilon, t, q, s, u, v)$-unp-private if there exists no adversary who can $(\epsilon, t, q, s, , u, v)$-break the unp-privacy of RS.

3.1.4   IMPROVEMENTS OF UNP-PRIVACY MODEL

Note that in the unp-privacy game, the adversary $\mathcal{A}_2$ does not get the full transcript of the RFID protocol execution between reader and challenge tag, but only r^* which is either a random message or the message sent by the challenge tag. As a result, an RFID protocol with protocol messages being traceable by an adversary can be shown unp-private, as confirmed by van Deursen and Radomirović [102]. To address this issue, Ma et al. proposed an improved unp-privacy model, named unp'-privacy [95]. In the unp'-privacy model, the adversary is given not only r^*, but also the last message f^* of the protocol.

Unp'-Privacy Model   Figure 3.6 illustrates the unp'-privacy experiment $\mathbf{Exp}_{\mathcal{A}}^{unp'}[\kappa, \ell, q, s, u, v]$ ($\mathbf{Exp}_{\mathcal{A}}^{unp'}$, for simplicity), in which an adversary comprised of a pair of algorithms $(\mathcal{A}_1, \mathcal{A}_2)$ runs in two stages. In the *learning stage*, algorithm $\mathcal{A}_1$ is required to select only one challenge tag $\mathcal{T}_c$ and a *test* message $c_0 \in P_{CH}$. It also outputs state information st which will be transmitted to algorithm $\mathcal{A}_2$. Throughout the experiment, adversary $\mathcal{A}$ is allowed to launch $O_1, O_2, O_3,$ and O_4 oracle queries without exceeding $q, s, u,$ and v overall calls respectively under the condition that $\mathcal{A}_1$ cannot query $\mathsf{SetTag}(\mathcal{T}_c)$. Next, the experiment selects a random bit b and sets a challenge message pair (r^*, f^*) to be random if $b = 0$, and taken from the output of $\pi(R, \mathcal{T}_c)$ with test message c_0 if $b = 1$. Then in the *guess stage*, algorithm $\mathcal{A}_2$ has oracle accesses to tags except $\mathcal{T}_c$

Experiment $\mathbf{Exp}_{\mathcal{A}}^{unp'}[\kappa, \ell, q, s, u, v]$
  1. setup the reader R and a set of tags $\mathcal{T}$ with $|\mathcal{T}| = \ell$;
  2. $\{\mathcal{T}_c, c_0, st\} \leftarrow \mathcal{A}_1^{O_1, O_2, O_3, O_4}(R, \mathcal{T})$; //learning stage
  3. set $\mathcal{T}' = \mathcal{T} - \{\mathcal{T}_c\}$;
  4. $b \in_R \{0, 1\}$;
  5. if $b = 0$ then $(r^*, f^*) \in_R P_{RS} \times P_{FR}$,
     else run the protocol with the challenge message c_0;
         get the transcripts of the protocol execution (c_0, r_0, f_0);
         set $(r^*, f^*) = (r_0, f_0)$;
  6. $b' \leftarrow \mathcal{A}_2^{O_1, O_2, O_3, O_4}(R, \mathcal{T}', st, r^*, f^*)$; //guess stage
  7. the experiment outputs 1 if $b' = b$, 0 otherwise.

Figure 3.6: Unp$'$-privacy experiment.

and is required to infer whether the challenge message pair (r^*, f^*) is chosen from the output of running the protocol $\pi(R, \mathcal{T}_c)$ with *test* message c_0.

Definition 3.14   The advantage of adversary $\mathcal{A}$ in experiment $\mathbf{Exp}_{\mathcal{A}}^{unp'}$ is defined as:

$$\mathrm{Adv}_{\mathcal{A}}^{unp'}(\kappa, \ell, q, s, u, v) = |\mathrm{Pr}[\mathbf{Exp}_{\mathcal{A}}^{unp'}[\kappa, \ell, q, s, u, v] = 1] - \frac{1}{2}|,$$

where the probability is taken over the choice of tag set $\mathcal{T}$ and the coin tosses of adversary $\mathcal{A}$.

Definition 3.15   An adversary $\mathcal{A}$ $(\epsilon, t, q, s, u, v)$-breaks the unp$'$-privacy of RFID system RS if the advantage $\mathrm{Adv}_{\mathcal{A}}^{unp'}(\kappa, \ell, q, s, u, v)$ of $\mathcal{A}$ in experiment $\mathbf{Exp}_{\mathcal{A}}^{unp'}$ is at least ϵ and the running time of $\mathcal{A}$ is at most t.

Definition 3.16 Unp$'$-Privacy   An RFID system RS is said to be $(\epsilon, t, q, s, u, v)$-unp$'$-private if there exists no adversary who can $(\epsilon, t, q, s, , u, v)$-break the unp$'$-privacy of RS.

A Counterexample   Ma et al. [95] introduced an efficient 2-round protocol and proved that it is unp$'$-private, where the adversary is provided with tag response r^* only in the guess stage. The unp$'$-privacy model is robust for 2-round RFID protocols, as demonstrated in [95]; however, this model has a deficiency when applied to 3-round protocols [96, 97].

To show this, the 2-round protocol of Ma et al. [95] is modified to a 3-round mutual authentication protocol as illustrated in Figure 3.7. This new protocol has a clear weakness with respect to privacy but can be proven to be unp$'$-private.

Let $F : \{0, 1\}^{l_k} \times \{0, 1\}^{l_d} \to \{0, 1\}^{l_r}$ be a PRF family. Let $ctr \in \{0, 1\}^{l_r}$ be a counter. Let $pad_1 \in \{0, 1\}^{l_{p1}}$ and $pad_2 \in \{0, 1\}^{l_{p2}}$ be two paddings such that $l_r + l_{p1} = l_d$. The RFID system is constructed as follows.

ReaderSetup(κ)   It sets up a reader R with $\sigma = \{F, pad_1, pad_2\}$ according to security parameter κ.

TagSetup(T_i, κ)   It sets up a tag T_i with a key $k_i \in \{0, 1\}^{l_k}$, a counter $ctr_i = 1$ and a 1-bit flag $s_i = 0$. It also stores a tuple (I_i, k_i, ctr_i, ID_i) in the reader's database, where $I_i = F_{k_i}(ctr_i \| pad_1)$ and ID_i is the tag's identity.

Protocol $\pi(R, T_i)$ R first sends a challenge $c \in_R \{0, 1\}^{l_c}$ to T_i, where $l_c + l_r + l_{p2} = l_d$. Upon receiving c, T_i executes the following steps:

1. randomly choose $r_2 \in \{0, 1\}^{l_{p2}}$ and compute $I_i = F_{k_i}(ctr_i \| pad_1)$;

2. set $r_1 = F_{k_i}(c \| I_i \| pad_2) \oplus ctr_i$ if $s_i = 0$, else set $r_1 = F_{k_i}(c \| I_i \| r_2) \oplus ctr_i$; and

3. respond with $(r_1 \| I_i, r_2)$, increment ctr_i by 1, and set $s_i = 1$.

Upon receiving the response $(r_1 \| I_i, r_2)$, R identifies the tag from its database as follows.

1. Search for the tuple (I_i, k_i, ctr_i', ID_i) using I_i as an index. If such a tuple exists, compute $F_{k_i}(c \| I_i \| pad_2)$ and then:

   (a) if $ctr_i' = F_{k_i}(c \| I_i \| pad_2) \oplus r_1$, update $ctr_i' = ctr_i' + 1$ and $I_i = F_{k_i}(ctr_i' \| pad_1)$, respond with $f = F_{k_i}(c \| ctr_i' \| r_2)$, and accept the tag; or

   (b) else abort the protocol.

2. Else look up the database for a tuple $(I_i', k_i, ctr_i', ID_i)$ in an exhaustive search such that $ctr_i = F_{k_i}(c \| I_i \| r_2) \oplus r_1$ and $F_{k_i}(ctr_i \| pad_1) = I_i$. Then:

   (a) if such a tuple exists, update $ctr_i' = ctr_i + 1$ and $I_i' = F_{k_i}(ctr_i' \| pad_1)$, respond with $f = F_{k_i}(c \| ctr_i' \| r_2)$, and accept the tag; or

   (b) else abort the protocol.

Upon receiving f, T_i checks whether $f = F_{k_i}(c \| ctr_i \| r_2)$. If not, T_i rejects the reader. Else, T_i sets $s_i = 0$ and accepts the reader.

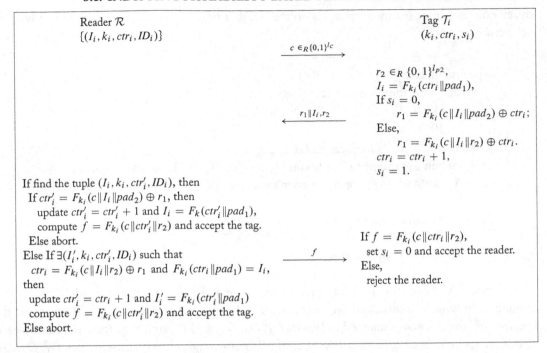

Figure 3.7: Counterexample.

A flaw of the protocol is that an active attacker can find out whether a tag's state is $s = 0$ or $s = 1$. If a tag is in state $s = 0$, the reader does not verify the integrity of r_2; while if the tag is in state $s = 1$, this verification occurs implicitly. Note that under normal circumstances tags will be in state $s = 0$. Hence, an active attacker can flag a tag by setting its state to $s = 1$ and trace the tag in subsequent protocol sessions. Nonetheless, the following theorem states that the protocol is unp'-private.

Theorem 3.17 The above mutual authentication RFID protocol is unp'-private, assuming that the function family $F : \{0, 1\}^{l_k} \times \{0, 1\}^{l_d} \to \{0, 1\}^{l_r}$ is a PRF family [97].

Unp*-Privacy   The limitation in the definition of unp'-privacy, as shown in the counterexample, is due to the constraint imposed on the adversary $\mathcal{A}_2$. In particular, $\mathcal{A}_2$ is not allowed to query oracles on the challenge tag $\mathcal{T}_c$. A remedy to this limitation is unp*-privacy model [96, 97].

The intuition of unp*-privacy model is that no adversary should be able to distinguish the output of a real tag from that of a virtual tag, given transcripts of multiple protocol sessions of both tags, where a virtual tag is defined as a tag without any secret information. This implies that no adversary can link a real tag and its behavior without learning its secret key. Note that unp*-

privacy does not impose any restrictions on the number of oracle queries issued by the adversary to the challenge tag.

Experiment $\mathbf{Exp}_{\mathcal{A}}^{unp^\star}[\kappa, \ell, q, s, u, v]$
1. setup the reader R and a set of tags $\mathcal{T}$ with $|\mathcal{T}| = \ell$;
2. $\{\mathcal{T}_c, st\} \leftarrow \mathcal{A}_1^{O_1, O_2, O_3, O_4}(R, \mathcal{T})$; //learning stage
3. $b \in_R \{0, 1\}$;
4. $b' \leftarrow \mathcal{A}_2^{O_1, O_2, O_4}(R, \mathcal{T}_c, st)$; //guess stage
   4.1 when $\mathcal{A}_2$ queries O_1, O_2 and O_4 oracles, if $b = 1$, run the algorithm
       ReaderStart, TagCompute, ReaderCompute respectively, and return the results;
   4.2 else $b = 0$, return a random element from P_{CH}, P_{FT}, P_{FR}, respectively.
5. the experiment outputs 1 if $b' = b$, 0 otherwise.

Figure 3.8: Unp*-privacy experiment.

Figure 3.8 illustrates the unp*-privacy experiment $\mathbf{Exp}_{\mathcal{A}}^{unp^\star}[\kappa, \ell, q, s, u, v]$ ($\mathbf{Exp}_{\mathcal{A}}^{unp^\star}$, for simplicity), in which an adversary $\mathcal{A}$ comprised of $(\mathcal{A}_1, \mathcal{A}_2)$ runs in two stages. Throughout the experiment, adversary $\mathcal{A}$ is allowed to launch O_1, O_2, O_3, and O_4 oracle queries without exceeding q, s, u, and v overall calls respectively. In the *learning stage*, algorithm $\mathcal{A}_1$ issues O_1, O_2, O_3, and O_4 oracle queries, and output an uncorrupted challenge tag $\mathcal{T}_c$. It also outputs state information st which will be transmitted to algorithm $\mathcal{A}_2$. Next, the experiment selects a random bit b. Algorithm $\mathcal{A}_2$ is allowed to query O_1, O_2, and O_4 oracles on R and $\mathcal{T}_c$. The experiment responds to $\mathcal{A}_2$ queries as follows.

InitReader If $b = 0$, generate a new session identifier sid, choose $c_{sid} \in_R P_{CH}$ and forward (sid, c_{sid}) to $\mathcal{A}_2$; else, run the algorithm ReaderStart, and forward the result to $\mathcal{A}_2$.

InitTag($\mathcal{T}_c, sid, c_{sid}$) If $b = 0$, choose $r_{sid} \in P_{FT}$ and forward r_{sid} to $\mathcal{A}_2$; else, run the algorithm TagCompute($\mathcal{T}_c, sid, c_{sid}$) and forward the result to $\mathcal{A}_2$.

SendRes(sid, c_{sid}, r_{sid}) If $b = 0$, choose $f_{sid} \in P_{FR}$ and forward f_{sid} to $\mathcal{A}_2$; else, run the algorithm ReaderCompute(sid, c_{sid}, r_{sid}) and forward the result to $\mathcal{A}_2$.

Finally, $\mathcal{A}_2$ is asked to make a guess on the value of the random bit b.

Definition 3.18 The advantage of adversary $\mathcal{A}$ in experiment $\mathbf{Exp}_{\mathcal{A}}^{unp^\star}$ is defined as:

$$\mathrm{Adv}_{\mathcal{A}}^{unp^\star}(\kappa, \ell, q, s, u, v) = |\mathrm{Pr}[\mathbf{Exp}_{\mathcal{A}}^{unp^\star}[\kappa, \ell, q, s, u, v] = 1] - \frac{1}{2}|,$$

where the probability is taken over the choice of tag set $\mathcal{T}$ and the coin tosses of the adversary $\mathcal{A}$.

Definition 3.19 An adversary $\mathcal{A}$ $(\epsilon, t, q, s, u, v)$-breaks the unp*-privacy of RFID system RS if the advantage $\text{Adv}_{\mathcal{A}}^{unp^\star}(\kappa, \ell, q, s, u, v)$ of $\mathcal{A}$ in experiment $\text{Exp}_{\mathcal{A}}^{unp^\star}$ is at least ϵ and the running time of $\mathcal{A}$ is at most t.

Definition 3.20 Unp*-Privacy An RFID system RS is said to be $(\epsilon, t, q, s, u, v)$-unp*-private if there exists no adversary who can $(\epsilon, t, q, s, , u, v)$-break the unp*-privacy of RS.

Note that the protocol given in Figure 3.7 does not satisfy unp*-privacy model. In the unp*-privacy experiment, if $b = 0$, the adversary modifies the second message randomly; with overwhelming probability, the third message of the protocol is empty. However, if $b = 1$, the third message is always a random value and not empty. Therefore, with overwhelming probability, the adversary can distinguish the two cases.

3.1.5 RELATION BETWEEN UNP*-PRIVACY AND IND-PRIVACY

Li et al. investigated the relation between ind-privacy and unp*-privacy [97]. A restricted ind-privacy model, called ind$'$-privacy, is introduced as a "bridge" to show that it is equivalent to ind-privacy and that unp*-privacy implies ind$'$-privacy. It is shown that ind-privacy does not imply unp*-privacy. Overall, unp*-privacy is stronger than ind-privacy.

While the notion of ind-privacy may suffice, it is difficult to use it in analyzing an RFID system. In fact, most of ind-privacy proofs known so far, including the proof in the original paper [99], use a notion similar to unp*-privacy as a bridge, showing that every PPT adversary is not able to distinguish the transcripts of protocol execution from random values. One technical challenge of applying ind-privacy is how to transfer the ability to distinguish between two tags to the ability to break a cryptographic primitive or to solve a hard problem. Another difference is that unp*-privacy restricts the adversary from making queries to any tags other than the target tag(s) in the second stage of the game. Such restriction can make a security proof more concise. Intuitively, ind-privacy implies that a tag cannot be distinguished from a group of tags in an RFID system, which may demonstrate a unique pattern as a group (e.g., with common prefix in protocol transcripts), while unp*-privacy requires that a tag's interaction with a reader does not have any such group patterns.

Ind$'$-Privacy Figure 3.9 shows the ind$'$-privacy experiment $\text{Exp}_{\mathcal{A}}^{ind'}[\kappa, \ell, q, s, u, v]$ ($\text{Exp}_{\mathcal{A}}^{ind'}$, for simplicity), which is identical to the ind-privacy experiment given in Figure 3.4 except that $\mathcal{A}_2$ in $\text{Exp}_{\mathcal{A}}^{ind'}$ is not allowed to query oracles on other tags except for $\mathcal{T}_c$.

Definition 3.21 The advantage of adversary $\mathcal{A}$ in the ind$'$-privacy experiment $\text{Exp}_{\mathcal{A}}^{ind'}$ is defined as:

$$\text{Adv}_{\mathcal{A}}^{ind'}(\kappa, \ell, q, s, u, v) = |\Pr[\text{Exp}_{\mathcal{A}}^{ind'} = 1] - \frac{1}{2}|,$$

Experiment $\mathbf{Exp}_{\mathcal{A}}^{ind'}[\kappa, \ell, q, s, u, v, w]$
1. setup the reader R and a set of tags $\mathcal{T}$ with $|\mathcal{T}| = \ell$;
2. $\{\mathcal{T}_i, \mathcal{T}_j, st\} \leftarrow \mathcal{A}_1^{O_1, O_2, O_3, O_4}(R, \mathcal{T})$; //learning stage
3. $b \in_R \{0, 1\}$;
4. if $b = 0$ then $\mathcal{T}_c = \mathcal{T}_i$, else $\mathcal{T}_c = \mathcal{T}_j$;
5. $b' \leftarrow \mathcal{A}_2^{O_1, O_2, O_4}(R, \mathcal{T}_c, st)$; //guess stage
6. the experiment outputs 1 if $b' = b$, 0 otherwise.

Figure 3.9: Ind$'$-privacy experiment.

where the probability is taken over the choice of tag set $\mathcal{T}$ and the coin tosses of the adversary $\mathcal{A}$.

Definition 3.22 An adversary $\mathcal{A}$ $(\epsilon, t, q, s, u, v)$-breaks the ind$'$-privacy of RFID system RS if its advantage $\mathrm{Adv}_{\mathcal{A}}^{ind'}(\kappa, \ell, q, s, u, v)$ in experiment $\mathbf{Exp}_{\mathcal{A}}^{ind'}$ is at least ϵ and its running time is at most t.

Definition 3.23 Ind$'$-Privacy An RFID system RS is said to be $(\epsilon, t, q, s, u, v)$-ind$'$-private if there exists no adversary $\mathcal{A}$ who can $(\epsilon, t, q, s, , u, v)$-break the ind$'$-privacy of RS.

Ind-Privacy $\Longleftrightarrow$ Ind$'$-Privacy   The only difference between ind-privacy and ind$'$-privacy is that, in ind-privacy an adversary can issue oracle queries to any tag in $\mathcal{T}' \cap \{\mathcal{T}_c\}$ in the guess stage, while in ind$'$-privacy, an adversary can only issue oracle queries on $\mathcal{T}_c$ in the guess stage. In other words, ind$'$-privacy puts more restrictions on the adversary, so ind-privacy implies ind$'$-privacy. However, in ind$'$-privacy, the adversary can issue O_3 queries to all tags in $\mathcal{T}' = \mathcal{T} - \{\mathcal{T}_i, \mathcal{T}_j\}$ in the learning stage, obtain the secret and state information of all tags in $\mathcal{T}'$ and store them in a list TagKey-List. In the guess stage, when the adversary wants to make O_1, O_2, O_3, O_4 queries to any tag in $\mathcal{T}'$, the adversary can obtain the corresponding query answers itself using TagKey-List. As a result, the restriction on the adversary does not weaken its power in the ind$'$-privacy model, and ind$'$-privacy implies ind-privacy.

Theorem 3.24 Ind-Privacy $\Longleftrightarrow$ Ind$'$-Privacy   For an RFID system $RS = (R, \mathcal{T}, \text{ReaderSetup}, \text{TagSetup}, \pi)$, ind-privacy is equivalent to ind'-privacy [97].

Unp^*-Privacy $\Longrightarrow$ Ind$'$-Privacy Recall that unp*-privacy indicates that no PPT adversary can distinguish the transcripts of protocol execution between reader and a real tag from those of protocol execution between reader and a virtual tag. In this latter case, protocol transcripts are random values. The underlying intuition of ind$'$-privacy is that no PPT adversary can distinguish the transcripts of protocol execution between reader and two distinct tags. It is obvious that no PPT adversary can distinguish between two random values. Therefore, if the transcripts of protocol execution between reader and each tag looks random, no adversary can distinguish the transcripts of protocol execution between reader and two distinct tags. In other words, unp*-privacy implies ind$'$-privacy.

Theorem 3.25 Unp^*-Privacy $\Longrightarrow$ Ind$'$-Privacy Assume that the RFID system $RS = (R, \mathcal{T},$ ReaderSetup, TagSetup, π) is $(\epsilon, t, q, s, u, v)$-unp*-private, then it is $(\epsilon, t, q, s, u, v)$-$ind'$-private [97].

Unp^*-Privacy $\Longrightarrow$ Ind-Privacy From Theorems 3.24 and 3.25, one can derive the following.

Theorem 3.26 Unp^*-Privacy $\Longrightarrow$ Ind-Privacy Assume that the RFID system RS is unp*-private, then it is ind-private.

Ind-Privacy $\nRightarrow$ Unp^*-privacy An ind-private RFID protocol implies that the distributions of protocol transcripts between reader and any two tags are computationally indistinguishable. Note that, the distribution could be any distribution, not necessarily random distribution. A unp*-privacy RFID protocol requires that the distribution of the protocol transcripts is random. Hence, ind-privacy does not imply unp*-privacy.

Let $RS = \{R, \mathcal{T}, \text{ReaderSetup, TagSetup}, \pi\}$ be any RFID system. A new RFID system $RS' = \{R, \mathcal{T}, \text{ReaderSetup, TagSetup}, \pi'\}$ can be constructed such that $(c, r||r, f) \leftarrow \pi'(R, T_i)$ holds for every protocol message $(c, r, f) \leftarrow \pi(R, T_i)$. Then, one can derive the following.

Theorem 3.27 If RFID system RS is ind-private, then RFID system RS' is also ind-private, but not unp*-private.

It is easy to see that RS' is ind-private if RS is ind-private. We proceed to show that it is not unp*-private. Since every protocol message of π' is in the form $(c, r||r, f) \in P_{CH} \times P_{RS}^2 \times P_{FR}$, an adversary can easily distinguish it from a random tuple $(c', r_1||r_2, f')$ chosen from $P_{CH} \times P_{RS}^2 \times P_{FR}$ by checking whether $r_1 = r_2$. Therefore, RS' is not unp*-private.

This theorem indicates that ind-privacy does not imply unp*-privacy. Ind-privacy does not necessarily mean that an adversary cannot distinguish a tag (or a group of tags) in an RFID system from a tag (or a group of tags) in another RFID system, while unp*-privacy does if the protocol messages have the same length.

3.1.6 MINIMAL REQUIREMENT ON RFID TAGS FOR UNP*-PRIVACY

Li et al. investigated the minimal requirement for RFID systems to achieve unp*-privacy [97]. Since an RFID reader is usually equipped with enough computational power, it is more meaningful to investigate the minimal requirement for RFID tags only. It is shown that the necessary and sufficient condition for enforcing unp*-privacy in an RFID system is to equip every tag with the power of computing a PRF. This result provides a theoretical foundation to explain why so many lightweight RFID protocols suffer from privacy vulnerabilities without implementing necessary cryptographic primitives.

Unp*-Privacy $\Longrightarrow$ PRF   Given an RFID system RS with unp*-privacy, each tag's computation function $F_{T_i}()$ can be used to construct a PRF family.

Without loss of generality, let $P_{CH} = \{0, 1\}^\alpha$, $P_K = \{0, 1\}^{\alpha_1}$, $P_{CN} = \{0, 1\}^{\alpha_2}$, $P_S = \{0, 1\}^{\alpha_3}$, and $P_{FT} = \{0, 1\}^{\alpha_2 + \alpha_3}$, where $\alpha, \alpha_1, \alpha_2$ and α_3 are four polynomials of κ. For an index $\lambda \in P_K \times P_{CN} \times P_S$, assume that λ can be uniquely represented by $\lambda_k \| \lambda_{cn} \| \lambda_s$ (i.e., $|\lambda_k| = \alpha_1, |\lambda_{cn}| = \alpha_2$ and $|\lambda_s| = \alpha_3$), where $\lambda_k \in P_K, \lambda_{cn} \in P_{CH}$ and $\lambda_s \in P_S$.

Given an RFID system $RS = (R, \mathcal{T}, \mathsf{ReaderSetup}, \mathsf{TagSetup}, \pi)$, choose a tag $\mathcal{T}_i \in_R \mathcal{T}$ and define a function family $G : \mathcal{K} \times \mathcal{D} \longrightarrow \mathcal{R}$ as

$$G_\lambda(x) = F_{T_i}(\lambda_k, \lambda'_{cn}, \lambda'_s, x), \tag{3.2}$$

where

$$\lambda \in \mathcal{K} = P_K \times P_{CN} \times P_S, \mathcal{D} = P_{CH} \text{ and } \mathcal{R} = P_{FT},$$
$$\lambda = \lambda_k \| \lambda_{cn} \| \lambda_s,$$
$$\lambda'_{cn} \| \lambda'_s = F_{T_i}(\lambda_k, \lambda_{cn}, \lambda_s, x).$$

The following theorem proves that the function family $G : \mathcal{K} \times \mathcal{D} \to \mathcal{R}$ is a PRF family.

Theorem 3.28   If the RFID system $RS = (R, \mathcal{T}, \mathsf{ReaderSetup}, \mathsf{TagSetup}, \pi)$ is complete, sound, and unp*-private, then the constructed function family $G : \mathcal{K} \times \mathcal{D} \to \mathcal{R}$ is a PRF family [97].

Unp*-Privacy $\Longleftarrow$ PRF   An RFID system with unp*-privacy can be constructed by implementing a PRF on each tag. Let $F : \{0, 1\}^{l_k} \times \{0, 1\}^{l_d} \to \{0, 1\}^{l_r}$ be a PRF family, $ctr \in \{0, 1\}^{l_r}$ be a counter, and $pad_1 \in \{0, 1\}^{l_{p1}}$ be a padding such that $l_r + l_{p1} = l_d$. The RFID system is constructed as follows and the protocol is illustrated in Figure 3.10.

$\mathsf{ReaderSetup}(\kappa)$ It sets up a reader R with $\sigma = \{F, pad_1, pad_2\}$ according to security parameter κ.

$\mathsf{TagSetup}(\mathcal{T}_i, \kappa)$ It sets up a tag $\mathcal{T}_i$ with a key $k_i \in \{0, 1\}^{l_k}$ and a counter $ctr_i = 1$. It also stores a tuple (I_i, k_i, ctr_i, ID_i) in the reader's database, where $I_i = F_{k_i}(ctr_i \| pad_1)$ and ID_i is the tag's identity.

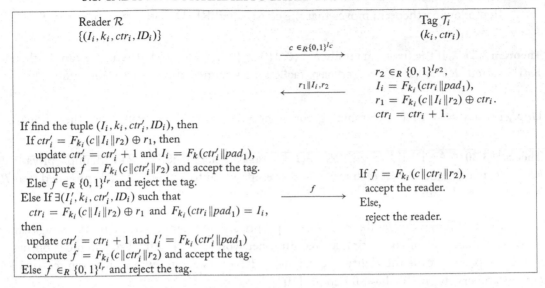

Figure 3.10: Mutual authentication protocol with unp*-privacy.

Protocol $\pi(R, \mathcal{T}_i)$ R sends a challenge $c \in_R \{0, 1\}^{l_c}$ to $\mathcal{T}_i$. Upon receiving c, $\mathcal{T}_i$ executes the following steps.

1. randomly choose $r_2 \in \{0, 1\}^{l_{p2}}$, where $l_c + l_r + l_{p2} = l_d$.

2. Compute $I_i = F_{k_i}(ctr_i \| pad_1)$ and $r_1 = F_{k_i}(c \| I_i \| r_2) \oplus ctr_i$.

3. Respond with $(r_1 \| I_i, r_2)$ and increment ctr_i by 1.

Upon receiving the response $(r_1 \| I_i, r_2)$, R identifies the tag from its database as follows.

1. Search for the tuple (I_i, k_i, ctr'_i, ID_i) using I_i as an index. If such a tuple exists, compute $F_{k_i}(c \| I_i \| r_2)$ and then:

   (a) If $ctr'_i = F_{k_i}(c \| I_i \| r_2) \oplus r_1$, update $ctr'_i = ctr'_i + 1$ and $I_i = F_{k_i}(ctr'_i \| pad_1)$, respond with $f = F_{k_i}(c \| ctr'_i \| r_2)$ and accept the tag.

   (b) Else, respond with $f \in_R \{0, 1\}^{l_r}$ and reject the tag.

2. Else look up the database for a tuple $(I'_i, k_i, ctr'_i, ID_i)$ in an exhaustive search such that $ctr_i = F_{k_i}(c \| I_i \| r_2) \oplus r_1$ and $F_{k_i}(ctr_i \| pad_1) = I_i$. Then:

   (a) If such a tuple exists, update $ctr'_i = ctr_i + 1$ and $I'_i = F_{k_i}(ctr'_i \| pad_1)$, respond with $f = F_{k_i}(c \| ctr'_i \| r_2)$ and accept the tag.

   (b) Else, respond with $f \in_R \{0, 1\}^{l_r}$ and reject the tag.

Upon receiving f, $\mathcal{T}_i$ checks whether $f = F_{k_i}(c \| ctr_i \| r_2)$. If not, $\mathcal{T}_i$ rejects the reader; otherwise, accepts.

The following theorem proves that the constructed RFID system is unp*-private.

Theorem 3.29   If the function family $F : \{0, 1\}^{l_k} \times \{0, 1\}^{l_d} \rightarrow \{0, 1\}^{l_r}$ is a PRF family, then the RFID system $RS = (R, \mathcal{T}, \mathsf{ReaderSetup}, \mathsf{TagSetup}, \pi)$ defined above is unp*-private [97].

Unp*-Privacy $\Longleftrightarrow$ PRF   Combining Theorems 3.28 and 3.29, one can derive the following.

Theorem 3.30   An RFID system $RS = (R, \mathcal{T}, \mathsf{ReaderSetup}, \mathsf{TagSetup}, \pi)$ with unp*-privacy can be constructed if and only if each tag $\mathcal{T}_i \in \mathcal{T}$ is empowered to compute a PRF, provided that RS is complete and sound.

This theorem indicates that to ensure unp*-privacy, the computational power of tags cannot be weaker than that of computing a PRF. In other words, the minimal requirement on tags to achieve unp*-privacy is the ability to compute a PRF or its equivalents such as symmetric block ciphers and cryptographic hash functions [103].

This minimal requirement highlights why many lightweight RFID protocols (e.g. [29, 34, 71, 104]) have privacy flaws [105, 106], as these protocols are constructed based on simple operations such as XOR, bit inner product, 16-bit pseudo-random number generator (PRNG), and cyclic redundancy checksum (CRC) without using any computation equivalent to PRF.

The RFID research community has in recent years realized the importance of implementing strong and yet lightweight cryptographic primitives for low-cost RFID tags [107] and significant progress has been made in this area. For instance, an efficient hardware implementation for the Advanced Encryption Standard (AES) requires 3,400 gate equivalents (GEs) [11]. A specially designed block cipher, PRESENT, can further reduce the hardware requirement to as few as 1,570 GEs with reasonable security (80 bits) and performance [43]. For asymmetric cryptography, a minimum 113-bit ECC can be realized in hardware with a much larger chip area (at least 10,000 GEs) [108].

Note that the minimal requirement does not imply that every RFID system constructed based on PRF or its equivalents is unp*-privacy. For example, the RFID systems given in [45, 109] are reported to have privacy vulnerabilities, though they are constructed based on symmetric encryption schemes or cryptographic hash functions. How to apply PRF or its equivalents in designing an efficient and low-cost RFID system with unp*-privacy remains interesting for further investigation.

The protocol illustrated in Figure 3.10 can be considered as an example of such design, which is motivated from the protocol given in [95]. One advantage of this protocol is that it is most efficient in identifying a tag in normal situations in which desynchronization does not happen frequently; it resorts occasionally to exhaustive search to identify a tag that has been desynchronized, but resumes to exact match of index again after a successful read of the tag until the next desynchronization attack.

The minimal condition reflects the equivalence between unp*-privacy and PRF family. PRF can also be used to construct RFID systems with ind-privacy. However, the other direction is uncertain. An open problem is to find the minimal condition for enforcing ind-privacy in RFID systems.

3.2 ZERO-KNOWLEDGE-BASED PRIVACY

Deng et al. proposed a zero-knowledge based RFID framework for RFID privacy, or zk-privacy for short [110, 111]. Intuitively, zk-privacy means that whatever information an adversary can obtain from interacting with a target tag can be derived by any simulator without interacting with the target tag. In other words, the interaction between the adversary and the target tag leaks zero/no information for the adversary to trace the tag.

ZK-privacy is defined in a rigorous and precise manner based on a zero-knowledge formulation [112, 113], and it incorporates the notions of adaptive completeness and mutual authentication. It is claimed to be more practical than unp-privacy, and stronger in terms of privacy than ind-privacy.

3.2.1 PRELIMINARIES

The mathematical notations, negligible function and pseudorandom functions used in defining zk-privacy are essentially the same as used in defining ind-privacy and unp-privacy in the previous section. A slight difference is that a security parameter κ is used consistently in defining and analyzing zk-privacy in this section. To be complete, we provide necessary preliminaries for defining zk-privacy even if there are some overlaps with the previous section.

A function $f : \mathbb{N} \to \mathbb{R}$ is said to be *negligible* if for every $c > 0$ there exits a number $m \in \mathbb{N}$ such that $f(\kappa) < \frac{1}{\kappa^c}$ holds for all $\kappa > m$, where $\mathbb{N}$ is the set of all non-negative integers, and $\mathbb{R}$ is the set of all real numbers. Two distribution ensembles $\{X(\kappa, z)\}_{\kappa \in \mathbb{N}, z \in \{0,1\}^*}$ and $\{Y(\kappa, z)\}_{\kappa \in \mathbb{N}, z \in \{0,1\}^*}$ are computationally indistinguishable, if for any probabilistic polynomial-time (PPT) algorithm D, and for sufficiently large $\kappa \in \mathbb{N}$ and any $z \in \{0, 1\}^*$, it holds that $|\Pr[D(\kappa, z, X) = 1] - \Pr[D(\kappa, z, Y) = 1]|$ is negligible in κ.

On a security parameter κ, let $m(\cdot)$ and $l(\cdot)$ be two positive polynomials in κ. Goldreich et al. defined pseudorandom functions [114] as follows:

$$\{F_k : \{0, 1\}^{m(\kappa)} \longrightarrow \{0, 1\}^{l(\kappa)}\}_{k \in_R \{0,1\}^\kappa}$$

is a PRF ensemble if the following two conditions hold:

1. efficient evaluation: There exists a polynomial-time algorithm that on input k and $x \in \{0, 1\}^{m(\kappa)}$ returns $F_k(x)$; and

2. pseudorandomness: A PPT oracle machine A (t, ϵ)-breaks the PRF ensemble, if

$$|\Pr[A^{F_\kappa}(\kappa) = 1] - \Pr[A^{H_\kappa}(\kappa) = 1]| \geq \epsilon$$

where F_κ is a random variable uniformly distributed over the multi-set $\{F_k\}_{k \in_R \{0,1\}^\kappa}$, H_κ is uniformly distributed among all functions mapping $m(\kappa)$-bit-long strings to $l(\kappa)$-bit-long strings, and the running time of A is at most t (here each oracle query accounts for one unit operation).

The PRF ensemble is (t, ϵ)-pseudorandom, if for all sufficiently large κ there exists no algorithm A that can (t, ϵ)-break the PRF ensemble. The PRF ensemble is pseudorandom, if for all sufficiently large κ's there exists no algorithm A that can (t, ϵ)-break the PRF ensemble, *for any t that is polynomial in κ and any ϵ that is non-negligible in κ.*

3.2.2   MODEL OF RFID SYSTEM

Deng et al. provided a formal description on RFID system and adversary [110, 111]. Compared to the previous section, it (i) generalizes the RFID protocol in multiple rounds (instead of three rounds), (ii) considers concurrent sessions, and (iii) provides a more detailed description on each session.

A probabilistic polynomial-time concurrent man-in-the-middle adversary is modeled for defining zk-privacy. The four oracles which an adversary can access, including InitReader, SendT, SendR, and Corrupt, are essentially the same as the ones used in the previous session, where SendT, SendR, and Corrupt correspond to InitTag, SendRes, and SetTag, respectively. A slight difference is that these oracles are defined with respect to a generalized RFID protocol and precise description on sessions.

In addition, an RFID system is defined to be "complete" in terms of adaptive completeness and "sound" in terms of mutual authentication.

RFID System Setting   Consider an RFID system comprising of a single legitimate reader (or multiple readers without distinguishing their identities) R and a set of ℓ tags $\mathcal{T} = \{\mathcal{T}_1, ..., \mathcal{T}_\ell\}$, where ℓ is a polynomial in security parameter κ. The reader and the tags are probabilistic polynomial time interactive Turing machines. An RFID system $(R, \mathcal{T})$ is setup by a procedure, denoted Setup(κ, ℓ). Specifically, on (κ, ℓ), this setup procedure generates a public system parameter σ_R, a reader secret-key k_R and initial internal state s_R^1 (if needed) for R. It may also setup an initial database DB^1 for R to store necessary information for identifying and authenticating tags. For each i, $1 \leq i \leq \ell$, this procedure generates a public parameter $\xi_{\mathcal{T}_i}$ and an initial secret-key $k_{\mathcal{T}_i}^1$ for tag $\mathcal{T}_i$ and sets the tag's initial internal state to be $s_{\mathcal{T}_i}^1$ (typically, $s_{\mathcal{T}_i}^1$ includes the public parameters σ_R and $\xi_{\mathcal{T}_i}$). It also associates each tag $\mathcal{T}_i$ with a unique ID, as well as other necessary information such as tag key and/or tag state information, and inserts it as a record in a database DB^1 of R. Note that $\xi_{\mathcal{T}_i}$ or/and $s_{\mathcal{T}_i}^1$ can be empty strings.

Let $para = (\sigma_R, \xi_1, \cdots, \xi_\ell)$ denote public system parameters. It is assumed that in the RFID system, the reader is secure, which is a "black-box" to an adversary.

A tag $\mathcal{T}_i$, $1 \leq i \leq \ell$, exchanges messages with reader R through a protocol $\pi(R, \mathcal{T}_i)$. Without loss of generality, it is assumed that a protocol run of π is always initiated by R and π consists of $2\gamma + 1$ rounds[1] for some $\gamma \geq 1$. Each protocol run of π is called a session. It is assumed that each tag interacts with the reader sequentially, but multiple tags can interact with the reader "concurrently" (with some anti-collision protocols). To allow and distinguish concurrent sessions (at the side of reader R), each session of protocol π is associated with a unique session identifier sid. In practice, sid is typically generated by the reader when it is invoked to send the first-round message. It is assumed that each message from tag to reader always bears a session-identifier.

Each tag $\mathcal{T}_i$, as well as reader R, uses fresh and independent random coins (generated on the fly) in each session, *in case it is an randomized algorithm.* It is assumed that the random coins used in each session are erased once the session is completed (whether successfully finished or aborted). Also, in each session run, the tag may update its internal state and secret-key, and the reader may update its internal state and database. It is assumed that the update process of new internal state and secret-key by an uncorrupted tag automatically overwrites (i.e., erases) its old internal state and secret-key.

Given security parameter κ, it is assumed that each tag $\mathcal{T}_i$ takes part in at most s (sequential) sessions in its life time[2] with R, and thus R involves at most $s\ell$ sessions, where s is some polynomial in κ. In practice, the value s can be a fixed constant (e.g., $s = 2^{28}$ [115]).

More precisely, for the j-th session (ordered by the session initiation time) where $1 \leq j \leq s\ell$, the reader R takes the input from the system parameters $para$, its secret-key k_R, current internal state s_R^j, database DB^j, random coins ρ_R^j, and a partial transcript T, where T is either an empty string (which indicates the starting of a new session) or a sequence of messages $(sid, c_1, \alpha_1, c_2, \alpha_2, \cdots, c_u, \alpha_u)$, $1 \leq u \leq \gamma$ (which indicates the on-going of session with sid). The reader R outputs the next message c_{u+1}. In the case of $T = (sid, c_1, \alpha_1, c_2, \alpha_2, \cdots, c_\gamma, \alpha_\gamma)$, besides sending back the last-round message $c_{\gamma+1}$, the reader R also updates its internal state to s_R^{j+1}, its database to DB^{j+1}, and stops the session by additionally outputting a bit, denoted by o_R^{sid}. This output bit indicates either acceptance ($o_R^{sid} = 1$) or rejection ($o_R^{sid} = 0$) of the current session.

Without loss of generality, it is assumed that the j-th session run by the reader R corresponds to the v-th session (of session-identifier sid) run by tag $\mathcal{T}_i$, where $1 \leq v \leq s$ and $1 \leq i \leq \ell$. In this session, $\mathcal{T}_i$ takes the input from the system parameters $para$, its current secret-key $k_{\mathcal{T}_i}^v$, current internal state $s_{\mathcal{T}_i}^v$, random coins $\rho_{\mathcal{T}_i}^v$, and a partial transcript $T = (sid, c_1, \alpha_1, \cdots, \alpha_{u-1}, c_u)$, where $1 \leq u \leq \gamma$. The tag $\mathcal{T}_i$ outputs the next message (sid, α_u). In the case of $T = (sid, c_1, \alpha_1, \cdots, c_\gamma, \alpha_\gamma, c_{\gamma+1})$ (i.e., $\mathcal{T}_i$ has received the last-round message of the session with sid), $\mathcal{T}_i$ updates its internal state to $s_{\mathcal{T}_i}^{v+1}$, its secret-key to $k_{\mathcal{T}_i}^{v+1}$, and stops the session by additionally outputting a bit, denoted by $o_{\mathcal{T}_i}^{sid}$. This output bit indicates either acceptance ($o_{\mathcal{T}_i}^{sid} = 1$) or rejection ($o_{\mathcal{T}_i}^{sid} = 0$) of the current session run by $\mathcal{T}_i$.

---

[1]For protocols of 2γ rounds with the last-round message sent by tag, we can define, by default, the $(2\gamma + 1)$-th round (from reader to tag) to be the output of R that indicates acceptation or rejection of the protocol run. Also, without loss of generality, it is assumed that R and $\mathcal{T}_i$ exchange some system public parameters in the first two rounds.

[2]It is assumed that s is large enough so that any tag can never run up to s sessions in its life time; otherwise, an adversary may distinguish two tags, thus violate their privacy, by running one tag more than s times while the other less than s times [99].

Note that in the above description, it is assumed that the reader and tags update their internal states, database, or keys *at the end of each protocol run*. In reality, this can be performed at any point of each protocol run. Also, for RFID protocol π with unidirectional authentication from tag to reader, the tag may not have a session output. In this case, the session output $o_{\mathcal{T}_i}^{sid}$ is set to "0".

Adversary   After an RFID system $(R, \mathcal{T})$ is setup by invoking Setup(κ, ℓ), An adversary $\mathcal{A}$ is modeled as a probabilistic polynomial-time concurrent man-in-the-middle (CMIM) against $(R, \mathcal{T})$, with adaptive tag corruption. Let $\hat{m}$ denote a message sent by adversary $\mathcal{A}$, and m denote the actual message sent by reader R or an uncorrupted tag. The adversary is given access to the following oracles:

InitReader(): $\mathcal{A}$ invokes R to start a session of protocol π and generate the first-round message c_1 which is also used as the session identifier sid. Supposing that the new session is the j-th session run by R, the reader R stores c_1 into its internal state s_R^j, and returns c_1 to the adversary.

SendT$(\mathcal{T}_i, \hat{m})$: Adversary $\mathcal{A}$ sends $\hat{m}$ to $\mathcal{T}_i$[3]. After receiving $\hat{m}$, $\mathcal{T}_i$ works as follows. (1) If $\mathcal{T}_i$ currently does not run any existing session, $\mathcal{T}_i$ initiates a new session with the session-identifier sid set to $\hat{m}$, treats $\hat{m}$ as the first-round message of the new session, and returns the second-round message (sid, α_1). (2) If $\mathcal{T}_i$ is currently running an incomplete session with session-identifier $sid = \hat{c}$, and is waiting for the u-th message from R, where $u \geq 2$, $\mathcal{T}_i$ works as follows: If $2 \leq u \leq \gamma$, it treats $\hat{m}$ as the u-th message from the reader and returns the next round message (sid, α_u). If $u = \gamma + 1$ (i.e., $\mathcal{T}_i$ is waiting for the last-round message of the session with sid), $\mathcal{T}_i$ returns its output $o_{\mathcal{T}_i}^{sid}$ to the adversary, and (internally) updates its internal state to $s_{\mathcal{T}_i}^{v+1}$, assuming that the session with sid is the v-th session run by $\mathcal{T}_i$, where $1 \leq v \leq s$.

SendR$(\widehat{sid}, \hat{\alpha})$: Adversary $\mathcal{A}$ sends $(\widehat{sid}, \hat{\alpha})$ to R. After receiving $(\widehat{sid}, \hat{\alpha})$, R checks from its internal state whether it is running a session with session identifier $sid = \widehat{sid}$, and works as follows. (1) If R is currently running an incomplete session with $sid = \widehat{sid}$ and is waiting for the u-th message from a tag, where $1 \leq u \leq \gamma$, R acts as follows: If $u < \gamma$, it treats $\hat{\alpha}$ as the u-th message from the tag, and returns the next round message c_{u+1} to $\mathcal{A}$. If $u = \gamma$, it returns the last-round message $c_{\gamma+1}$ and the output o_R^{sid} to $\mathcal{A}$, and internally updates its internal state to s_R^{j+1} and the database to DB^{j+1}, assuming that the session with sid corresponds to the j-th session run by R. (2) In all other cases, R returns a special symbol $\perp$ (indicating invalid query).

Corrupt$(\mathcal{T}_i)$: Adversary $\mathcal{A}$ obtains the secret-key and internal state information (as well as the random coins) currently held by $\mathcal{T}_i$. Once tag $\mathcal{T}_i$ is corrupted, all its actions are controlled and performed by the adversary $\mathcal{A}$.

Let O_1, O_2, O_3, and O_4 denote the above oracles, respectively. These oracles fully capture the capability of any PPT CMIM adversary with adaptive tag corruption.[4] Let $\mathcal{O}$ denote the set of

---

[3]For simplicity, notation $\mathcal{T}_i$ is abused to denote any virtual identity of a tag in $\mathcal{T}$ (not the tag's real identity) labeled by $\mathcal{A}$ when $\mathcal{A}$ selects the tag from $\mathcal{T}$.

[4]For simplicity, it is assumed that all tags are always within the attack scope of adversary. In practice, some tags may be in or out from the attack scope of adversary at different time [116].

the four oracles $\{O_1, O_2, O_3, O_4\}$ specified above. *An adversary is a (t, n_1, n_2, n_3, n_4)-adversary, if it works in time t and makes oracle queries to O_μ without exceeding n_μ times, where $1 \leq \mu \leq 4$.* Each oracle call is treated as a unit operation, and thus for a t-time adversary it holds that $\Sigma_{\mu=1}^4 n_\mu \leq t$. Let $A^O(R, \mathcal{T}, para)$ denote a PPT algorithm A that, on input of some system public parameter *para*, concurrently interacts with R and the tags in $\mathcal{T}$ via the four oracles in $\mathcal{O}$, where $(R, \mathcal{T})$ is setup by $\mathsf{Setup}(\kappa, \ell)$.

Note that in this formulation, the output bits of protocol participants (which indicate authentication success or failure) are *publicly* accessible to the adversary. The reason is that, in reality, such outputs can be publicly observed from the behaviors of protocol participants during/after the protocol run or can be learnt by some other side channels.

Adaptive Completeness and Mutual Authentication   Roughly speaking, adaptive completeness means, after any attacks (*particularly the desynchronizing attacks*) made by an adversary $\mathcal{A}$,[5] the protocol execution between reader R and any uncorrupted tag is still complete (e.g., being able to recover from desynchronization). In other words, after undergoing arbitrary attacks, the uncorrupted parties in an RFID system can still recover *whenever the attacks stop*.

Definition 3.31   Adaptive Completeness   For an RFID system $(R, \mathcal{T})$ setup by $\mathsf{Setup}(\kappa, \ell)$, denote by

$$(sid, c_1^{sid}, \alpha_1^{sid}, \cdots, o_R^{sid}, o_{\mathcal{T}_i}^{sid}) \leftarrow \pi(R, \mathcal{T}_i)$$

the running of a session with identifier *sid* of protocol π between R and an uncorrupted tag $\mathcal{T}_i \in \mathcal{T}$. Suppose that the session with *sid* corresponds to the v-th session at the side of $\mathcal{T}_i$ and the j-th session at the side of R, where $1 \leq v \leq s$ and $1 \leq j \leq s\ell$. Consider the case that the two sessions are of the same round messages, and that all the exchanged messages in these two sessions are all honestly generated by R and $\mathcal{T}_i$. Denote by E the event that $o_R^{sid} = 0$ holds (or $o_{\mathcal{T}_i}^{sid} = 0$ holds if protocol π is for mutual authentication)[6] or R identifies a different tag $\mathcal{T}_{i'} \neq \mathcal{T}_i$ in its j-th session.

A PPT CMIM adversary $\mathcal{A}$ $(t, \epsilon, n_1, n_2, n_3, n_4)$-breaks the adaptive completeness of the RFID system against an uncorrupted tag $\mathcal{T}_i$, if the probability that event E occurs is at least ϵ and $\mathcal{A}$ is a (t, n_1, n_2, n_3, n_4)-adversary. The probability is taken over the coins used by $\mathsf{Setup}(\kappa, \ell)$, the coins of $\mathcal{A}$, the coins used by R (*up to finishing the j-th session*), and the coins used by $\mathcal{T}_i$ (*up to finishing the v-th session*). An RFID system $(R, \mathcal{T})$ satisfies adaptive completeness, if for all sufficiently large κ and for any uncorrupted tag $\mathcal{T}_i$, there exists no adversary $\mathcal{A}$ that can $(t, \epsilon, n_1, n_2, n_3, n_4)$-break the adaptive completeness against $\mathcal{T}_i$, for any (t, ϵ), where t is polynomial in κ and ϵ is non-negligible in κ.

Now consider mutual authentication of RFID protocols. Roughly speaking, for protocol π of RFID system $(R, \mathcal{T})$, the authentication from reader to tag (resp., from tag to reader) means

---

[5]Here, for presentation simplicity, we model message losses caused by the underlying network also as a kind of adversarial attack.

[6]In the case of $o_R^{sid} = 0$ or $o_{\mathcal{T}_i}^{sid} = 0$, the session with *sid* may not be complete.

that a CMIM adversary $\mathcal{A}$ cannot impersonate reader R (resp., an uncorrupted tag $\mathcal{T}_i \in \mathcal{T}$) to an uncorrupted tag $\mathcal{T}_i \in \mathcal{T}$ (resp., reader R), unless $\mathcal{A}$ honestly relays messages actually generated and sent by R and tag $\mathcal{T}_i$. To make this formal, a notion of matching sessions should be defined.

Definition 3.32   Matching Sessions   Denote by $(sid, c_1^{sid}, \alpha_1^{sid}, \cdots, \alpha_\gamma^{sid}, c_{\gamma+1}^{sid})$ the transcript of exchanged round messages (except the session outputs) of a *successfully completed* session with *sid* of protocol π run by a tag $\mathcal{T}_i$, where $1 \le i \le \ell$. This session has a matching session at the side of reader R, if R ever successfully completed a session with identical session transcript.

Denote by $(sid', c_1^{sid'}, \alpha_1^{sid'}, \cdots, \alpha_\gamma^{sid'}, c_{\gamma+1}^{sid'})$ the transcript of exchanged round messages (except the session outputs) of a *successfully completed* session sid' run by R. This session has a matching session at the side of some tag $\mathcal{T}_i$, where $1 \le i \le \ell$, if either of the following conditions holds:

- $\mathcal{T}_i$ ever *completed*, whether successfully finished or aborted, a session of the identical transcript *prefix* $(sid', c_1^{sid'}, \alpha_1^{sid'}, \cdots, \alpha_\gamma^{sid'})$; or

- $\mathcal{T}_i$ is now running a session with partial transcript $(sid', c_1^{sid'}, \alpha_1^{sid'}, \cdots, \alpha_\gamma^{sid'})$ and is waiting for the last-round message of session sid'.

The matching-session definition, for a successfully completed session run by reader R, takes into account the following "cutting-the-last-message" attack: A CMIM adversary $\mathcal{A}$ relays the messages exchanged by R and an uncorrupted tag $\mathcal{T}_i$ for a protocol run of π until receiving the last-round message $c_{\gamma+1}^{sid'}$ from R; after this, $\mathcal{A}$ sends an arbitrary message $\hat{c}_{\gamma+1}^{sid'} (\ne c_{\gamma+1}^{sid'})$ to $\mathcal{T}_i$ (which typically causes $\mathcal{T}_i$ to abort the session), or, just drops the session at the side of $\mathcal{T}_i$ without sending $\mathcal{T}_i$ the last-round message. Such "cutting-the-last-message" attacks are unpreventable.

Figure 3.11 shows the authentication experiment $\mathbf{Exp}_{\mathcal{A}}^{auth}[\kappa, \ell]$. A CMIM adversary $\mathcal{A}$ interacts with R and tags in $\mathcal{T}$ via the four oracles in $\mathcal{O}$. At the end of the experiment, $\mathcal{A}$ outputs the transcript, *trans*, of a session. Denote by E_1 the event that *trans* corresponds to the transcript of a successfully completed session run by R in which R successfully identifies an *uncorrupted* tag $\mathcal{T}_i$, but this session has no matching session at the side of the uncorrupted tag $\mathcal{T}_i$. Denote by E_2 the event that *trans* corresponds to the transcript of a successfully completed session run by some *uncorrupted* tag $\mathcal{T}_i \in \mathcal{T}$, and this session has no matching session at the side of R.

Experiment $\mathbf{Exp}_{\mathcal{A}}^{auth}[\kappa, \ell]$
1. run Setup(κ, ℓ) to setup the reader R and a set of tags $\mathcal{T}$;
    denote by *para* the public system parameters;
2. *trans* $\leftarrow \mathcal{A}^{\mathcal{O}}(R, \mathcal{T}, para)$.

Figure 3.11: Authentication experiment.

Definition 3.33 **Authentication** Given security parameter κ, an adversary $\mathcal{A}$ $(\epsilon, t, n_1, n_2, n_3, n_4)$-breaks the authentication of an RFID system $(R, \mathcal{T})$ against reader R (resp., an uncorrupted tag $\mathcal{T}_i \in \mathcal{T}$) if the probability that event E_1 (resp., E_2) occurs is at least ϵ and $\mathcal{A}$ is a (t, n_1, n_2, n_3, n_4)-adversary.

The RFID system $(R, \mathcal{T})$ satisfies tag-to-reader authentication (resp., reader-to-tag authentication), if for all sufficiently large κ there exists no adversary $\mathcal{A}$ that can $(\epsilon, t, n_1, n_2, n_3, n_4)$-break the authentication of $(R, \mathcal{T})$ against reader R (resp., any uncorrupted tag $\mathcal{T}_i \in \mathcal{T}$), for any (t, ϵ), where t is polynomial in κ and ϵ is non-negligible in κ. An RFID system satisfies mutual authentication, if it satisfies both tag-to-reader authentication and reader-to-tag authentication.

There exist some differences between adaptive completeness and (mutual) authentication. On the one hand, adaptive completeness is formulated w.r.t. the session transcript between R and an honest uncorrupted tag $\mathcal{T}_i$ (that corresponds to the j-th (resp., v-th) session at the side of R (resp., $\mathcal{T}_i$)), while in the authentication experiment, the session transcript (*output by adversary* $\mathcal{A}$) is typically between adversary $\mathcal{A}$ and reader R or an honest tag. On the other hand, in the definition of adaptive completeness, the probability is taken over the coins of R *up to finishing the j-th session* and the coins of $\mathcal{T}_i$ *up to finishing the v-th session*, while in the definition of (mutual) authentication, the probability is taken over the coins of R and tags in all sessions (besides the coins used by $\mathcal{A}$ and Setup(κ, ℓ)).

3.2.3 ZK-PRIVACY

To formally define zk-privacy, it is necessary to clarify the notion of blind access to tags and the notion of clean tags.

Let $A^{\mathcal{O}}(R, \widehat{\mathcal{T}}, \mathcal{I}(\mathcal{T}_g), aux)$ be a PPT algorithm A that, given input $aux \in \{0, 1\}^*$ (typically, aux includes system parameters and historical state information of A), concurrently interacts with R and a set of tags $\widehat{\mathcal{T}}$ via the four oracles $\mathcal{O} = \{O_1, O_2, O_3, O_4\}$. A is said to have *blind access* to a *challenge* tag $\mathcal{T}_g \notin \widehat{\mathcal{T}}$ if A interacts with $\mathcal{T}_g$ via a special interface $\mathcal{I}$. Specifically, $\mathcal{I}$ is a PPT algorithm that runs $\mathcal{T}_g$ internally, and interacts with A externally. To send a message $\hat{c}$ to $\mathcal{T}_g$, A sends to $\mathcal{I}$ a special O_2 oracle query of the form SendT$(challenge, \hat{c})$; after receiving this special O_2 query, $\mathcal{I}$ invokes $\mathcal{T}_g$ with SendT$(\mathcal{T}_g, \hat{c})$, and returns to A the output of $\mathcal{T}_g$. From the viewpoint of A, it does not know which tag it is interacting with. It is also required that A interacts with $\mathcal{T}_g$ via O_2 queries only.

Next, the notion of clean tags is defined. A tag $\mathcal{T}_i$ is called *clean*, if it is not corrupted (i.e., no adversary has made any O_4 query to $\mathcal{T}_i$), and is not currently running an incomplete session with reader R, i.e., the last session of the tag has been either finished or aborted. In other words, a clean tag is an uncorrupted tag that is currently at the status of waiting for the first-round message from reader R to start a new session.

ZK-privacy is defined in terms of two worlds in a zk-privacy experiment. Figure 3.12 illustrates the real world of a zk-privacy experiment, $\mathbf{Exp}_A^{zkp}[\kappa, \ell]$ ($\mathbf{Exp}_A^{zkp}$, for simplicity), in which a PPT CMIM adversary $\mathcal{A}$ is comprised of a pair of algorithms $(\mathcal{A}_1, \mathcal{A}_2)$ and runs in two stages. In the *first stage*, algorithm $\mathcal{A}_1$ is concurrently interacting with R and all the tags in $\mathcal{T}$ via the four oracles in $\mathcal{O}$, and is required to output a set $\mathcal{C}$ of *clean* tags at the end of the first stage, where $\mathcal{C} \subseteq \mathcal{T}$ consists of δ *clean* tags, denoted as $\{\mathcal{T}_{i_1}, \cdots, \mathcal{T}_{i_\delta}\}$. The algorithm $\mathcal{A}_1$ also outputs state information st, which will be transmitted to algorithm $\mathcal{A}_2$. Between the first stage and the second stage, a challenge tag, denoted as $\mathcal{T}_g$, is taken uniformly at random from $\mathcal{C}$. Note that if $\delta = 0$, then no challenge tag is selected, and $\mathcal{A}$ is reduced to $\mathcal{A}_1$ in this experiment. In the *second stage*, on input st, $\mathcal{A}_2$ concurrently interacts with reader R and the tags in $\widehat{\mathcal{T}} = \mathcal{T} - \mathcal{C}$ via the four oracles in $\mathcal{O}$, and additionally has blind access to $\mathcal{T}_g$. Note that $\mathcal{A}$ cannot corrupt any tag (particularly $\mathcal{T}_g$) in $\mathcal{C}$, and $\mathcal{A}$ does not have access to tags in $\mathcal{C} - \{\mathcal{T}_g\}$ in the second stage. Finally, $\mathcal{A}_2$ outputs its view, denoted by $view_{\mathcal{A}}$, at the end of the second stage. Specifically, $view_{\mathcal{A}}$ is defined to include system public parameter *para*, the random coins used by $\mathcal{A}$, $\rho_{\mathcal{A}}$, and the (ordered) list of all oracle answers to the queries made by $\mathcal{A}$ in experiment $\mathbf{Exp}_{\mathcal{A}}^{zkp}$. Note that $view_{\mathcal{A}}$ does not explicitly include the oracle queries made by $\mathcal{A}$ and $\mathcal{A}$'s output at the first stage, as all these values are implicitly determined by the system public parameter *para*, $\mathcal{A}$'s coins and all oracle answers to $\mathcal{A}$'s queries. The output of experiment $\mathbf{Exp}_{\mathcal{A}}^{zkp}$ is defined to be $(g, view_{\mathcal{A}})$. Denote by $(g, view_{\mathcal{A}}(\kappa, \ell))$ the random variable describing the output of experiment $\mathbf{Exp}_{\mathcal{A}}^{zkp}[\kappa, \ell]$.

Experiment $\mathbf{Exp}_{\mathcal{A}}^{zkp}[\kappa, \ell]$
1. run Setup(κ, ℓ) to setup the reader R and a set of tags $\mathcal{T}$; denote by *para* the public system parameter;
2. $\{\mathcal{C}, st\} \leftarrow \mathcal{A}_1^{\mathcal{O}}(R, \mathcal{T}, para)$, where $\mathcal{C} = \{\mathcal{T}_{i_1}, \mathcal{T}_{i_2}, \cdots, \mathcal{T}_{i_\delta}\} \subseteq \mathcal{T}$ is a set of *clean* tags, $0 \le \delta \le \ell$;
3. $g \in_R \{1, \cdots, \delta\}$, set $\mathcal{T}_g = \mathcal{T}_{i_g}$ and $\widehat{\mathcal{T}} = \mathcal{T} - \mathcal{C}$;
4. $view_{\mathcal{A}} \leftarrow \mathcal{A}_2^{\mathcal{O}}(R, \widehat{\mathcal{T}}, \mathcal{I}(\mathcal{T}_g), st)$;
5. output $(g, view_{\mathcal{A}})$.

Figure 3.12: ZK-privacy experiment: real world.

Figure 3.13 illustrates the simulated world of zk-privacy experiment, $\mathbf{Exp}_{\mathcal{S}}^{zkp}[\kappa, \ell]$ ($\mathbf{Exp}_{\mathcal{S}}^{zkp}$, for simplicity), in which a PPT simulator $\mathcal{S}$ is comprised of a pair of algorithms $(\mathcal{S}_1, \mathcal{S}_2)$ and runs in two stages. In the *first stage*, algorithm $\mathcal{S}_1$ concurrently interacts with R and all the tags in $\mathcal{T}$ via the four oracles in $\mathcal{O}$, and outputs a set, denoted $\mathcal{C}$, of *clean* tags, where $|\mathcal{C}| = \delta$ and $0 \le \delta \le \ell$. It also outputs state information st, which will be transmitted to algorithm $\mathcal{S}_2$. Between the two stages, a value g is taken uniformly at random from $\{1, \cdots, |\mathcal{C}|\}$ (which is unknown to $\mathcal{S}$). In the *second stage* of $\mathcal{S}$, on input st, $\mathcal{S}_2$ concurrently interacts with reader R and the tags in $\widehat{\mathcal{T}} = \mathcal{T} - \mathcal{C}$, and outputs a simulated view, denoted *sview*, at the end of the second stage. It is required that all oracle answers to the queries made by $\mathcal{S}$ (in both the first stage and the second stage) in experiment

---

Experiment $\mathbf{Exp}_{\mathcal{S}}^{zkp}[\kappa, \ell]$

1. run Setup(κ, ℓ) to setup the reader R and a set of tags $\mathcal{T}$; denote by *para* the public system parameter;
2. $\{\mathcal{C}, st\} \leftarrow \mathcal{S}_1^{\mathcal{O}}(R, \mathcal{T}, para)$, where $\mathcal{C} = \{T_{i_1}, T_{i_2}, \cdots, T_{i_\delta}\} \subseteq \mathcal{T}$ is a set of *clean* tags, $0 \le \delta \le \ell$;
3. $g \in_R \{1, \cdots, \delta\}$, and set $\widehat{\mathcal{T}} = \mathcal{T} - \mathcal{C}$;
4. $sview \leftarrow \mathcal{S}_2^{\mathcal{O}}(R, \widehat{\mathcal{T}}, st)$, where *sview* particularly includes all oracle answers to queries made by $\mathcal{S}$;
5. output $(g, sview)$.

Figure 3.13: ZK-privacy experiment: simulated world.

$\mathbf{Exp}_{\mathcal{S}}^{zkp}$ are included in *sview*. The output of experiment $\mathbf{Exp}_{\mathcal{S}}^{zkp}$ is defined as $(g, sview)$. Denote by $(g, sview(\kappa, \ell))$ the random variable describing the output of experiment $\mathbf{Exp}_{\mathcal{S}}^{zkp}[\kappa, \ell]$.

Informally, an RFID protocol π satisfies zk-privacy, if whatever can be derived from interacting with a challenge tag $\mathcal{T}_g$ in the second-stage of $\mathcal{A}$ can actually be derived by $\mathcal{A}$ itself *without interacting with* $\mathcal{T}_g$. In this sense, the interaction between $\mathcal{A}_2$ and $\mathcal{T}_g$ leaks "zero knowledge" to $\mathcal{A}$.

Definition 3.34 ZK-Privacy An RFID protocol π satisfies computational (resp., statistical) zk-privacy, if for any PPT CMIM adversary $\mathcal{A}$ there exists a polynomial-time simulator $\mathcal{S}$ such that for all sufficiently large κ and any ℓ which is polynomials in κ (i.e., $\ell = poly(\kappa)$, where $poly(\cdot)$ is some positive polynomial), the following ensembles are computationally (resp., statistically) indistinguishable:

- $\{g, view_{\mathcal{A}}(\kappa, \ell)\}_{\kappa \in N, \ell \in poly(\kappa)}$

- $\{g, sview(\kappa, \ell)\}_{\kappa \in N, \ell \in poly(\kappa)}$.

That is, for any polynomial-time (resp., any power unlimited) algorithm D, it holds that

$$|Pr[D(\kappa, \ell, g, view_{\mathcal{A}}(\kappa, \ell)) = 1] - Pr[D(\kappa, \ell, g, sview(\kappa, \ell)) = 1]| = \varepsilon,$$

where ε is negligible in κ. The probability is taken over the random coins used by Setup(κ, ℓ), the random coins used by $\mathcal{A}$, $\mathcal{S}$, reader R, and all (uncorrupted) tags, the choice of g, and the coins used by the distinguisher algorithm D.

ZK-privacy can be extended to forward and backward zk-privacy. Denote by $(k_{T_g}^f, s_{T_g}^f)$ (resp., $(k_{T_g}^1, s_{T_g}^1)$) the final (resp., initial) secret-key and internal state of $\mathcal{T}_g$ at the end of (resp., beginning) of the experiment $\mathbf{Exp}_{\mathcal{A}}^{zkp}$. An RFID protocol π is of *forward* (resp., *backward*) zk-privacy, if for any PPT CMIM adversary $\mathcal{A}$ there exists a polynomial-time simulator $\mathcal{S}$ such that for all sufficiently large κ and any $\ell = poly(\kappa)$, the following distributions are indistinguishable: $\{k_{T_g}^f, s_{T_g}^f (resp., k_{T_g}^1, s_{T_g}^1), g, view_{\mathcal{A}}(\kappa, \ell)\}$ and $\{k_{T_g}^f, s_{T_g}^f (resp., k_{T_g}^1, s_{T_g}^1), g, sview(\kappa, \ell)\}$. For forward/backward zk-privacy, it is required that the challenge tag T_g should remain *clean* at the end of experiment $\mathbf{Exp}_{\mathcal{A}}^{zkp}$. Note that the adversary is allowed to corrupt the challenge tag after the end of $\mathbf{Exp}_{\mathcal{A}}^{zkp}$.

3.2.4 DISCUSSIONS

Why allow $\mathcal{A}_1$ to output an arbitrary set $\mathcal{C}$ of tags, and limit $\mathcal{A}_2$ to blind access to a challenge tag chosen randomly from $\mathcal{C}$? The definition of zk-privacy implies that adversary $\mathcal{A}$ cannot distinguish any challenge tag T_g from any set $\mathcal{C}$ of tags; otherwise, $\mathcal{A}$ can figure out the identity of T_g in $\mathcal{C}$ from its view $view_{\mathcal{A}}$, while this tag's identity cannot be derived from any simulator's view $sview$ (a formal proof of this in case of $|\mathcal{C}| = 2$ is provided in Section 3.2.5). If $\mathcal{C}$ is removed from the definition of zk-privacy, it is possible for the adversary to distinguish any two tags under its attack, even if each of the tags can be perfectly simulated by a simulator. A special case is that each tag has an upper-bound of sessions in its life time so that an adversary can distinguish any two tags by setting one tag to be run out of sessions in the learning stage [99]. In addition, we do not restrict $\mathcal{C}$ to two tags so as to take into account the case that any number of tags may be correlated.

Why limit $\mathcal{A}_1$ to output of clean tags? If $\mathcal{A}_1$ is allowed to output "unclean tags", $\mathcal{A}_2$ can trivially violate the zk-privacy. Consider that $\mathcal{A}_1$ selects two tags that are waiting for different round message (e.g., one tag is clean and the other is not), then $\mathcal{A}_2$ can trivially distinguish them by forwarding to T_g different round messages.

Why allow $\mathcal{S}$ to have access to oracles in $\mathcal{O}$? Suppose that $\mathcal{S}$ simulates a tag from scratch and $\mathcal{A}$ (run by $\mathcal{S}$ as a subroutine) requests to corrupt the tag in the middle of the simulation. Without oracle access, it is difficult or even impossible for $\mathcal{S}$ to continue its simulation and keep it consistent with its previous simulation for the same tag.

Why limit $sview$ to include all oracle answers to queries made by $\mathcal{S}$? This is to restrict $\mathcal{S}$ not to access the oracles in $\mathcal{O}$ more than $\mathcal{A}$ does. The indistinguishability between the simulated view $sview$ and the real view $view_{\mathcal{A}}$ of adversary $\mathcal{A}$ in zk-privacy implies that for any (t, n_1, n_2, n_3, n_4)-adversary $\mathcal{A}$, with overwhelming probability, $\mathcal{S}$ cannot query O_1, O_2, O_3, O_4 more than n_1, n_2, n_3, n_4 times, respectively.

Why require T_g to remain clean at the end of $\mathbf{Exp}_{\mathcal{A}}^{zkp}$ for forward/backward privacy? In general, forward/backward privacy cannot be achieved if an adversary is allowed to corrupt the challenge tag before the end of its sessions in $\mathbf{Exp}_{\mathcal{A}}^{zkp}$ (i.e., the tag is not clean at the moment of corruption); otherwise, the adversary is able to derive certain protocol messages from the tag's internal state, secret-key, random coins, and partial session transcript.

More on backward privacy. In general, backward privacy means that even if $\mathcal{A}$ learns the internal state and secret-key of a tag for the v-th session, it still cannot distinguish the run of $(v + 1)$-th session run by this tag from a simulated session run. Without loss of generality, we assume that the internal state and secret-key known to $\mathcal{A}$ are the initial ones (i.e., $k_{T_g}^1$ and $s_{T_g}^1$).

For most RFID protocols in practice, the internal state and the secret-key of any tag at any time t can be determined by the tag's initial state, initial secret-key, and the session transcript related to the tag up to time t. In such a case, the indistinguishability between the simulated view $sview$ of S and the real view $view_A$ of A relies upon the random coins used by T_g in experiment $\mathbf{Exp}_A^{zkp}$. These random coins are not disclosed to A since the random coins used by an uncorrupted tag in any session are erased once the session is completed, and the challenge tag T_g is required to be clean at the end of $\mathbf{Exp}_A^{zkp}$.

Why disallow A_2 to corrupt tags in C in zk-privacy formulation? For any tag $T_i \in C$ corrupted by A_2, it can distinguish whether T_i is the challenge tag T_g or not, which can nullify any polynomial-time successful simulation by the simulator S *unless S can also corrupt the corresponding tags in C.* However, allowing the simulator S to corrupt (or just get access to) tags in C weakens simulatability (e.g., in case tags have correlated states) and can even make it meaningless (e.g., in case S corrupts the challenge tag T_g), as such simulator is too powerful. Recall that A_2 and the simulator should, in particular, not know which tag in C is the challenging tag. For conceptual simplicity, A_2 is not allowed to have access to tags in C other than blind access to the challenge tag T_g. As it shall be clear that, zk-privacy is still very powerful.

Special cases in zk-privacy experiments. One special case is that in experiment $\mathbf{Exp}_A^{zkp}$, A_1 outputs $C = T$. In this case, the simulator S_2 does not have oracle access to any tag. The zk-privacy is analogue to auxiliary-input zero-knowledge [113], where the view of A_1/S_1 corresponds to the auxiliary input. Another special case is that A_1 outputs only a single tag in C, and all other tags can be corrupted by A_1 and A_2. In this case, the forward/backward zk-privacy implies that both adversary A and simulator S have access to certain secret information of all tags.

Suppose an RFID system consists of a single tag T_i, and consider a special adversary A_1 that simply outputs $C = \{T_i\}$ without any interaction with T_i, zk-privacy ensures that all actions of T_i can be simulated efficiently. In general, if an RFID system consists of a single tag, as long as the single tag is clean, all its actions can be simulated efficiently.

Comparison with traditional formulation of zero-knowledge. The notion of zk-privacy is defined based on the traditional zero-knowledge formulation [112, 113] with the following differences. First, in zk-privacy, the simulator S is allowed to have access to oracles in O (where the actions of these oracles may depend upon some secret values such as secret-keys and internal states), while traditional zk-simulator is a polynomial-time algorithm without oracle access to players of secret values. Second, the zk-privacy is formulated against a structured adversary A which is divided into two phases, while the traditional zk is formulated against any polynomial-time adversary. Third, in zk-privacy, the random challenge g is unknown to A, but is presented to the distinguisher, which renders extra power to the distinguisher; in comparison, in the traditional zero-knowledge formulation, the distinguisher and the adversary essentially have the same power and advantage. Lastly, for forward (resp., backward) zk-privacy, the final (resp., initial) secret-key and internal state of the challenge tag T_g are disclosed to A, while for the traditional zero-knowledge formulation, no secret values of the knowledge prover are assumed to be leaked to the adversary.

3.2.5 COMPARISONS WITH IND-PRIVACY AND UNP-PRIVACY

Comparison with Ind-Privacy   Ind-privacy proposed in [99] describes the indistinguishability between any two tags by an adversary. It was mentioned in [99] that an important area for future research is to study stronger RFID privacy notions. It can be proven that zk-privacy is strictly stronger than a revised version of ind-privacy after some subtleties are clarified. The revised version of ind-privacy is given below (which is later compared to the original version as given in section 3.1.2).

Figure 3.14 illustrates the ind-privacy experiment $\mathbf{Exp}_{\mathcal{A}}^{ind}[\kappa, \ell, n_1, n_2, n_3, n_4]$ ($\mathbf{Exp}_{\mathcal{A}}^{ind}$, for simplicity). In $\mathbf{Exp}_{\mathcal{A}}^{ind}$, an adversary $\mathcal{A}$ is comprised of a pair of algorithms $(\mathcal{A}_1, \mathcal{A}_2)$ and runs in two stages. Throughout the experiment, adversary $\mathcal{A}$ is allowed to launch O_1, O_2, O_3, and O_4 oracle queries without exceeding n_1, n_2, n_3, and n_4 overall calls, respectively. The experiment proceeds as follows. At first, the experiment runs $\mathsf{Setup}(\kappa, \ell)$ to setup an RFID system $(R, \mathcal{T})$. Then, in the *learning stage*, algorithm $\mathcal{A}_1$ outputs a piece of state information st and a pair of *clean tags* $\{\mathcal{T}_{i_0}, \mathcal{T}_{i_1}\}$ to which it has not made Corrupt queries. Next, the experiment selects a random bit g and sets the challenge tag to be $\mathcal{T}_{i_g}$. Finally, in the *guessing stage*, algorithm $\mathcal{A}_2$ is asked to make a guess on the random bit g by outputting a bit b'. During the second stage, $\mathcal{A}_2$ can interact with R and the tags in $\widehat{\mathcal{T}} = \mathcal{T} - \{\mathcal{T}_{i_0}, \mathcal{T}_{i_1}\}$, and get blind access to (but cannot corrupt) the challenge tag $\mathcal{T}_{i_g}$ via an interface $\mathcal{I}$. (In [99], it is stated that $\mathcal{A}_2$ is still allowed to access the challenge tag $\mathcal{T}_{i_g}$ but cannot corrupt $\mathcal{T}_{i_g}$, without formally formulating the interface entity $\mathcal{I}$.)

Experiment $\mathbf{Exp}_{\mathcal{A}}^{ind}[\kappa, \ell, n_1, n_2, n_3, n_4]$

1. run $\mathsf{Setup}(\kappa, \ell)$ to setup the reader R and a set of tags $\mathcal{T}$; denote by *para* the system public parameters;
2. $\{\mathcal{T}_{i_0}, \mathcal{T}_{i_1}, st\} \leftarrow \mathcal{A}_1^{\mathcal{O}}(R, \mathcal{T}, para)$; //*learning stage*
3. set $\widehat{\mathcal{T}} = \mathcal{T} - \{\mathcal{T}_{i_0}, \mathcal{T}_{i_1}\}$;
4. $g \in_R \{0, 1\}$;
5. $b' \leftarrow \mathcal{A}_2^{\mathcal{O}}(R, \widehat{\mathcal{T}}, \mathcal{I}(\mathcal{T}_{i_g}), st)$; //*guess stage*
6. the experiment outputs 1 if $b' = g$, 0 otherwise.

Figure 3.14: Ind-privacy experiment revisited.

Definition 3.35 **Ind-Privacy Revisited** The advantage of $\mathcal{A}$, denoted $\text{Adv}_{\mathcal{A}}^{ind}(\kappa, \ell, n_1, n_2, n_3, n_4)$, in experiment $\text{Exp}_{\mathcal{A}}^{ind}[\kappa, \ell, n_1, n_2, n_3, n_4]$ is defined as:

$$|\Pr[\text{Exp}_{\mathcal{A}}^{ind}[\kappa, \ell, n_1, n_2, n_3, n_4] = 1] - \frac{1}{2}|.$$

An adversary $\mathcal{A}$ $(\epsilon, t, n_1, n_2, n_3, n_4)$-breaks the ind-privacy of an RFID system $(R, \mathcal{T})$ if the advantage of $\mathcal{A}$ in experiment $\text{Exp}_{\mathcal{A}}^{ind}$, i.e., $\text{Adv}_{\mathcal{A}}^{ind}(k, \ell, n_1, n_2, n_3, n_4)$, is at least ϵ and the running time of $\mathcal{A}$ is at most t.

An RFID system $(R, \mathcal{T})$ is said to satisfy ind-privacy, if there exists no adversary who can $(\epsilon, t, n_1, n_2, n_3, n_4)$-break the RFID system for some non-negligible ϵ and some polynomials t, n_1, n_2, n_3, n_4 (all of them are in κ).

In the original definition of ind-privacy (see Section 3.1.2), it is not explicitly specified that the two tags output by $\mathcal{A}_1$ must be clean tags. In the definition of forward ind-privacy [99], the time point of tag corruption and the actions of adversary after tag corruption are not precisely specified.

Now compare zk-privacy with ind-privacy in an RFID system with only one tag. In such a case, any RFID protocol, even if it reveals the tag's secret-key, trivially satisfies ind-privacy. The reason is that in this special scenario, the view of $\mathcal{A}$ is independent of the random bit g (as the challenge tag $\mathcal{T}_{i_g}$ is always the unique tag regardless of the choice of g), and thus $\Pr[b' = g]$ is $\frac{1}{2}$ for any adversary. In comparison, zk-privacy in such case essentially degenerates to the traditional zero-knowledge definition, which still provides reasonable privacy guarantee. In general, zk-privacy is stronger than ind-privacy as shown below.

Theorem 3.36 zk-privacy is stronger than ind-privacy.

First, zk-privacy implies ind-privacy, which holds unconditionally. In other words, if an RFID system $(R, \mathcal{T})$ does not satisfy ind-privacy, then it also does not satisfy zk-privacy. To prove this, we show that if there exists a PPT adversary $\mathcal{A} = (\mathcal{A}_1, \mathcal{A}_2)$ which can $(\epsilon, t, n_1, n_2, n_3, n_4)$-break the ind-privacy of the RFID system $(R, \mathcal{T})$, then we can construct another PPT adversary $\mathcal{A}'$ such that no PPT simulator exists for $\mathcal{A}'$.

In the experiment $\text{Exp}_{\mathcal{A}'}^{zkp}$, let $\mathcal{A}'$ run $\mathcal{A}$ and do whatever $\mathcal{A}$ does. In particular, $\mathcal{A}'$ and $\mathcal{A}$ take the same parameters (t, n_1, n_2, n_3, n_4). Since $\mathcal{A}$ run by $\mathcal{A}'$ always outputs a *pair* of clean tags at the end of its first stage, $\text{Exp}_{\mathcal{A}'}^{zkp}$ outputs $(g, view_{\mathcal{A}'})$, where $g \in \{0, 1\}$ is a random bit, and $view_{\mathcal{A}'}$ implicitly determines the output of $\mathcal{A}$ (i.e., the guessed bit b'). That is, the guessed bit b' can be computed from $view_{\mathcal{A}'}$ in polynomial-time. Since it is assumed that $\mathcal{A}$ $(\epsilon, t, n_1, n_2, n_3, n_4)$-breaks ind-privacy, it holds that $\Pr[b' = g]$ is at least $\frac{1}{2} + \epsilon$ for the output of $\text{Exp}_{\mathcal{A}'}^{zkp}$. However, the simulated view *sview* in the output of experiment $\text{Exp}_{\mathcal{S}}^{zkp}$ is independent of g (recall that random value g is unknown to simulator $\mathcal{S}$). Therefore, for the guessed bit b' implied by *sview* (which can be computed from *sview* in polynomial-time), it always holds that $Pr[b' = g] = \frac{1}{2}$. This shows that for the above $\mathcal{A}'$ and for any polynomial-time simulator, there exists a polynomial-time distinguisher that can distinguish the output of $\mathsf{Exp}_{\mathcal{A}}^{zkp}$ from that of $\mathsf{Exp}_{\mathcal{S}}^{zkp}$ with nonnegligible probability at least ϵ.

Next, several protocol examples are provided to show that it is possible to satisfy ind-privacy but not zk-privacy.

Consider a special RFID system which consists of only one tag $\mathcal{T}_1$ (and reader R). The secret-key of $\mathcal{T}_1$ is the signature on $\mathcal{T}_1$'s ID, denoted s_{ID}, signed by R under the public-key of R. Consider an RFID protocol π in which $\mathcal{T}_1$ reveals its secret-key s_{ID} to R. As the RFID system consists of only one tag, the protocol π satisfies ind-privacy. However, π clearly does not satisfy zk-privacy. Specifically, considering an adversary $\mathcal{A} = (\mathcal{A}_1, \mathcal{A}_2)$ where $\mathcal{A}_1$ simply outputs $\mathcal{C} = \{\mathcal{T}_1\}$ and then $\mathcal{A}_2$ invokes $\mathcal{T}_g = \mathcal{T}_1$ to get the signature s_{ID}, no PPT simulator can output s_{ID} due to the security of the underlying signature scheme. Note that any secure one-time signature can be used to show that this protocol does not satisfy zk-privacy, where secure one-time signature can be constructed based on any one-way function [118].

Given any ind-private two-round RFID protocol $\pi = (c, a)$ for an RFID system $(R, \mathcal{T})$, where $\mathcal{T}$ consists of polynomially many tags, c is the first-round message from the reader and a is the response from a tag, π can be transformed into a new protocol π' as follows: In the protocol π', besides their respective secret-keys, all tags in $\mathcal{T}$ also share a unique pair of public-key PK and secret-key SK in a CPA-secure public-key encryption scheme. For a protocol run of π' between reader R and a tag $\mathcal{T}_i$, R sends $c' = E_{PK}(c)$ in the first-round, and $\mathcal{T}_i$ decrypts c' to get c and then sends back $a' = c\|a$. The protocol π' could appear in the scenario of tag group authentication, where the ability of sending back c demonstrates the membership of a group identified due to public-key PK. Furthermore, in the scenario of anonymizer-enabled RFID systems [119], the decryption operation can be performed by the anonymizer. As in protocol π' all tags share the same public-key PK, the ind-privacy of π' is inherited from that of π. Specifically, the session transcripts of π' can be computed in polynomial-time from the session transcripts of π and public-key PK. However, π' does not satisfy zk-privacy. Specifically, consider an adversary $\mathcal{A} = (\mathcal{A}_1, \mathcal{A}_2)$, where $\mathcal{A}_1$ simply outputs the set of clean tags $\mathcal{C} = \mathcal{T}$ (in particular, $\mathcal{A}$ never corrupts tags) and then $\mathcal{A}_2$ blindly interacts with the challenge tag $\mathcal{T}_g$ for only one session. Due to the CPA-security of the underlying public-key encryption scheme, no PPT simulator can handle the $\mathsf{SendT}(challenge, \hat{c})$ queries made by $\mathcal{A}_2$, as such ability implies the ability of ciphertext decryption. Note that CPA security is sufficient here, as the adversary $\mathcal{A}$ involves only one session with the challenge tag $\mathcal{T}_g$.

Although the above two protocol examples may not seem very realistic, they clearly show the differences between zk-privacy and ind-privacy. It remains an interesting question to find more interesting protocols that are ind-private but not zk-private.

Comparison with Unpredictability-Based Privacy Notions   The RFID privacy notions given in [95, 96, 97, 101] are formulated based on the unpredictability of protocol output. For convenience, these privacy notions (including unp-privacy [101], *unp'*-privacy [95], and *unp**-privacy

[96, 97]) are generally referred to as "unp-based privacy notions." The unp-based privacy notions are formulated with respect to RFID protocols with a 3-round canonical form, denoted as $\pi = (c, r, f)$, where c, r, f stand for the first, second, and third round message, respectively. Note that zk-privacy is not confined to this protocol structure.

The unp-based privacy notions require that the second-round message sent from a tag must be pseudorandom (i.e., indistinguishable from a truly random string). This requirement has certain limitations. First, any RFID protocol $\pi = (c, r, f)$ satisfying unp-based privacy notions can be modified to $\pi' = (c, r||1, f)$, where "$||$" denotes the string concatenation operation. That is, the modified protocol π' is identical to π except that in the second-round, the tag additionally concatenates a bit "1" to r. This modified RFID-protocol π' does not satisfy unp-based privacy notions, as the second-round message $r||1$ is clearly not pseudorandom. However, intuitively, the tags' privacy should be preserved since the same bit "1" is appended to all second-round messages for all tags. Notice that when RFID-protocols are implemented in practice, the messages being exchanged between reader and tags normally bear some nonrandom information such as version number of RFID standard. Another limitation is that the unp-based privacy notions may exclude the use of public-key encryption in RFID-protocols, as public-key generated ciphertexts are typically *not* pseudorandom.

Another point is that the adversaries considered in the definition of unp-based privacy notions are not allowed to access protocol outputs. If an adversary $\mathcal{A}$ has access to protocol outputs, it can simply distinguish between real protocol messages and random messages in the guess stage of privacy experiments. What $\mathcal{A}$ needs to do is to forward a second (or third) protocol message to reader (or uncorrupted tag). If the message is generated by an uncorrupted tag (or by the reader in a matching session), the reader (or the tag) will always output "accept." On the other hand, if the message is just a random value, with overwhelming probability the reader (or the tag) will reject the message due to authentication soundness.

In summary, it is argued that zk-privacy is more reasonable than unp-based privacy notions in practice. It allows for more general protocol structure, more powerful adversary, and nonpseudorandom protocol messages.

3.2.6 AN RFID MUTUAL AUTHENTICATION PROTOCOL WITH ZK-PRIVACY

Deng et al. proposed an RFID mutual authentication protocol with zk-privacy [111], which is illustrated in Figure 3.15. Let $F_k: \{0, 1\}^{2\kappa} \rightarrow \{0, 1\}^{2\kappa}$ be a pre-specified keyed PRF and F_k^0 (resp., F_k^1) the κ-bit prefix (resp., suffix) of the output of F_k, where κ is the system security parameter. When a tag $\mathcal{T}_i$ with identity *ID* registers to the reader R, it is assigned a secret-key $k \in_R \{0, 1\}^\kappa$, and a counter *ctr* of length l_{ctr} with initial value 1. Reader R pre-computes an initial index $I = F_k^0(1||pad_1)$ for the tag, where $pad_1 \in \{0, 1\}^{2\kappa - l_{ctr}}$ is a fixed padding, and stores the tuple (I, k, ctr, ID) into its database.

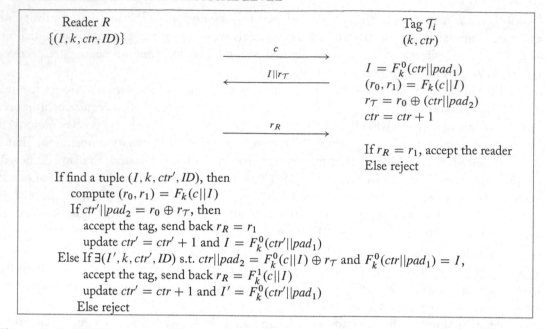

Figure 3.15: RFID mutual authentication protocol with ZK-privacy.

At the start of a new protocol session, R sends a challenge string $c \in_R \{0, 1\}^\kappa$ to $\mathcal{T}_i$, which also serves as the session identifier. To simplify the presentation, the session identifier and the corresponding verification of the identifier by protocol players are implicitly implied and will not be explicitly mentioned in the following.

Upon receiving c from R, $\mathcal{T}_i$ computes $I = F_k^0(ctr\|pad_1)$, $(r_0, r_1) = F_k(c\|I)$ (where $r_0 = F_k^0(c\|I)$ and $r_1 = F_k^1(c\|I)$), and $r_T = r_0 \oplus (ctr\|pad_2)$. $\mathcal{T}_i$ sends (I, r_T) to R and then updates its counter $ctr = ctr + 1$, where $pad_2 \in \{0, 1\}^{\kappa - l_{ctr}}$ is another predetermined padding string.

After receiving (I, r_T), R searches its database to find a tuple indexed by I.

- If R finds such a tuple, say (I, k, ctr', ID), it computes $(r_0, r_1) = F_k(c\|I)$, and checks whether $ctr'\|pad_2 = r_0 \oplus r_T$: If yes, R accepts $\mathcal{T}_i$ by outputting "1", sends $r_R = r_1$ to the tag, updates the tuple (I, k, ctr', ID) with $ctr' = ctr' + 1$ and $I = F_k^0(ctr'\|pad_1)$; if not, R searches for the next tuple including I (to avoid potential collision of index I, i.e., two different tuples are of the same index I, which though occurs with negligible probability due to the pseudorandomness of PRF). If all tuples indexed by I fail in the above checks, R rejects the tag and outputs "0".

- If no tuple is found to have an index I (which indicates counter desynchronization between R and $\mathcal{T}_i$), for each tuple (I', k, ctr', ID) in its database, R computes $(r_0, r_1) = F_k(c\|I)$ and $ctr\|pad_2 = r_0 \oplus r_T$, and checks whether $I = F_k^0(ctr\|pad_1)$: If yes (which indicates ctr is the correct counter value at $\mathcal{T}_i$), R accepts $\mathcal{T}_i$, outputs "1", sends back $r_R = r_1$ as the third message, and updates the tuple (I', k, ctr', ID) with $ctr' = ctr+1$ and $I' = F_k^0(ctr'||pad_1)$. In the case that R fails with all the tuples in its database, it rejects the tag and outputs "0".

Upon receiving r_R, T_i checks whether $r_R = r_1$: If yes, T_i accepts the reader and outputs "1"; otherwise, it rejects the reader and outputs "0".

The design of this protocol is motivated by the design of protocol with unp^*-privacy (see Figure 3.10). In this protocol, each tag performs only two PRF operations. In the normal case without counter desynchronization, with overwhelming probability the reader mainly performs two PRF operations. In the worst case with counter desynchronization, the reader needs to performs about $2n$ PRF operations where n is the number of entries in the reader's database. Note that in practice, PRFs which are constructed based on lightweight stream/block ciphers or hashing [120, 121, 122, 123, 124] can be implemented very efficiently. Further note that the tags in this protocol are deterministic without secret-key updating (for presentation simplicity, such protocols are referred to as deterministic RFID authentication protocols). This protocol is not backward/forward private in accordance with the backward/forward zk-privacy formulation presented in Section 3.2.3. This is because no *deterministic* RFID authentication protocols *without proper secret-key update mechanisms* can be backward/forward private in any existing RFID privacy framework. The above proposed scheme can be easily modified to satisfy backward or forward privacy by introducing appropriate secret-key update mechanisms, which is left for future exploration. Since zk-privacy is strictly stronger than ind-privacy, this protocol also satisfies ind-privacy.

Theorem 3.37   Assuming F_k is a pseudorandom function, the protocol specified above satisfies adaptive completeness, mutual authentication and zk-privacy [111].

3.3   VAUDENAY'S PRIVACY FRAMEWORK

Vaudenay proposed a comprehensive privacy framework for RFID tag authentication [116], which is further extended for mutual authentication [117]. In Vaudenay's privacy framework, an RFID system of one reader (or multiple readers without distinguishing their identities) and multiple tags is defined below.

Definition 3.38   RFID System   An RFID system consists of the following components.

- A setup scheme $SetupReader(1^s)$ which generates a private/public key pair (K_S, K_P) for the reader depending on a security parameter s. K_S is stored in the reader's backend, while K_P is publicly released. It is assumed that s is implicitly specified in K_P.

- A polynomial-time algorithm $SetupTag_{K_P}(ID)$ which returns (K, S) for a tag, where K is the tag's secret and S is the tag's initial state. The pair (K, S) is stored in the reader's backend if the tag is legitimate.

- A polynomial-time interactive protocol between the reader and a tag in which the reader ends with a tape *Output*.

It is required that the reader's output is correct except with a negligible probability for any polynomial-time experiment which can be described as follows:

- set up the reader;

- create multiple tags including a target one named *ID*; and

- execute a complete protocol between reader and tag *ID*.

The reader's output is correct if and only if *Output* $= \perp$ and tag *ID* is not legitimate, or *Output* $=$ *ID* and *ID* is legitimate.

Oracles   At any time, a tag can be either free tag (which is out of access from an adversary) or drawn tag (which an adversary can communicate with). A virtual tag (or vtag) is a unique reference to the action of drawing a tag (from free tag to drawn tag). A virtual tag plays the same role as a temporary identity or pseudonym for a drawn tag. In Vaudenay's privacy framework, the following eight oracles are used to capture the capabilities of an adversary given public key K_P as input.

1. *CreateTag^b(ID)*: It creates a free tag, either legitimate ($b = 1$) or not ($b = 0$), with unique identifier *ID*. This oracle uses *SetupTag$_{K_P}$* to set up the tag and (for $b = 1$ only) update the reader's database.

2. *DrawTag(distr)* $\rightarrow$ *(vtag$_1$, b$_1$, ..., vtag$_n$, b$_n$)*: It moves from the set of free tags to the set of drawn tags a tuple of tags at random according to distribution *distr*. This oracles returns a vector of virtual tags *(vtag$_1$, ... vtag$_n$)* which anonymously designate these tags. It also returns a bit vector *(b$_1$, ... b$_n$)* to indicate whether the drawn tags are legitimate or not. In addition, this oracle keeps a hidden table $\mathcal{T}$ such that $\mathcal{T}(vtag)$ is the *ID* of *vtag*.

3. *Free(vtag)*: It moves the virtual tag *vtag* back to the set of free tags.

4. *Launch* $\rightarrow$ π: It makes the reader launch a new protocol instance π.

5. *SendReader(m, π)* $\rightarrow$ *m'*: It sends a message *m* to a protocol instance π for the reader and receives a reply *m'*.

6. *SendTag(m, vtag)* $\rightarrow$ *m'*: It sends a message *m* to a virtual tag *vtag* and receives a reply *m'*.

7. *Result(π)* $\rightarrow$ *x*: When π is complete, this oracle returns 1 if *Output* $\neq \perp$ and 0 otherwise.

8. *Corrupt(vtag)* $\rightarrow$ *S*: It returns the current state *S* of the tag *vtag*. If *vtag* is no longer used after this oracle call, *vtag* is said to be destroyed.

For convenience, let *Execute*(*vtag*) → (π, *transcript*) group a *Launch* query and successive use of *SendReader* and *SendTag* to execute a complete protocol between the reader and the tag *vtag*. It returns the transcript of the protocol π, which is the list of successive protocol messages.

Adversary Classes   In Vaudenay's privacy framework, an adversary can be categorized into the following classes.

- Weak adversary: It cannot corrupt any tags.

- Forward adversary: It can corrupt tags under the limitation that once the adversary corrupts a tag, it can do nothing subsequently except for corrupting more tags.

- Destructive adversary: It can do anything after a tag corruption, but with the limitation that the adversary cannot reuse a tag after corrupting it. Specifically, once a tag is corrupted it will be virtually destroyed. In particular, a destructive adversary cannot observe or interact with a corrupted tag nor can the adversary impersonate a corrupted tag to the reader.

- Strong adversary: It has no limitations on corrupting tags, and can do anything at its wish.

For each category of adversary defined above, a *narrow* variant is defined, where a narrow adversary cannot access the output of any protocol run.

Definition 3.39   Strong, Destructive, Forward, Weak, and Narrow Adversary   Consider polynomial-time adversaries. Let *Strong* be the class of adversaries who have access to all eight oracles. Let *Destructive* be the class of adversaries who never use *vtag* again after a *Corrupt*(*vtag*) query. Let *Forward* be the class of adversaries in which *Corrupt* queries can only be followed by other *Corrupt* queries. Let *Weak* be the class of adversaries who make no *Corrupt* query. Let *Narrow* be the class of adversaries who make no *Result* query.   It is clear that *Strong* $\Longrightarrow$

Destructive $\Longrightarrow$ *Forward* $\Longrightarrow$ *Weak*, and that any of these classes is stronger than its narrow variant.

Privacy   The privacy notion in Vaudenay's framework is defined in terms of adversary's capability of inferring non-trivial ID relations from protocol messages. Informally, an adversary is trivial if it makes no effective use of protocol messages; in other words, these protocol messages can be simulated without significantly affecting the success probability of the adversary.

Definition 3.40   Consider an adversary which launches its attacks in two phases: attack phase and analysis phase. In the attack phase, the adversary can make appropriate oracle queries according to the adversary's class, while in the analysis phase, the adversary make no oracle query. In between, the adversary is provided with the hidden table $\mathcal{T}$ of the *DrawTag* oracle. The adversary outputs either *true* or *false* at the end of the analysis phase. The adversary wins if the output is *true*.

Definition 3.41   Blinder, Trivial Adversary   A blinder B for an adversary A is a polynomial-time algorithm which sees the same messages as A and simulates the *Launch*, *SendReader*, *SendTag*, and *Result* oracles to A. The blinder does not have access to the reader's tapes so does not know the reader's secret key or database. A blinded adversary A^B is itself an adversary which does not use the *Launch*, *SendReader*, *SendTag*, and *Result* oracles. An adversary is trivial if there exists a blinder B such that $|Pr[A \text{ wins}] - Pr[A^B \text{ wins}]|$ is negligible.

Definition 3.42   Privacy   An RFID system is P-private if all such adversaries which belong to class P are trivial, where P can be any of *Strong, Destructive, Forward, Weak*, and their *Narrow* variants.

The privacy notion measures the privacy loss in the wireless link but not in tag corruption as *Corrupt* queries are not blinded. It can be proven that narrow-weak privacy is equivalent to weak privacy, and narrow-forward privacy is equivalent to forward privacy provided that whenever a legitimate tag and the reader have some matching conversation, the reader does not output $\perp$ [116]. Another conclusion is that no RFID system can be destructive-private and at the same time narrow-strong private, which implies that strong privacy is not possible [116].

Case Studies   Three typical RFID authentication protocols are investigated under Vaudenay's privacy framework [116]. The first one is a simple challenge response protocol. Let $(F_K)_{K \in \{0,1\}^{k(s)}}$ be a pseudorandom function family (PRF) from $\{0,1\}^{\delta(s)}$ to $\{0,1\}^{\gamma(s)}$ where $k(s), \delta(s), \gamma(s)$ are polynomially bounded and $2^{-\delta(s)}$ and $2^{-\gamma(s)}$ are negligible. The algorithm *SetupTag(ID)* picks a random k-bit key K and sets tag state $S = K$. A challenge-response protocol can be constructed as follows:

- reader picks a random $\frac{\gamma}{2}$-bit string a and sends it to tag;

- tag with state S sends a random $\frac{\gamma}{2}$-bit string b and $c = F_S(a,b)$ to reader; and

- reader searches for (ID, K) in its database such that $c = F_K(a,b)$; it returns ID or $\perp$ if (ID, K) is not found.

It can be proven that this protocol is secure (in terms of soundness of tag authentication) and weak-private [116].

The second protocol involves update of tag state so that it is narrow-destructive private. Let F and G are two oracles running random functions from $\{0,1\}^{\alpha+k}$ and $\{0,1\}^k$ to $\{0,1\}^k$, respectively. The algorithm *SetupTag(ID)* picks a random k-bit key K and sets tag state $S = K$. The protocol works as follows:

- reader picks a random α-bit string a and sends it to tag;

- tag with state S sends $c = F(S,a)$ to reader, and then updates its state S with $G(S)$; and

- reader searches for (ID, K) in its database such that $c = F(G^i(K), a)$ for any $i < t$, where t is a predetermined threshold. The reader returns ID or $\perp$ if (ID, K) is not found.

It can be proven that the above protocol is secure (in terms of soundness of authentication) and narrow-destructive private in the random oracle model provided that k and t are polynomially bounded and that 2^{-k} is negligible [116]. This protocol is not complete since after t iterations without the reader a tag can no longer be identified.

This protocol can be tweaked to get narrow-forward privacy but not narrow-destructive privacy. In the tweaked protocol, all tags share an additional common secret K_s in their states such that when a tag receives a special query $a = K_s$ (instead of normal query where a is a random bit string), the tag replies with its unique secret $c = K$. This tweaked protocol is not narrow-destructive private because K_s can be obtained by an adversary in corrupting a tag, and thus used in querying other tags after the corruption. It is still narrow-forward private since the adversary cannot query any other tags except corruption after corruption.

The last protocol is constructed using public key cryptography (PKC). A PKC system consists of a key generator, a probabilistic encryption algorithm, and a deterministic decryption algorithm. A PKC system is IND-CPA secure (IND-CCA secure, respectively) if the advantage of polynomial-time adversaries winning the IND-CPA (IND-CCA, respectively) game is negligible. In the IND-CPA game, a polynomial-time adversary is given a public key, generates two equal-length messages m_1 and m_2, and submits them to a challenge oracle along with the public key. The challenge oracle selects one of the messages with probability 1/2, encrypts the message with the public key, and returns the ciphertext c_0 to the adversary. The adversary wins the game if it can determine which message was chosen by the oracle with a probability greater than 1/2. In the IND-CCA game, a polynomial-time adversary can further access a decryption oracle which returns the plaintext of any ciphertext except c_0.

The PKC-based RFID system is initiated by generating a private/public key pair (K_S, K_P) for a PKC system with encryption algorithm Enc_{K_P} and decryption algorithm Dec_{K_S}. A master secret key K_M is also generated in the RFID system. The tag generation algorithm $SetupTag(ID)$ selects a random k-bit key K for a tag ID and sets the tag's initial state as $S = (K_P, ID, K)$, where $K = F_{K_M}(ID)$ is generated using a PRF F parameterized with the master key. The RFID reader stores the private key K_S and the master key K_M. Assuming k and α are polynomial, the PKC-based protocol works as follows:

- reader picks an α-bit random a and sends it to tag;

- tag sends ciphertext $c = Enc_{K_P}(ID||K||a)$ to reader; and

- reader decrypts $Dec_{K_S}(c) = ID||K||a'$, and checks whether $a' = a$ and $K = F_{K_M}(ID)$; if so, it outputs ID; else it outputs $\perp$.

It can be proven that this protocol is narrow-strong private if the PKC system is IND-CPA secure. It is further forward private if the PKC system is IND-CCA secure [116].

Discussions   In Vaudenay's privacy framework, an adversary is categorized into (i) weak, (ii), forward, (iii) destructive, and (iv) strong. For each category, it also defines a narrow variant. Suppose that P is one of the adversary categories. Informally, an RFID protocol is called P-private if for any adversary $\mathcal{A} \in P$, there exists a simulator $\mathcal{S}$ such that $\mathcal{A}$ cannot distinguish its interactions with the actual RFID system or with the simulator.

Compared to zk-privacy, the simulator in Vaudenay's privacy framework is not required to handle tag corruption queries by the adversary. In other words, the simulator works only for those adversaries which do not make tag corruption queries. It is not clear how such simulator acts upon tag corruption queries made by an adversary. Suppose that $\mathcal{S}$ simulates a tag from scratch and $\mathcal{A}$ (typically run by $\mathcal{S}$ as a subroutine) requests to corrupt the tag in the middle of simulation (possibly in the middle of a session run). Without access to tag corruption queries, it is difficult or even impossible for $\mathcal{S}$ to continue its simulation for the tag and keep it consistent with its previous simulation for the same tag.

The adversary considered in zk-privacy essentially corresponds to strong adversary Vaudenay's privacy framework, with the difference in that the adversary cannot corrupt any tag in set C of clean tags before the end of zk-privacy experiment $\mathbf{Exp}_{\mathcal{A}}^{zkp}$. In comparison, Vaudenay's privacy framework poses no restriction on tag corruption (though it is not clear how the simulator handles such adversaries), which implies that an adversary can corrupt any tag at any time (possibly in the middle of session). However, in such a case, forward/backward privacy may not be achievable if the challenge tag is corrupted in the middle of a session; this is the reason why it is required that the challenge tag $\mathcal{T}_g$ must remain *clean* at the moment of corruption in zk-privacy, while this point is not very clear in Vaudenay's privacy framework.

Compared to zk-privacy, the matching session concept defined in Vaudenay's privacy framework is restricted to identical session transcript, without clarifying some subtleties such as the "cutting-the-last-message" attacks for tag authentication. The completeness notion is defined for honest protocol execution only, with no adversarial desynchronizing attacks taken into account.

Another difference is that eight oracles are used in Vaudenay's privacy framework to model an adversary's capabilities, while four oracles are used in zk-privacy. Note that, with the formulation of oracles SendT and SendR in zk-privacy, adversary $\mathcal{A}$ can have access to the protocol outputs once a party (the reader or a tag) sends its last-round message. This is necessary if, in reality, such outputs can be publicly observed from the behaviors of protocol participants during/after the protocol run or can be learnt from other side channels. This issue is treated in Vaudenay's privacy framework by separately rendering an additional oracle Result to the adversary, while such Result oracle is implicitly embedded into the formulations of the SendR and SendT oracles in zk-privacy. The other three additional oracles considered in Vaudenay's privacy framework are CreatTag, Draw-Tag and FreeTag. It should not be difficult to add these oracles to zk-privacy. To keep it succinct and without loss of generality, it is assumed in zk-privacy that all tags are always within the attack scope of the adversary, and $\mathcal{T}_i$ is used to denote the virtual identity of a tag in $\mathcal{T}$ (not its real identity) *labeled by* $\mathcal{A}$ when $\mathcal{A}$ selects the tag from the tag set $\mathcal{T}$.

3.4 UNIVERSAL COMPOSIBILITY-BASED PRIVACY

A universal composability (UC)-based privacy framework for RFID authentication was proposed in [125, 126, 127]. UC is a powerful notion proposed by Canetti [128] to describe cryptographic protocols that behave like ideal functionality, and can be composed with other protocols. The UC framework considers the indistinguishability between the real world protocol execution with an arbitrary adversary and the simulation in the ideal world. There is a so-called environment $\mathcal{Z}$ who can set inputs to all parties and can interact with the adversary. In the ideal world, both the reader and tags send inputs to a trusted party which executes according to the ideal functional specification and sends the outputs to the corresponding parties. In the real world, the reader and tags run a real RFID authentication protocol in the presence of an efficient adversary. Roughly speaking, a protocol is UC secure, if for any efficient adversary $\mathcal{A}$ in the real world there exists an efficient simulator S, which corresponds to an adversary in the ideal world, such that no efficient environment $\mathcal{Z}$ can distinguish whether it is interacting with protocol players and $\mathcal{A}$ in the real world or protocols players and the simulator S in the ideal world. Note that, unlike other frameworks, the UC framework for RFID authentication allows reader corruption.

Although the UC framework renders very strong security and privacy guarantee, the formulation of UC security usually results in more complex system design and analysis. The UC framework is also more abstract and may be less easy to understand and apply in comparison with other RFID privacy notions. The original goal of the UC framework aims for strong composability *against arbitrary external protocols*; however, as pointed out in [129, 130, 131], the actual security guarantee of UC is quite subtle. Specifically, UC security implicitly assumes that external arbitrary protocols, with which the protocol in question (e.g., RFID authentication protocol here) is composed, are "independent" of the protocol in question in the sense that they do not share common states [129, 130, 131].[7] This requirement is quite strong for protocol composition in reality. In particular, UC does not imply, *by definition*, concurrent nonmalleability against concurrent man-in-the-middle adversary, which is a focus in zk-privacy framework [110, 111].

3.5 PRIVACY IN PATH AUTHENTICATION

Now consider an RFID system with multiple readers which may have different identities or they are owned by different parties. We call it multi-reader system, which can be seen in many applications such as RFID-enabled supply chains. Note that the privacy notions presented in the previous sections are defined in the setting of a single reader (or multiple readers without distinguishing their identifies). While these privacy notions can still be used in a multi-reader system, new privacy notions can be defined, including privacy in path authentication and ownership transfer. We

[7]Some stronger versions of UC framework allow limited state sharing via specified interfaces.

focus on privacy in path authentication in this section, and leave ownership transfer to the next section.

Section 2.3 addresses the problem of path authentication, which is used for a valid reader to accept only those tags which have passed through valid paths in a multi-reader system, where a valid path is a legitimate sequence of steps (valid readers) which a valid tag could pass. In RFID path authentication, it is typical to have additional privacy requirement, preventing an adversary from learning any information about the internal processes within the multi-reader system. In particular, an adversary (e.g., competitor in an RFID-enabled supply chain) should not attain any knowledge about tags' paths, nor trace tags through subsequent steps in the system. To formalize the privacy requirement, several privacy notions are defined in this section for path authentication. In addition, the complete versions of typical path authentication solutions (see Section 2.3) are provided to meet the additional privacy requirement.

3.5.1   MULTI-READER SYSTEM AND ADVERSARY MODEL

A multi-reader system is defined as a digraph $G = (V, E)$, where V is a set of vertices, and E is a set of edges. Each vertex $v \in V$ represents one *step* in the system. A vertex/step in the system is uniquely associated with a reader. Each directed edge $e = \overrightarrow{v_i v_j} \in E$ denotes that step v_j is a possible next step to step v_i in the system. It is allowed to have loops and reflexible edges in the system. A *path* is a finite sequence of steps $P = (v_{i_0}, \cdots, v_{i_\ell})$, where $(v_{i_j}, v_{i_{j+1}}) \in E$ for $j \in \{0, \ell - 1\}$. An empty path consists of an empty set of steps. The meaning of "a tag T_i following path P (or moving T_i through P)" is that starting from the current position of tag T_i in the system, the tag will go through path P with v_{i_0} as its next step. The last step v_{i_ℓ} of a valid path $P_{valid_i} = (v_{i_0}, \cdots, v_{i_\ell})$ represents a *check point*. When a tag arrives at a check point, the manager of system needs to verify the tag and its path.

A path authentication scheme consists of an issuer I, a set of managers[8] $\mathcal{M}$ and a set of normal readers $\mathcal{R}$. The issuer I is the starting point of the multi-reader system; a manager from $\mathcal{M}$ is placed at the end of each valid path; and normal readers from $\mathcal{R}$ are placed at other places of the system. The issuer I initializes a tag by storing certain state information in the tag. While a tag goes through the system, each reader in its path updates the state of the tag. Eventually, the tag arrives at a manager, which reads out the state of the tag and verifies its validity. Formally, a path authentication scheme consists of the following functions.

- Initialize(κ): Given a security parameter κ, it setups a multi-reader system G with an issuer I, a set of l managers $\mathcal{M}$, a set of m readers $\mathcal{R}$, a set of n tags $\mathcal{T}$, a set of ν valid path P_{valid}, and public system parameter *para*.

- Read(T_i): It returns the current state S_{T_i} of tag T_i.

- Write(T_i): It writes a new state to tag T_i. For valid readers, it is assumed that they update a tag only if the tag is authenticated.

---

[8]Note that this is generalized from one manager in TRACKER [86].

- PathCheck(S_{T_i}): Given a tag's state S_{T_i}, it verifies whether tag T_i has passed through a valid path. If it is the case, it returns the valid path P_{valid}; else it returns $\emptyset$.

An adversary $\mathcal{A}$ against RFID path authentication is given access to four oracles $\mathcal{O} = \{O_1, O_2, O_3, O_4\}$, where O_1, O_2, O_3 denote Read, Write, PathCheck functions, respectively. Oracle O_4 denotes a new function Move($T_i, k, \mathcal{K}, b$), where k is a positive integer, $\mathcal{K} \in \{P, G\}$ is either path P or the whole system G, and $b \in \{0, 1\}$ is a single bit. Move $(T_i, k, \mathcal{K}, b)$ is defined as follows.

- If $\mathcal{K} = G$, no matter whether $b = 0$ or $b = 1$, starting from the current step of T_i with internal state $S_{T_i}^j$, move the tag T_i forward k steps arbitrarily in the system G.

- If $\mathcal{K} = P$, it works as follows: If $b = 1$, from the current step of T_i with internal state $S_{T_i}^j$, move the tag T_i forward k steps through the designated path $\mathcal{P}$. If $b = 0$, move tag T_i forward k steps along any path.

- The reader in each step updates the tag's state. Finally, Move(T_i, k, P, b) returns the state transcript $\{S_{T_i}^{j+1}, \cdots, S_{T_i}^{j+k}\}$ of T_i from step $j + 1$ to $j + k$. In case there exists no path along which T_i can move k steps in the above definition, an empty path is used and the returned state transcript is empty.

Oracle O_4 is first introduced in [91] so as to precisely model various kinds of tag movement at path level (we refine it to be more general in the above definition). In earlier works [86, 88], the concept of path is not explicitly defined, and the operations on tag movement are specified through step-level oracles. With O_4, any tag movement can be described by adjusting the parameters of the oracle, thus making it easier to define security and privacy notions.

The four oracles capture an adversary's capabilities to read from a tag, write into a tag, check the validity of a tag, and follow a tag through a designated path P (for the case of $\mathcal{K} = P$) or simply update the state of the tag by forwarding it arbitrarily in the system G (for the case of $\mathcal{K} = G$). Let $\mathcal{A}^{\mathcal{O}}(para)$ denote a probabilistic polynomial-time (PPT) adversary $\mathcal{A}$ which, on the input of system public parameter $para$, runs a multi-reader system via the four oracles in $\mathcal{O}$. An adversary is a (t, n_1, n_2, n_3, n_4)-adversary if it works in time t and makes oracle queries to O_μ without exceeding n_μ times, where $1 \leq \mu \leq 4$.

3.5.2 TAG UNLINKABILITY AND STEP UNLINKABILITY

Two privacy notions, tag unlinkability and step unlinkability, can be defined for path authentication [87]. Tag unlinkability defines the privacy of a tag's identity, while step unlinkability models the privacy of a tag's path. Note that in the older version of TRACKER [86], there is another privacy notion, named path unlinkability, which is proven to be weaker than step unlinkability [87].

Tag Unlinkability   Intuitively, tag unlinkability means that an adversary cannot link a tag's state to the tag's identity. A formal definition is given in [91] through a tag-unlinkability experiment

$Exp_{\mathcal{A}}^{Tag-Unlinkability}[\kappa]$, which is shown in Figure 3.16. In the learning phase of the experiment, the adversary is allowed to access oracles O_1, O_2, O_3, O_4 without exceeding n_1, n_2, n_3, n_4 times, respectively. Then, the adversary outputs two tags T_0 and T_1 (which have not reached any checkpoints) together with a transcript st, where st is the information it has gathered. In the challenge phase, the experiment tosses a coin $\delta \in_R \{0, 1\}$, moves the tag T_δ one step forward arbitrarily in the system G, and provides the state transcript $\mathcal{S}_\delta$ of tag T_δ to the adversary. Given $\mathcal{S}_\delta$ and st, the adversary guesses the value of δ, and outputs its guessed value δ'. If $\delta = \delta'$, the experiment outputs 1; otherwise, the experiment outputs 0.

Experiment $\mathbf{Exp}_{\mathcal{A}}^{Tag-Unlinkability}[\kappa]$
1. run Setup(κ) to setup $I, \mathcal{R}, \mathcal{T}, \mathcal{M}, para$.
2. $\{T_0, T_1, st\} \leftarrow \mathcal{A}_1^{\mathcal{O}}(para)$.
3. $\delta \xleftarrow{} _R \{0, 1\}$.
4. $\mathcal{S}_\delta \leftarrow \mathsf{Move}(T_\delta, 1, G, 1)$.
5. $\delta' \leftarrow \mathcal{A}_2^{\mathcal{O}}(\mathcal{S}_\delta, st)$.
6. output 1 if $\delta' = \delta$; 0 otherwise.

Figure 3.16: Tag unlinkability experiment.

Definition 3.43   The advantage of $\mathcal{A}$, denoted $Adv_{\mathcal{A}}^{Tag-Unlinkability}(\kappa)$, in the tag unlinkability experiment is $\left| \Pr[\mathbf{Exp}_{\mathcal{A}}^{\mathbf{Tag-Unlinkability}}[\kappa] = 1] - \frac{1}{2} \right|$.

Definition 3.44   Tag Unlinkability   An   RFID   path   authentication   scheme   is $(t, n_1, n_2, n_3, n_4, \epsilon)$-tag-unlinkable, if $Adv_{\mathcal{A}}^{Tag-Unlinkability}(\kappa) < \epsilon$ holds for any (t, n_1, n_2, n_3, n_4)-adversary $\mathcal{A}$, where ϵ is negligible in κ.

The above definition is slightly different from the original tag unlinkability notion [87] in that the challenge tags T_0 and T_1 are selected by the experiment in the original notion, while they are selected by the adversary in the above definition. Tag unlinkability is also different from the privacy notions given earlier in this chapter (e.g., ind-privacy, unp-privacy, zk-privacy) which do not require that a challenge tag be processed by a valid reader before or during the challenge phase. Essentially, tag unlinkability means that an adversary cannot link to a tag from its state updated by a valid reader. In comparison, the previous privacy notions require that a tag be untraceable no matter whether the tag is updated by a valid reader or not. In this sense, tag unlinkability is weaker.

Step Unlinkability Another privacy notion, step unlinkability, requires that no efficient adversary can tell whether two different tags share a common step or not. The step unlinkability experiment (which is refined from [91] to be more general) $Exp_{\mathcal{A}}^{Step-Unlinkability}[\kappa]$ is shown in Figure 3.17. The experiment starts by setting the system $I, \mathcal{R}, \mathcal{T}, \mathcal{M}$ through Setup(κ). An adversary $\mathcal{A}$ runs two algorithms $\mathcal{A}_1$ and $\mathcal{A}_2$, respectively, in two phases. In the learning phase, $\mathcal{A}_1$ queries the oracle set $\mathcal{O}$ and outputs a tag T, positive integer k, and transcript st (which includes T's path obtained by $\mathcal{A}_1$ in the learning phase). In the challenge phase, the experiment creates a new tag T_c, and tosses a coin $\delta \in_R \{0, 1\}$. Then, the experiment selects a path P as follows: if $\delta = 0$, the path P does not have any common step with T's path; else the path P has one or more common steps with T's path. After getting the path P, the experiment moves T_c along path P by k steps (if possible) and outputs state transcript $\mathcal{S}_{T_c}$. Then, in the challenge phase, the experiment provides adversary $\mathcal{A}_2$ with $\mathcal{S}_{T_c}$ and st. The adversary makes a guess on the value of δ and outputs the guessed value δ'. The experiment outputs 1 if $\delta' = \delta$, and 0 otherwise.

Experiment $\mathbf{Exp}_{\mathcal{A}}^{Step-Unlinkability}[\kappa]$
1. run Setup(κ) to setup $I, \mathcal{R}, \mathcal{T}, \mathcal{M}, para$.
2. $\{T, k, st\} \leftarrow \mathcal{A}_1^{\mathcal{O}}(para)$.
3. create a new tag T_c.
4. randomly select a bit $\delta \in \{0, 1\}$.
5. select a path P as follows:
   if $\delta = 0$, then P dose not have any common step with T's path;
   else, P has one or more common steps with T's path.
6. $\mathcal{S}_{T_c} \leftarrow$ Move($T_c, k, P, 1$)
7. $\delta' \leftarrow \mathcal{A}_2^{\mathcal{O}}(\mathcal{S}_{T_c}, st)$
8. output 1 if $\delta' = \delta$, 0 otherwise.

Figure 3.17: Step unlinkability experiment.

Definition 3.45 The advantage of $\mathcal{A}$, denoted $Adv_{\mathcal{A}}^{Step-Unlinkability}(\kappa)$, in the step unlinkability experiment is $\left| \Pr[\mathbf{Exp}_{\mathcal{A}}^{\mathbf{Step-Unlinkability}}[\kappa] = 1] - \frac{1}{2} \right|$.

Definition 3.46 **Step Unlinkability** An RFID path authentication scheme is $(t, n_1, n_2, n_3, n_4, \epsilon)$-step-unlinkable, if $Adv_{\mathcal{A}}^{Step-Unlinkability}(\kappa) < \epsilon$ holds for any (t, n_1, n_2, n_3, n_4)-adversary $\mathcal{A}$, where ϵ is negligible in κ.

Note that the above definition is different from the original notion of step unlinkability [87] in that there is no restriction on the path taken by the challenge tag T_c in the original definition. An implicit assumption in the original notion is that it is equally likely tag T_c in the challenge phase and tag T in the learning phase share a common step or share no common step. However, this may not be the case in practical settings. Consider a toy example where a multi-reader system consists of three paths P_a, P_b, P_c, and every tag will go through these three paths with equal probability. Assume that P_a and P_b share a common step v, while P_c shares no common step with the other two paths. Further assume that an adversary learns that tag T passes through path P_a in the learning phase. If there is no restriction on the path taken by the challenge tag, the adversary can easily make a guess that tag T_c in the challenge phase shares a common step with T with probability 2/3, which is significantly higher than 1/2. In such a scenario, step unlinkability cannot be achieved (no matter how the path authentication scheme is designed). In comparison, the step unlinkability notion given above is more generic as a challenge tag T_c is restricted to take, with exact probability 1/2, either a path sharing a common step with T or a path sharing no common step with T in the unlinkability experiment.

3.5.3   PATH PRIVACY

Cai et al. proposed another privacy notion, named path-privacy, for path authentication [91]. This notion captures the privacy requirement for both tag identity and tag path in a single experiment, which is shown in Figure 3.18.

In the path privacy experiment $\mathbf{Exp}_{\mathcal{A}}^{Path-Privacy}[\kappa]$, an adversary $\mathcal{A}$ runs two algorithms $\mathcal{A}_1$ and $\mathcal{A}_2$ in learning phase and challenge phase, respectively. The experiment runs $\mathsf{Setup}(\kappa)$ to setup a multi-reader system with $I, \mathcal{R}, \mathcal{T}, \mathcal{M}$. In the learning phase, $\mathcal{A}_1$ queries the four oracles without exceeding n_1, n_2, n_3, n_4 times, respectively. At the end of the learning phase, $\mathcal{A}_1$ outputs two tags T_0 and T_1, a path P, a positive integer k, and state information st. In the challenge phase, the experiment first flips a coin δ. If $\delta = 1$, the experiment moves T_1 forward k steps along path P (if possible) and outputs state transcript S_1. If $\delta = 0$, the experiment moves T_0 forward k steps along any path, and outputs state transcript S_0. Note that the Move operation is performed by the experiment, during which the adversary has no access to individual readers and tags. In the challenge phase, the experiment provides $\mathcal{A}_2$ with S_δ and st. Adversary $\mathcal{A}_2$ makes a guess on the value of δ as δ'. If $\delta' = \delta$, the experiment outputs 1; else the experiment outputs 0.

Experiment $\mathbf{Exp}_{\mathcal{A}}^{Path-Privacy}[\kappa]$
 1. run $\mathsf{Setup}(\kappa)$ to setup $I, \mathcal{R}, \mathcal{T}, \mathcal{M}, para$.
 2. $\{T_0, T_1, P, k, st\} \leftarrow \mathcal{A}_1^{\mathcal{O}}(para)$,
 3. $\delta \leftarrow \{0, 1\}$.
 4. $S_\delta \leftarrow \mathsf{Move}(T_\delta, k, P, \delta)$.
 5. $\delta' \leftarrow \mathcal{A}_2^{\mathcal{O}}(S_\delta, st)$.
 6. output 1 if $\delta' = \delta$, 0 otherwise.

Figure 3.18: Path privacy experiment.

Definition 3.47 The advantage of $\mathcal{A}$, denoted $Adv_{\mathcal{A}}^{Path-Privacy}(\kappa)$, in the path privacy experiment is $\left| \Pr[\mathbf{Exp}_{\mathcal{A}}^{\mathbf{Path-Privacy}}[\kappa] = 1] - \frac{1}{2} \right|$

Definition 3.48 Path Privacy An RFID path authentication scheme is $(t, n_1, n_2, n_3, n_4, \epsilon)$-path-private, if $Adv_{\mathcal{A}}^{Path-Privacy}(\kappa) < \epsilon$ holds for any (t, n_1, n_2, n_3, n_4)-adversary $\mathcal{A}$, where ϵ is negligible in κ.

It is claimed that path privacy implies both tag unlinkability and step unlinkability [91] as shown below.

Theorem 3.49 Path privacy implies tag unlinkability.

It can be proven that if a path authentication scheme is $(t, n_1, n_2, n_3, n_4, \epsilon)$-path-private, then it is $(t, n_1, n_2, n_3, n_4, 2\epsilon)$-tag-unlinkabile. Assuming that a path authentication scheme is not $(t, n_1, n_2, n_3, n_4, 2\epsilon)$-tag-unlinkabile, there exists a (t, n_1, n_2, n_3, n_4)-adversary $\mathcal{B}$ in the tag unlinkability experiment who can choose two specific tags T_0 and T_1 in the learning phase such that (without loss of generality) when T_1 moves a specific step further, denoted by path P_1, the adversary's advantage $Adv_{\mathcal{B}}^{Tag-Unlinkability}(\kappa)$ is at least 2ϵ in the challenge phase.

Now consider a (t, n_1, n_2, n_3, n_4)-adversary $\mathcal{A}$ in the path privacy experiment which runs $\mathcal{B}$ as its subroutine. In the learning phase, assume that this adversary chooses to output $\{T_0, T_1, P_1, 1, st\}$ to the experiment after getting the output from $\mathcal{B}$. The experiment flips a coin $\delta \leftarrow \{0, 1\}$, and runs $S_\delta \leftarrow \mathsf{Move}(T_\delta, 1, P_1, \delta)$. If $\delta = 0$, the adversary can simply make a random guess about the output with probability $1/2$ (thus its advantage is zero in this case); if $\delta = 1$, the adversary $\mathcal{A}$ can forward S_1, st to the adversary $\mathcal{B}_2$ as input, and get its output with an advantage at least 2ϵ. The overall advantage of $\mathcal{A}$ is thus at least ϵ. Therefore, the path authentication scheme is not $(t, n_1, n_2, n_3, n_4, \epsilon)$-path-private.

Theorem 3.50 Path privacy implies step unlinkability.

It can be proven that if a path authentication scheme is $(t, n_1, n_2, n_3, n_4, \epsilon)$-path-private, then it is $(t, n_1, n_2, n_3, n_4, 2\epsilon)$-step-unlinkabile. Assuming that a path authentication scheme is not $(t, n_1, n_2, n_3, n_4, 2\epsilon)$-step-unlinkabile, there exists a (t, n_1, n_2, n_3, n_4)-adversary $\mathcal{B}$ in the step unlinkability experiment who can choose a specific tag T and a positive integer k in the learning phase such that in the challenge phase when given a specific path P_0 which does not have any common step with T's path, and a specific path P_1 which has one or more common steps with T's path, and (without loss of generality) when a newly created tag T_c moves k steps along path P_1, the adversary's advantage $Adv_{\mathcal{B}}^{Step-Unlinkability}(\kappa)$ is at least 2ϵ.

Now consider a (t, n_1, n_2, n_3, n_4)-adversary $\mathcal{A}$ in the path privacy experiment which runs $\mathcal{B}$ as its subroutine. In the learning phase, assume that this adversary chooses to output $\{T_0, T_1, P_1, k, st\}$ to the experiment after getting the output from $\mathcal{B}$, where T_0 can be any tag different from T_c and $T_1 = T_c$. The experiment flips a coin $\delta \leftarrow \{0, 1\}$, and runs $\mathcal{S}_\delta \leftarrow$ Move$(T_\delta, k, P_1, \delta)$. If $\delta = 0$, the adversary can simply make a random guess about the output with probability $1/2$ (thus its advantage is zero in this case); if $\delta = 1$, the adversary $\mathcal{A}$ can forward $\mathcal{S}_1, st$ to the adversary $\mathcal{B}_2$ as input, and get its output with an advantage at least 2ϵ. The overall advantage of $\mathcal{A}$ is thus at least ϵ. Therefore, the path authentication scheme is not $(t, n_1, n_2, n_3, n_4, \epsilon)$-path-private.

Note that the notions of step unlinkability and path privacy are defined based on the structure of G. In some cases, these notions cannot be achieved simply due to the structure of G regardless of path authentication scheme. For an extreme example, assuming that there is only one path in G, it is impossible to achieve step unlinkability or path privacy.

3.5.4 PATH AUTHENTICATION SCHEMES WITH PRIVACY

Typical path authentication schemes given in Section 2.3 are extended below to meet privacy requirements.

TRACKER In Section 2.3.1, TRACKER is presented to meet the security (soundness) requirement. It can be easily extended to meet tag unlinkability and step unlinkability requirements.

Recall that the initial state of tag T in TRACKER is $s_T^0 = (ID, \phi^0, \sigma^0)$, where ID is the tag's ID, $\phi^0 = a_0$ is the path mark for step v_0, and $\sigma^0 = HMAC_{k_0}(ID)$ is an HMAC signature combining ID and step v_0. When tag T arrives at step v_i, reader R_i reads out the tag's current state $s_T^{i-1} = (ID, \phi^{i-1}, \sigma^{i-1})$ and writes a new state $s_T^i = (ID, \phi^i, \sigma^i)$ into T, where $\phi^i = \phi^{i-1} x_0 + a_i$, and $\sigma^i = HMAC_{k_i}(\sigma^{i-1})$.

To meet tag unlinkability and step unlinkability requirements, the tag's state s_T^i is changed from (ID, ϕ^i, σ^i) to $(c_{ID}^i, c_\phi^i, \sigma^i)$, where c_{ID}^i and c_ϕ^i are encrypted versions of tag ID and path mark ϕ^i, respectively. The encryption is performed in an elliptic curve ElGamal cryptosystem given below.

Let $\mathcal{E}$ be an elliptic curve over a finite field $\mathbf{F}_p$. Let P be a point on $\mathcal{E}(\mathbf{F}_p)$ of a large prime order q such that the discrete logarithm problem is intractable for $\mathcal{G} = \langle P \rangle$, where p and q are two security parameters (e.g., $|p| = |q| = 160$ bits). Let $sk \in \mathbf{F}_q$ be a secret key, and $pk = (P, Y)$ be the corresponding public key, where $Y = sk \cdot P$. The encryption of message $m \in \mathcal{E}$ is performed as $E(m) = (U, V)$, where $U = r \cdot P$ and $V = m + r \cdot Y$ given any random $r \in \mathbf{F}_q$. The decryption of cipher text $c = (U, V)$ is performed as $D(c) = U - sk \cdot V = m$.

Let $\mathcal{M}$ be a reversible mapping which is used to map a tag's ID to a point in $\mathcal{E}$. Let $\mathcal{M}_\phi$ be a additively homomorphic mapping from $\mathbf{F}_q$ to $\mathcal{E}$ (one-to-one, but not reversible) to map a path mark to a point in the elliptic curve. In particular, $\mathcal{M}_\phi(\phi(\mathcal{P})) = \phi(\mathcal{P}) \cdot P \in \mathcal{E}$ for any path mark $\phi(\mathcal{P}) \in \mathbf{F}_q$.

In the initialization stage, issuer I sets up an elliptic curve ElGamal cryptosystem and generates a secret key sk and public key $pk = (P, Y)$. It sends the secret key sk to manager M via a secure channel. For each new tag T, I chooses two random numbers $r_\phi^0, r_{ID}^0 \in \mathbf{F}_q$ and writes the initial state $s_T^0 = (c_{ID}^0, c_\phi^0, \sigma^0)$ into T, where $c_{ID}^0 = E(ID) = (r_{ID}^0 \cdot P, \mathcal{M}(ID) + r_{ID}^0 \cdot Y)$, $c_\phi^0 = E(\phi^0) = (r_\phi^0 \cdot P, a_0 \cdot P + r_\phi^0 \cdot Y)$, and $\sigma^0 = HMAC_{k_0}(ID)$.

When tag T arrives at step v_i, reader R_i reads out the tag's current state $s_T^{i-1} = (c_{ID}^{i-1}, c_\phi^{i-1}, \sigma^{i-1})$, where $c_{ID}^{i-1} = (U_{ID}^{i-1}, V_{ID}^{i-1})$ and $c_\phi^{i-1} = (U_\phi^{i-1}, V_\phi^{i-1})$. Then, reader R_i computes

$$U_\phi^{\prime i} = x_0 \cdot U_\phi^{i-1} = (x_0 r_\phi^{i-1}) \cdot P$$

$$V_\phi^{\prime i} = x_0 \cdot V_\phi^{i-1} + a_i = (a_0 x_0^i + \sum_{j=1}^{i} a_j x_0^{i-j}) \cdot P + (x_0 r_\phi^{i-1}) \cdot Y.$$

Then, reader R_i picks two random numbers $r_{ID}', r_\phi' \in \mathbf{F}_q$, and re-encrypts ID and path mark:

$$c_{ID}^i = (U_{ID}^i, V_{ID}^i) = (r_{ID}' \cdot P + U_{ID}^{i-1}, r_{ID}' \cdot Y + V_{ID}^{i-1})$$

$$c_\phi^i = (U_\phi^i, V_\phi^i) = (r_\phi' \cdot P + U_\phi^{\prime i}, r_\phi' \cdot Y + V_\phi^{\prime i}).$$

Let $r_\phi^i = r_\phi' + x_0 r_\phi^{i-1}$; then,

$$U_\phi^i = r_\phi^i \cdot P$$

$$V_\phi^i = (a_0 x_0^i + \sum_{j=1}^{i} a_j x_0^{i-j}) \cdot P + r_\phi^i \cdot Y.$$

Reader R_i also updates the signature $\sigma^i = HMAC_{k_i}(\sigma^{i-1})$ (note that in a later version of paper [86], the updated signature is encrypted in the same way as tag ID is encrypted [87]). Finally, R_i writes the new state $s_T^i = (c_{ID}^i, c_\phi^i, \sigma^i)$ into tag T.

With $|p| = |q| = 160$ bits and HMAC of output size of 160 bits, the storage requirement on each tag is $2 \cdot 160 + 2 \cdot 160 + 160 = 800$ bits, which is feasible for EPC Gen 2 tags.

For path verification, manager M pre-computes a list of pairs $(\mathcal{P}_{valid}, \mathcal{M}_\phi(\phi(\mathcal{P}_{valid})))$ for all valid paths. Upon receive a tag T, the manager readers out the tag's state $s_T^\ell = (c_{ID}^\ell, c_\phi^\ell, \sigma^\ell)$. First, M decrypts c_{ID}^ℓ to get plaintext ID and checks it for cloning with DB_{clone}. If the tag ID is in DB_{clone}, M rejects the tag and outputs nothing; otherwise, M decrypts c_ϕ^ℓ to get a point $\pi = \phi(\mathcal{P}) \cdot P$. Then, M checks whether π is in the list of valid path mappings $\mathcal{M}_\phi(\phi(\mathcal{P}_{valid}))$. If there is no match, M rejects the tag and outputs nothing; otherwise, M checks the tag's signature σ^ℓ according to the matched valid path. If the tag's signature is incorrect, manager M rejects the tag and outputs nothing; otherwise, M accepts the tag, outputs its valid path, and updates DB_{clone}.

CHECKER Recall in CHECKER (see Section 2.3.2), a tag's state $s_T^j = (ID, \sigma_\mathcal{P}(ID))$ consists of both tag ID and path signature. To meet tag unlinkability and step unlinkability requirements, an encryption step is added: after the tag's state is verified and updated by its current reader R_k, it is encrypted by R_k using the public key of the tag's next reader R_{k+1}. When R_{k+1} receives the tag, it first decrypts the tag's state using its own private key before it verifies the tag's state as stated in Chapter 2.3.2.

PRF-Based Path Authentication   In the path authentication scheme proposed by Cai et al. [91], tag T_i's state is (ID_i, v_i) given path $\mathcal{P}_i = (R_{i_0}, R_{i_1}, \ldots R_{i_j})$, where $v_i = PRF_{k_{i_j}}(PRF_{k_{i_{j-1}}}(\cdots PRF_{k_0}(ID_i)))$. To meet path privacy requirement, an encrypted version of tag ID (i.e., ID_i), instead of tag ID itself, is stored in tag (along with path signature v_i); the tag's ID is encrypted by issuer I, re-encrypted by each reader, and decrypted by manager M in an elliptic curve ElGamal cryptosystem the same way as in TRACKER [86].

Distributed Path Authentication   In the distributed path authentication scheme proposed by Cai et al. [89], each tag's state consists of a tag ID, a path mark, and a path signature on tag ID. To meet privacy requirements, the tag's state is encrypted with a random secret key by each reader in a symmetric cryptosystem such as Blowfish. To solve the key distribution problem, the same encryption key is used for a batch of tags, and the Tiny Secret Sharing (TSS) scheme [73] is adopted to divide the encryption key into a number of shares, with one share per tag in the batch. A share of the key is stored in each tag along with the ciphertext of the tag's state.

A "hit-and-run" adversary is assumed to have no capability of collecting enough shares in each batch; therefore, the adversary cannot recover the encryption key. Without decrypting a tag's state, an adversary cannot link a tag's state to the tag's identity (i.e., tag unlinkability), neither can tell whether two different tags share a common step in their paths (i.e., step unlinkability). A valid reader, who has full access to the tags, can nonetheless recover the encryption key and decrypt all tags in a batch.

The privacy requirements are met in this solution by encrypting tag states in a symmetric cryptosystem where a random encryption key is distributed by the current reader to the next reader via a secret sharing scheme. In comparison, tag states are re-encrypted by the manager's public key in TRACKER and PRF-based path authentication such that only the manager can decrypt tag states and verify them. In CHECKER, tag states are encrypted by the current reader using the next reader's public key so that the next reader can decrypt and verify tag states.

3.6   PRIVACY IN OWNERSHIP TRANSFER

Ownership transfer of RFID tags involve multiple readers with different identities, where the readers may be owned by different parties in many applications such as supply chain management. The ownership of a tag usually means the capability of authenticating the tag. Ownership transfer of tag T from reader R_1 to R_2 means that the capability of authenticating T is given to R_2 by R_1. This can be achieved by sending necessary tag secrets from the current owner R_1 to the new owner R_2. In terms of security, ownership transfer is nothing but tag authentication plus key distribution.

The major issue in ownership transfer is to ensure old owner's privacy and new owner's privacy. The old owner's privacy requires that the new owner of a tag cannot trace the tag according to the tag's communication records with its previous owner after the tag's ownership is transferred, while the new owner's privacy means that the current owner cannot trace a tag once the ownership of the tag is transferred to the new owner.

The old owner's privacy can be achieved by updating tag secrets in a way similar to achieving forward privacy. This updating process should be performed by the current owner right before distributing tag secrets to the new owner [132] and it should be resilient to desynchronization attacks [133].

New owner's privacy can be achieved in the presence of an external trusted third party, which coordinates the ownership transfer process, or it can be achieved in an isolated environment where the new owner can update tag secrets right after receiving them without being eavesdropped by the previous owner [134]. Note that new owner's privacy is weaker than backward privacy since the latter does not require new ownership to be established.

Besides old owner's privacy and new owner's privacy, other features which have been identified relevant to ownership transfer include (i) ownership delegation: the current owner delegates its ownership to an authorized reader under certain constraint or until it revokes the delegation [135]; (ii) authorized recovery: after ownership transfer, the current owner allows the previous owner to recover its ownership [132]; (iii) tag assurance: the new owner can verify the tags being transferred according to the descriptions provided by the current owner [136]; (iv) undeniable ownership transfer: after ownership transfer, the previous owner cannot deny its ownership for the tags being transferred [136]; (v) current ownership proof: the current owner can generate a proof to convince a third party about its ownership [136]; and (vi) owner initiation: ownership transfer can only be initialized by the current owner but not anyone else [136].

CHAPTER 4

RFID Security at the Network Level

At the network level, tag IDs collected at the physical level are incorporated with other information (e.g., location, time, business step) to form RFID events, which are stored in each party's database and shared among networked parties. We investigate security and privacy issues at the network level in EPCglobal Network, which is a standard architecture created by EPCglobal for sharing RFID information in many applications such as supply chain management. An EPC-global Network architecture (see Section 1.3) consists of (i) multiple EPC Information Services (EPCISes), which manage RFID/EPC events under individual parties' control, (ii) an EPC Discovery Service (EPCDS), which stores the indexing information of EPC events registered by each party/EPCIS and handles other parties' queries about the indexing information, and (iii) an EPC Object Name Service (ONS), which is a simplified version of EPCDS.

RFID Security in EPCglobal Network concerns how to protect each networked party's information in EPCIS and EPCDS so that the information is shared with authorized parties only.

Sometimes we do not distinguish a party with its EPCIS. In an EPCglobal Network, an EPCIS is the owner of all EPC events stored in it; it is also the owner of the indexing information of EPC events it registers to EPCDS. To share its information, EPCIS allows users, who are either EPCISes or public users (e.g., consumers who do not represent any EPCIS in EPCglobal Network), to query its information in EPCIS and EPCDS. In particular, the following security issues in EPCglobal Network are addressed in this book.

- Access control in EPCDS

    - Policy: How an EPCIS specifies which users are authorized to access its indexing information of EPC events in EPCDS.

    - Enforcement: How to enforce all EPCISes' policies in EPCDS efficiently.

- Access control in EPCIS

    - Policy: How an EPCIS specifies which users are authorized to access its EPC events in EPCIS.

    - Enforcement: How to enforce the EPCIS' policy in EPCIS efficiently.

Since the information stored and shared in EPCglobal Network is mostly sensitive (which may reveal inventory levels, trading partners, and business plans), the security requirements in EPCglobal Network have been unanimously identified [4, 5, 6]. Consequently, EPC Security Services is considered as the fourth component in EPCglobal Network, which "allow a secured access to the information of the EPCglobal Network in accordance to the access rights of the participants [7]." However, there is still a lack of designs to meet the security requirements identified [3, 4, 5]. Moving to fill the gap, we present some new research results on access control policies and enforcement mechanisms in EPCglobal Network. We focus on authorization only and assume that authentication has been performed appropriately [143].

4.1   BACKGROUND

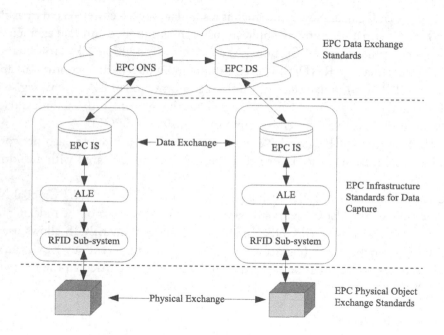

Figure 4.1: EPCglobal Network [138].

The architecture of the EPCglobal Network is described in a standard document [3]. Figure 4.1 illustrates EPCglobal Network, including EPC Discovery Service (EPCDS), EPC Information Service (EPCIS), EPC Object Naming Service (ONS), and underlying RFID subsystems. In EPCglobal Network, each component plays a unique and important role. The RFID sub-system is in charge of capturing event information when physical objects move across different parties such as manufacturers, suppliers, and retailers. The event information includes product/EPC information (what), date and time (when), event location (where), and business context (why) [4]. The event information is delivered to EPCIS systems via the Application Level Events (ALE) interface.

The delivered event information is stored in the EPCIS repository and accessed by users through the EPCIS query interface. To ensure that only authorized users can access its event information, EPCIS defines access control policies and enforce them when answering user queries. With EPCIS querying service, any authorized users, who know the address of EPCIS service, can get access to its EPC repository.

To facilitate information sharing across EPCglobal Network, EPCDS and EPC ONS are both designed to help users locate EPCIS systems for interested EPC events. Given an EPC, ONS returns the address of a single EPCIS which originally assigns the EPC code[1], while EPCDS returns all pointers to the EPCISes which hold detailed event information about the EPC. Since ONS is a simplified version of EPCDS, we focus on EPCDS only.

EPCDS can be considered as a search engine in EPCglobal Network, allowing users to find EPCISes which store detailed event information about EPCs of interest. While the standardization of EPCDS design is still an open direction [3], three typical EPCDS models have been proposed, including Directory Service model, Query Relay model, and Aggregating Discovery Service model [137]. The former two models are designed in the BRIDGE project [139], and the latter is proposed by Muller et al [140].

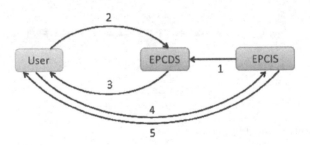

Figure 4.2: Directory Service Model [137].

Directory Service Model   In Directory Service model, EPCDS stores a directory of EPC numbers and corresponding EPCIS addresses. Figure 4.2 illustrates the steps of this Directory Service model:

1. EPCIS registers at EPCDS with the EPC numbers it handles, together with its service address or URL. EPCDS stores the pairs of EPC numbers and EPCIS addresses in a lookup table;

[1]In the current design, ONS provides discovery of manufacturer EPCIS for a given class-level EPC, though it is feasible in theory to deal with item-level EPC as in EPCDS.

2. user sends a query to EPCDS with a specific EPC number or a range of EPC numbers as parameters;

3. EPCDS uses the lookup table to search for queried EPC numbers, locates relevant EPCIS addresses and returns them to the user;

4. with the returned addresses, the user queries directly to EPCIS repositories for desired EPC event information; and

5. EPCIS repositories return the required EPC event information to the user according to their access control policies.

One of main problems in Directory Service model is that EPCDS returns all relevant EPCIS addresses to each user who queries. Access control is not specified in detail.

Based on the query result, every user knows exactly which EPCIS repositories handle which EPC numbers. Availability of EPCIS addresses indicates ownership of EPC information. Therefore, any parties, who consider their possession of EPC numbers as proprietary, may not want to expose their EPCIS addresses to the public, especially to their competitors. Without proper access control at EPCDS, such parties would be reluctant to register data on EPCDS.

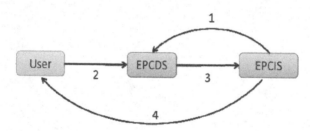

Figure 4.3: Query Relay model [137].

Query Relay Model   In the Query Relay model, EPCDS does not return the service addresses of EPCIS repositories upon request. Instead, it redirects the query to corresponding EPCIS repositories. Figure 4.3 shows the steps of this Query Relay model:

1. EPCIS registers at EPCDS with the EPC numbers it handles, together with its service address or URL. Then, EPCDS stores the pairs of EPC numbers and EPCIS addresses in a lookup table;

2. user sends a query to EPCDS with a specific EPC number or a range of EPC numbers as well as the user's credentials;

3. EPCDS uses the lookup table to search for queried EPC numbers, locates relevant EPCIS addresses and relays the user's query and credentials to those EPCIS resources; and

4. each relevant EPCIS checks the user's credentials for authentication and returns the query result to the user according to its access control policy.

In the Query Relay model, a user's query can be of two types. The first one is full query, directly requesting EPCIS to return EPC event information. The second query type is resource query, where EPCIS returns only the service addresses that user should query so as to get required EPC event information. Different from the Directory Service model, the Query Relay model does not return any EPCIS addresses to users; instead, the users' queries are relayed to relevant EPCISes. As long as each EPCIS defines and enforces its access control policy appropriately, there is no need of enforcing any additional access control at EPCDS from security point of view (of course, EPCDS should ensure that no user can access to its look-up table). Nonetheless, access control can still be enforced at EPCDS so as to restrict the queries relayed to EPCISes.

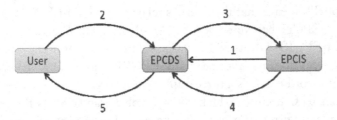

Figure 4.4: Aggregating Discovery Service Model [137].

Aggregating Directory Service Model   Aggregating Discovery Service (ADS) model is defined based on the Query Relay model. In this model, instead of returning EPC event information directly to a user, each EPCIS returns its result back to EPCDS. After getting all replies from relevant EPCIS repositories, EPCDS aggregates the replies and sends them back to the user. Figure 4.3 shows the steps of ADS model.

1. EPCIS registers at EPCDS with the EPC numbers it handles, together with its service address or URL. Then, EPCDS stores the pairs of EPC numbers and EPCIS addresses in a lookup table.

2. User sends a query to EPCDS with a specific EPC number or a range of EPC numbers as well as the user's credentials.

3. EPCDS uses the lookup table to search for queried EPC numbers, locates relevant EPCIS addresses and relays the user's query and credentials to those EPCIS resources.

4. Each EPCIS resource checks the user's credentials for authentication and returns the query result to EPCDS according to its access control policy.

5. EPCDS aggregates the results from EPCISes and relays them back to the user.

Similar to the Query Relay model, the ADS model does not require any additional access control to be enforced at EPCDS unless it is for the purpose of reducing communication traffic from EPCDS to EPCISes.

4.2 ACCESS CONTROL POLICIES IN EPCGLOBAL NETWORK

Access control policies should be defined by each EPCIS to enable its information to be shared with authorized parties only. At EPCIS level, access control policies should specify which users are authorized to get access to which EPC numbers and EPC events stored in EPCIS. At EPCDS level, access control policies should specify which users' queries about EPCIS addresses should be granted. A user's query being granted by EPCDS in the Directory Service model means that the query result (a set of EPCIS addresses) is returned to the user, while in the Query Relay model and the ADS model it means that the query is relayed to relevant EPCISes.

Consider an EPCglobal Network with a single EPCDS D and a set I of EPCISes (we do not distinguish an EPCIS with its address). Let U be the set of users, where each user is either EPCIS or public who does not represent any EPCIS; that is, $U = I \cup \{public\}$. At EPCIS $I_i \in I$, each event record $r \in I_i$ is a three-tuple $(epc, event, time)$, where epc is an EPC number, $event$ represents an EPC event in which epc is involved, and $time$ is the time when $event$ happens. EPCIS I_i may register an event indexing record $(epc, time)$ in EPCDS D for its event $(epc, event, time)$. Such event indexing record can be used by other users to discover event records at EPCIS I_i. Let D_i denote the set of all event indexing records registered by an EPCIS $I_i \in I$ at D. Note that an EPCIS may not register all its events, especially for those with the same EPC numbers; on the other hand, it is not meaningful for EPCIS to register a single event multiple times. A primitive query q to EPCDS or EPCIS is a two-tuple (epc, u), where epc is an EPC number[2] and $u \in U$ is a user.[3] With this notation, we define the following access control policy which can be enforced at both EPCDS and EPCIS.

Definition 4.1 Access Control Policy in EPCglobal Network An access control policy $p(r, I_i, q)$ specifies whether the content of data record r owned by EPCIS I_i (at EPCDS D or at EPCIS I_i) can be used to answer a query q. In general, policy $p(r, I_i, q) \implies allow$ iff the following conditions are satisfied:

- EPC-match: $r.epc = q.epc$;

- partner-relationship: $q.u$ and I_i satisfy certain relationship w.r.t. $r.epc$. In particular, we consider the following *chain-based relationships* which are commonly used in supply chain management practice:

---

[2]Note that primitive queries can be easily extended to involve a range of EPC numbers.
[3]It is assumed that a user has already been authenticated or can be authenticated with proper credentials.

- whole-chain: $q.u$ has ever registered an event indexing record r' in D such that $r'.epc = r.epc$ (i.e., $q.u$ and I_i have ever registered the same $r.epc$ in D; in other words, they are in the same supply chain for handling $r.epc$);

- up-stream: $q.u$ has ever registered an event indexing record r' in D such that $r'.epc = r.epc$ and $r'.time < r.time$ (i.e., $q.u$ is in the upstream of I_i for handling $r.epc$);

- down-stream: $q.u$ has ever registered an event indexing record r' in D such that $r'.epc = r.epc$ and $r'.time > r.time$ (i.e., $q.u$ is in the downstream of I_i for handling $r.epc$);

- public: No constraint on the relationship between $q.u$ and I_i w.r.t. $r.epc$.

- Attribute-logic: The attributes of r, I_i, and q satisfy certain logic expression. Different types of attribute-based logic expressions can be defined [141, 142]; however, it would be highly costly to verify them with a large number of data records in EPCIS or EPCDS. In particular, we consider the following white list and black list expressions which can be efficiently implemented:

  - white-list $W_{EPC}(I_i)$ for EPC: $q.epc \in W_{EPC}(I_i)$, where $W_{EPC}(I_i)$ is a set of EPC numbers. I_i can define $W_{EPC}(I_i)$ so as to restrict queries to the EPC numbers defined in $W_{EPC}(I_i)$ only;

  - black-list $B_{EPC}(I_i)$ for EPC: $q.epc \notin B_{EPC}(I_i)$, where $B_{EPC}(I_i)$ is a set of EPC numbers. I_i can define $B_{EPC}(I_i)$ so as to block any queries to the EPC numbers defined in $B_{EPC}(I_i)$);

  - white-list $W_U(I_i)$ for user: $q.u \in W_U(I_i)$, where $W_U(I_i)$ is a set of users. I_i can define $W_U(I_i)$ so as to ensure that only users in $W_U(I_i)$ (e.g., trusted parties or business partners) can get query answers;

  - black-list $B_U(I_i)$ for user: $q.u \notin B_U(I_i)$, where $B_U(I_i)$ is a set of users. I_i can define $B_U(I_i)$ so as to ensure that no user in $B_U(I_i)$ (e.g., competitors) can get query answers.

The white lists and black lists are global parameters defined by I_i for all q sent to query I_i's data. By default, $W_{EPC}(I_i) = EPC$, $B_{EPC}(I_i) = \emptyset$, $W_U(I_i) = U$, and $B_U(I_i) = \emptyset$, where EPC denotes the set of all possible EPC numbers. The attribute logic is always true in this default case. In practice, I_i may choose to use white-lists and/or black-lists by revising the default values. In case both white-lists and black-lists are used and their intersections are nonempty, black-lists generally take precedence over white-lists to resolve conflicts.

A policy $p(r, I_i, q)$ is called list and chain based access control (List-Chain-BAC) if $p(r, I_i, q) \Longrightarrow allow$ means *EPC-match* AND *partner-relationship* $\in$ {*whole-chain, up-stream, down-stream, public*} AND *attribute-logic*$(W_{EPC}(I_i), B_{EPC}(I_i), W_U(I_i), B_U(I_i))$. Specifically, a policy is called list based access control (List-BAC) if the partner-relationship is public; it is called chain based access control (Chain-BAC) if the attribute-logic is always true; and it is called bare-match access control if the partner-relationship is public and the attribute-logic is always true.

If a bare-match policy is defined for an event indexing record $r \in D_i$ in EPCDS, it means that given a user's query about $r.epc$, the address of EPCIS I_i (which is the owner of r in D) can always be returned to the user in the Directory Service model, or the user's query can always be forwarded to EPCIS I_i in the Query Relay model and ADS model. If a bare-match policy is defined for an event record in EPCIS, it means that the record can be accessed by any external user.

Given an EPC number epc, there could be multiple event records $r = (epc, event, time)$ stored in an EPCIS I_i which handles epc, and there could be one or more event-indexing records $r' = (epc, time)$ registered by I_i in EPCDS D to facilitate queries to r in EPCIS. All of these records share the same epc, but not necessarily the same $time$ value. In general, I_i may define different access control policies for different r at EPCIS and for different r' at EPCDS; also, it is possible for I_i to define different access control policies for r in EPCIS and r' in EPCDS even if $r.time = r'.time$.

Note that the policy in Definition 4.1 is defined for EPCIS I_i to protect its information against external users. Other access control policies (e.g., role-based access control) may be used for protecting its information against internal users. At EPCIS I_i, the policy is enforced by I_i in full control, while at EPCDS D, the policy defined by I_i is enforced by D. In this chapter, it is assumed that EPCDS is fully trusted by all EPCISes which register events to it.

4.3   ACCESS CONTROL ENFORCEMENT IN EPCDS

It is common in RFID-enabled supply chain management where a large number of tagged product items are handled in fast pace by many supply chain parties at different locations. To meet practical requirements, access control policies should be enforced in a highly efficient and scalable manner. Algorithm 1 is designed to process queries in EPCDS under List-Chain-BAC.

The efficiency of algorithm 1 relies on how to proceed with line 5, which is to determine whether $q.u$ and I_i satisfy partner-relationship w.r.t. $r.epc$ defined in $p(r, I_i, q)$. Except for public partner-relationship, this process requires searching for an event indexing record r' registered by $q.u$ in EPCDS such that $r'.epc = r.epc$ (for whole-chain) and $r'.time < r.time$ (for up-stream) or $r'.time > r.time$ (for down-stream). It is not necessary to do this each time when line 5 is proceeded. Notice that $r.epc = q.epc$ is fixed in line 5 for different r and I_i; a better solution is to "search for all event indexing records r' registered by $q.u$ in D such that $r'.epc = q.epc$" right before the for-loop (line 2) starts. Then in line 5, the partner-relationship can be verified directly by comparing r and r' according to policy $p(r, I_i, q)$.

To further improve the efficiency of query process in EPCDS under List-Chain-BAC, we propose to use a tag-chain structure to organize the data records in EPCDS.

Algorithm 1 User query process in EPCDS under List-Chain-BAC.

Input : user query $q = (epc, u)$
Output : set of EPCISes S

1: $S = \emptyset$
2: **for all** EPCIS $I_i \in I$ such that $I_i \neq q.u$ **do**
3:     **if** $q.epc \in W_{EPC}(I_i)$ and $q.epc \notin B_{EPC}(I_i)$ and $q.u \in W_U(I_i)$ and $q.u \notin B_U(I_i)$ **then**
4:        **for all** $r \in D_i$ such that $r.epc = q.epc$ and $I_i \notin S$ **do**
5:           **if** $q.u$ and I_i satisfy partner-relationship w.r.t. $r.epc$ defined in $p(r, I_i, q)$ **then**
6:             add I_i in S
7:           **end if**
8:        **end for**
9:     **end if**
10: **end for**
11: return S

Definition 4.2 Tag-Chain Given an EPC number *epc*, a tag-chain $C(epc)$ in EPCDS D is a set of pairs (r, I_i) for all data records $r \in D$ such that $r.epc = epc$, where I_i is the owner of r.

With tag-chain structure, EPCDS can be considered as a set of tag-chains indexed by EPC numbers. When a new event indexing record r is registered to D, tag-chain $C(r.epc)$ is updated accordingly. Algorithm 2 shows the query process with tag-chains in EPCDS under List-Chain-BAC.

The efficiency of algorithm 2 relies on how to proceed with line 4, which is to determine whether $q.u$ and I_i satisfy partner-relationship w.r.t. $r.epc$ defined in $p(r, I_i, q)$. Except for public partner-relationship, this process requires searching for all pairs $(r', q.u) \in C(q.epc)$ and comparing r and r' according to policy $p(r, I_i, q)$. The process of searching for all pairs $(r', q.u) \in C(q.epc)$ can be performed right before the for-loop (line 2) starts. Then in line 4, the partner-relationship can be verified directly by comparing r and r' according to policy $p(r, I_i, q)$.

Algorithm 2 is more efficient and scalable than algorithm 1 due to the use of tag-chain structure. Our on-going work is to evaluate the performance of these two algorithms with various parameters, including number of EPCISes, number of EPC numbers, size and distribution of tag-chains, distribution of queries, and type of access control policies.

Algorithm 2 User query process with tag-chains in EPCDS under List-Chain-BAC.

Input : user query $q = (epc, u)$
Output : set of EPCISes S

1: $S = \emptyset$
2: **for all** $(r, I_i) \in C(q.epc)$ such that $I_i \neq q.u$ and $I_i \notin S$ **do**
3:    **if** $q.epc \in W_{EPC}(I_i)$ and $q.epc \notin B_{EPC}(I_i)$ and $q.u \in W_U(I_i)$ and $q.u \notin B_U(I_i)$ **then**
4:       **if** $q.u$ and I_i satisfy partner-relationship w.r.t. $r.epc$ defined in $p(r, I_i, q)$ **then**
5:          add I_i in S
6:       **end if**
7:    **end if**
8: **end for**
9: return S

4.4   ACCESS CONTROL ENFORCEMENT IN EPCIS

Access control enforcement in EPCIS is not the same as access control enforcement in EPCDS. The main reason is that an EPCIS may not have a global view on which EPCISes have ever registered a particular EPC number which is queried.

Consider a typical scenario where a user $u \in U$ would like to know all event information about a particular EPC number epc. To know who has event information about epc, user u sends a query $q = (epc, u)$ to EPCDS, which outputs a set S of EPCISes which have event information about epc (see Section 4.3). The output S is returned to u in the Directory Service model, while in the Query Relay model and ADS model S is used by EPCDS for query relay. The user's query q is then sent to all EPCIS $I_i \in S$ for event information. The user's query is either sent by u directly in the Directory Service model or relayed by D in the Query Relay model and ADS model. In the latter case, it is assumed that the user's authentication credential is relayed together with q. Algorithm 3 shows how to process query q in EPCIS I_i under List-Chain-BAC.

In the Directory Service model and Query Relay model, the output E of event information about $q.epc$ is returned to user $q.u$, while in the ADS model, E is returned to EPCDS, which aggregates outputs from all EPCISes in S before returning the aggregated result to user $q.u$.

The efficiency of algorithm 3 relies on how to proceed with line 4, which is to determine whether $q.u$ and I_i satisfy partner-relationship w.r.t. $r.epc$ defined in $p(r, I_i, q)$. Except for public partner-relationship, this process requires to know *whether there exists an event indexing record r' registered by $q.u$ in EPCDS such that $r'.epc = r.epc$ (for whole-chain) and $r'.time < r.time$ (for up-stream) or $r'.time > r.time$ (for down-stream)*. In general, I_i may not know what $q.u$ has registered in D. In such a case, line 4 can be proceeded with a relationship query sent by I_i to D, which is shown in algorithm 4. The relationship query sent by I_i to D has input I_i and $q = (epc, u)$,

---

Algorithm 3 User query process in EPCIS I_i under List-Chain-BAC.

Input : user query $q = (epc, u)$
Output : set of events E

1: $E = \emptyset$
2: **if** $q.epc \in W_{EPC}(I_i)$ and $q.epc \notin B_{EPC}(I_i)$ and $q.u \in W_U(I_i)$ and $q.u \notin B_U(I_i)$ **then**
3:    **for all** $r \in I_i$ such that $r.epc = q.epc$ **do**
4:       **if** $q.u$ and I_i satisfy partner-relationship w.r.t. $r.epc$ defined in $p(r, I_i, q)$ **then**
5:          add $r.event$ in E
6:       **end if**
7:    **end for**
8: **end if**
9: return E

---

as well as optional input $\bowtie$ and *r.time*. If there is no optional input in the relationship query, EPCDS checks for whole-chain partner-relationship; otherwise, the optional input symbol $\bowtie$ would be either $<$ for up-stream relationship, or $>$ for down-stream relationship.

In case the tag-chain structure is used in EPCDS, algorithm 4 remains the same except for line 1, which should be revised to

---

Algorithm 4 Relationship query process in EPCDS under List-Chain-BAC.

Input : EPCIS I_i, forwarded user query $q = (epc, u)$
Optional input : $\bowtie$, *r.time*
Output : true or false

1: **for all** $r' \in D$ registered by $q.u$ such that $r'.epc = q.epc$ **do**
2:    **if** $p(r', q.u, (q.epc, I_i)) \implies allow$ **then**
3:       **if** there is no optional input **then**
4:          return true
5:       **else if** $r'.time \bowtie r.time$ **then**
6:          return true
7:       **end if**
8:    **end if**
9: **end for**
10: return false

---

    1. **for all** $(r', q.u) \in C(q.epc)$ **do**

where $C(q.epc)$ is the tag-chain for $q.epc$. Note that in algorithm 4, EPCIS I_i is the query issuer asking to access data records r' owned by $q.u$ in EPCDS. Line 2 checks for the access control policy defined by $q.u$ to ensure that I_i has the permission to access relevant data records in D. This means when $q.u$ sends query q to I_i, $q.u$ should ensure that I_i has the permission to query its related data records in EPCDS (this can be done easily by inserting I_i in $q.u$'s white list $W_U(q.u)$); otherwise, $q.u$ would get an empty reply from I_i.

    Since the user query process in EPCIS shown in algorithm 3 consults EPCDS for partner-relationship status, it may result in performance bottleneck for EPCDS serving many EPCISes. This issue can be addressed when an EPCIS has the same access control policy for protecting its EPC records in EPCIS and relevant event indexing records in EPCDS; in such case, it may not be necessary for EPCIS to verify its access control policy again if the user's query has already been checked at EPCDS[4]. If EPCIS chooses to trust EPCDS on policy verification, then algorithm 3 can be simplified significantly. To do so, EPCDS should return $S = \{I_i, sig_D(q, I_i, time)\}$ instead of $S = \{I_i\}$ in algorithm 1 or algorithm 2, where $sig_D(q, I_i, time)$ is EPCDS' signature on q, I_i, and the signing time (which could be verified within certain time period). Then, algorithm 3 can be simplified to algorithm 5

Algorithm 5 Simplified user query process in EPCIS I_i without policy checking.

Input: user query $q = (epc, u)$, EPCDS' signature $sig_D(q, I_i, time)$
Output: set of events E

1: $E = \emptyset$
2: **if** $sig_D(q, I_i, time)$ is verified correctly **then**
3:     **for all** $r \in I_i$ such that $r.epc = q.epc$ **do**
4:         add $r.event$ in E
5:     **end for**
6: **end if**
7: return E

    In more general cases, it is still possible to enable each EPCIS to answer user queries without consulting with EPCDS. We are currently working on this and hope to include our design in a future edition of this book.

A Note on User Authentication in EPCglobal Network   Note that we focus on access control in EPCglobal Network and assume that user authentication has been performed appropri-

---

[4]Clearly, whole-chain relationship does not need to be verified again at EPCIS if it is verified at EPCDS already; however, it is subtle for up-stream relationship and down-stream relationship since the timestamps of EPCIS events could be different from the timestamps of relevant EPCDS records.

ately. Traditional user authentication solutions may be used in EPCglobal Network. For example, password-based authentication is one choice for user authentication at EPCDS, while Kerberos or PKI can be used for user authentication at EPCIS. Kerschbaum and Sorniotti proposed a cryptographic scheme for two users to authenticate each other that they have processed the same tag in EPCglobal Network, assuming that a trusted third party exists for supporting users in updating each tag's content before its delivery to the next owner [143]. This solution can be used to secure user query process at EPCIS for whole-chain partnership only.

4.5   DEFENCE AGAINST FALSE EVENT INJECTION IN EPCDS

In EPCglobal Network, EPCDS allows users to search for EPC event information from possibly unknown partners and facilitates information sharing among different information resources. As EPCDS contains critical business information about partner relationship and product movement, user authentication and authorization have been considered in EPCDS design for protecting the information stored in EPCDS. As it is shown in the previous sections of this chapter, access control can be defined and enforced based on partner relationship in a sense that only parties which have handled the same EPC products are allowed to access related EPC event information from other parties. However, no solution has been proposed to authenticate the registered EPC events and verify that the registering parties have indeed owned and processed the claimed EPC products at the claimed time. This vulnerability may lead to false EPC event injection attack [145], where forged EPC event information is registered to EPCDS by malicious parties. Following the false event injection attack, malicious parties may impersonate as legitimate partners, bypass the access control of EPCDS, and get unauthorized event information from other parties. This attack would also lower the quality of EPC information stored in EPCDS.

Threat Model   Assume that EPCDS D is protected with proper user authentication and access control so that the event indexing records registered by each EPCIS in D cannot be access by unauthorized users. However, user authentication and access control in EPCDS do not prevent an EPCIS from registering false event indexing records from the first place. In practice, forged EPC events may be created and registered in EPCDS due to the following reasons.

- **To access unauthorized data**: In secure EPCDS, access control policies are defined based on partner relationships for handling certain EPC numbers, such as up-stream or down-stream partnerships. Without authentication of EPC events, any party/EPCIS can register any EPC events in EPCDS. This allows a malicious party to register forged EPC numbers in EPCDS and claim that it owns these EPC products and is part of supply chain. In this way, the malicious party can easily bypass chain based access control at EPCDS and access sensitive information registered by other parties who actually handled the products with the forged EPC numbers.

- **To inspect business interest of querying parties**: After registering some forged EPC numbers submitted by an adversary from certain EPCIS address, EPCDS would return the adversary's EPCIS address to querying parties. Thereafter, the adversary would receive queries from other parties which have interest in the injected EPC numbers. By analyzing the queries, the adversary can observe the interests of the querying parties and gain insights about their business.

- **To give false information to competitors**: An adversary in this category may register forged EPC events in EPCDS and make them open to user queries. When queried by competitors, it may provide false information about EPC products.

Note that the above threats may be mitigated by setting up proper black-lists and white-lists in List-Chain-BAC. However, this solution does not work well for unknown supply chain partners which cannot be included in black-lists or white-lists, especially in dynamic supply chains. While Chain-BAC is a convenient approach to protecting dynamic supply chains, it can be bypassed due to false event injection attacks. Two types of adversaries can be considered in such a scenario.

- **Weak Adversary**: A weak adversary is not part of supply chain. It obtains EPC numbers indirectly, such as from eavesdropping. Except for EPC numbers, other EPC event information, including time and locations of EPC tags, is made up by the adversary.

- **Strong Adversary**: A strong adversary is a legitimate party that processes EPC products and is part of supply chain. It may manipulate the time of EPC tags being read so as to bypass certain access control policies.

Clearly, a strong adversary is more powerful than weak adversary since it is a legitimate party in EPCglobal Network. In particular, a strong adversary may change an event's time when it registers the event to EPCDS. Consider a simple example where party B has some event information about epc and it defines an up-stream policy such that only upstream parties can access its event information. Assume that party A is at B's downstream which should not be able to access B's events about epc according to B's policy. To bypass this restriction, A may predate the time of its event on epc in event registration so that A appears to be B's up-stream party.

General Defence Process   A general defense process against false EPC event injection involves three steps: prevention, detection and punishment [145]. The properties of individual steps are summarized in Figure 4.5 and explained below.

- Prevention: The prevention of false event injection can be achieved using cryptographic techniques such that an adversary cannot inject false event data unless it breaks the underlying cryptographic primitives. Normally, cryptographic techniques require shared secrets to be stored and processed in RFID tags, which may not be suitable for low-cost tags with limited storage and computational power. Moreover, key distribution and management should be addressed when cryptographic measures are applied.

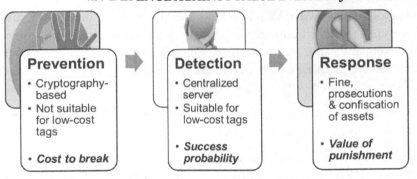

Figure 4.5: Process of defending against false EPC event injection [145].

- Detection: The detection of false event injection aims to detect false event data when or after false event data are injected into EPCDS. Normally, it requires a centralized trusted server (e.g., EPCDS) which has a global view of RFID tags to perform or assist the detection of false events registered in EPCDS. The effectiveness of detection-based approaches can be measured by false positive/alarm and false negative/miss rates in various application scenarios. For practical reasons, detection-based approaches should be suitable for low-cost tags (e.g., EPC Gen 2 tags) with limited storage and possibly no computational power.

- Punishment: As an additional line of thwarting false event injection, appropriate punishment such as monetary fines, prosecutions and confiscation of assets should be given to attackers after their attacks are detected. The reliability of attacker identification in false event injection depends on the effectiveness of user authentication in EPCglobal Network, detection of false event injection, and integrity of EPCDS data records. It is also important to convince a third party (e.g., a judge) with highly reliable evidence so as to enforce any punishment against false event injection.

Although the most effective defense process is to use all of the described steps, individual steps can be applied separately depending on application requirements. We focus on prevention and detection based solutions in the following discussions.

Prevention   One way to prevent an EPCIS from injecting false EPC events into EPCDS is to require that the EPCIS provide "proof of ownership" when it registers its EPC events in EPCDS. The "proof of ownership" aims to prove that an EPCIS owns a claimed EPC event, including the following.

- **Proving identity of tag**: When an EPC event is registered in EPCDS, the EPC number in the event should be authenticated. In other words, the EPC number belongs to a genuine RFID tag.

- **Proving identity of owner**: When an EPC event is registered in EPCDS, the owner/EPCIS of the event should be authenticated. This may involve confirming the owner's attributes, such as company name and its role in a supply chain. There could be one or more authentication servers in an EPCglobal Network which perform such authentication services to EPCDS.

- **Proving timeliness**: When an EPC event is registered in EPCDS, the owner of the event should prove to EPCDS that it generates the true EPC event at its claimed time.

A number of cryptographic techniques have been proposed to authenticate RFID tags (see Section 2.1). Any RFID tag authentication solution can be directly used to prove tag identity to EPCDS, assuming that it is performed between tag and EPCDS, instead of between tag and EPCIS.[5] In addition, the timeliness of event should be proved to EPCDS when an event is registered.

Two such solutions are discussed in [145], assuming that each tag shares a secret k with EPCDS and can perform a pseudo-random function (e.g., AES and SHA-3) $F_k()$. One solution is timer-based, in which a tag with EPC value epc generates a pseudo-random number $r = F_k(epc, time)$ whenever it is processed by an EPCIS in an event at $time$; when the event is registered at EPCDS, both pseudo-random number r and event indexing record $(epc, time)$ are submitted so that EPCDS can verify epc and $time$ by checking r based on the shared secret k. The second solution is counter-based, in which a tag with epc generates a pseudo-random number $r = F_k(epc, counter)$ in an EPC event, where $counter$ is a positive integer stored in a tag and automatically incremented upon each read. When EPC event $(epc, event, time)$ is registered, both r and $(epc, counter)$ are submitted so that EPCDS can verify epc and $counter$ by checking r based on k. In this case, $counter$ can be used as time-stamp for registered EPC event (Chain-BAC policies can be enforced with event time in such counter format).

We note that such tag authentication would not be scalable if each tag shares a different key with EPCDS due to a large number of tags in EPCglobal Network. On the other hand, if it is assumed that all tags share the same key with EPCDS, then it is a single point of failure in a sense that the corruption of a single tag would enable an adversary to inject false events about any tags. A better solution is that EPCDS keeps a master key k_m in its storage and shares a different secret $k = F_{k_m}(epc)$ with each epc.

Another solution is to use RFID path authentication (see Section 2.3), in which EPCDS authenticates a registered event according to tag path, assuming that EPCDS knows all valid paths leading to each EPCIS before path authentication. Using this approach, EPCDS may not be able to verify the exact time of registered EPC event but it can verify that the involving tag has passed through a valid path; consequently, the length of tag path can be used as time-stamp for registered EPC event (Chain-BAC policies can be enforced with event time in such path-length format).

---

[5]RFID tag authentication with EPCIS may be performed independently to tag authentication with EPCDS based on different secrets.

Detection   It is possible to detect false event injection by closely monitoring the movement of each RFID tag in EPCglobal Network. A falsely injected EPC event may demonstrate certain anomaly patterns, which could be detected using statistical, machine learning, data mining, or pattern matching approaches. A promising approach is tailing [94], which is situated for clone tag detection in practical settings (with low-cost tags, blind zones, and reader failures). In this approach, each EPC tag contains a tag tail and a tail pointer. In each EPC event, an RFID reader increments the tail pointer and overwrites the random bits at which the pointer points. An illustrative example would be $\langle AXC, 2 \rangle$ at the first reader, $\langle AXY, 3 \rangle$ at the second reader and $\langle WXY, 1 \rangle$ at the third reader, where the first part represents the tag tail and the second part represents the tail pointer. Clone tag detection can be performed by checking the consistency of tails and tail pointers in a sequence of EPC events (see Section 2.4 for detail).

If the tailing approach is applied to detecting false event injection in EPCDS, the tailing information of each tag should be read and updated by an EPCIS and reported to EPCDS whenever a related event is registered by the EPCIS to EPCDS. Different from clone tag detection, a tag's tailing information should not be read or updated if no EPC event is reported to EPCDS even if some EPC events are generated about the tag within an EPCIS. The detection of false event injection can be performed the same way as clone tag detection at EPCDS. A high detection rate can be achieved by reducing the probabilities of mis-event, mis-read, and mis-write and increasing the length of tag tails. It is also possible to leverage on batch processing in supply chain for more efficient detection of false event injection at EPCDS.

A Note on Other Security Issues   Note that defending against false event injection within EPCIS is relatively easier due to weak adversary model. All existing tag authentication solutions can be directly applied in such case. If EPCDS is not fully trusted, or access control is not fully effective, integrity measurement should be taken by each EPCIS so as to protect its data at EPCDS. Similarly, integrity measurement should be taken at each EPCIS as well due to ineffective access control and possible insider attacks. The privacy concerns in such scenarios will be addressed in the next chapter.

CHAPTER 5

RFID Privacy at the Network Level

While RFID Security in EPCglobal Network ensures that each networked party's information in EPCIS and EPCDS is shared with authorized parties only, RFID privacy at the network level further ensures that no adversary can obtain any unauthorized information in EPCglobal Network. In the previous chapter, EPCDS is assumed to be fully trusted to enforce access control so that the valuable information registered by EPCISes is shared with authorized users only. Now we relax this assumption such that EPCDS is not fully trusted, which is more realistic, as EPCDS could be (i) penetrated by hacking activities (consequently, access control may not be fully effective at EPCDS), (ii) honest-but-curious, and (iii) in collusion with some users (possibly due to Trojan attacks). Even though EPCDS operator itself is honest, we still use EPCDS to represent all possible passive adversaries and assume it is honest-but-curious in this chapter.

If EPCDS is not fully trusted, it is crucial to protect the information registered by each networked party at EPCDS, as the information can be used for creating inventory lists and deriving business intelligence on the flow of goods. However, no sufficient privacy mechanisms have been proposed to address the privacy concerns in EPCglobal Network. We hope that the initial results summarized below would inspire more research effort in this field.

5.1 ANONYMITY OF TAG ID IN EPCDS

Since EPCDS is an adversary, it is essential to prevent it from knowing the EPC numbers from the data registered by EPCISes, or from user queries. Otherwise, the adversary would be able to identify EPC products and derive who are inventorying the products, who are trading the products, and who are interested in the products. To address such privacy concerns, Fabian et al. proposed a privacy-enhanced discovery service, named SHARDIS, in which cryptographic hash values of EPC numbers, instead of plaintext EPC numbers, are stored in EPCDS data items and used in user queries [146].

SHARDIS is designed in a peer-to-peer paradigm where the discovery service consists of a number of storage nodes and gateway nodes. In SHARDIS, a data item registered by an EPCIS, which is called SHARIDS address document in [146], is partitioned into n shares using Shamir's (k, n) threshold scheme [147] and each share s_i is stored in a storage node according to an overlay key $H(epc, i, time)$, where H is a cryptographic hash function, epc is an EPC number (other product identification number can be used in SHARDIS; we focus on EPC number in our discussion), and *time* is a time interval during which the share is available. When a user queries for an EPC number *epc*, the user generates the same overlay key for each share, locates storage nodes, and retrieve enough shares for recovering relevant data items.

The major privacy threat to SHARDIS is querying attacks, which can be easily launched by any user or EPCDS. Assuming that any user or EPCDS is interested in the data items about certain EPC number, he can simply generate all overlay keys for the EPC number, query SHARDIS, and obtain interested data items in plaintext. Even if the adversary does not know the exact EPC number, it is not very difficult to make a guess according to EPC Tag Data Standard [1]. Also, for the storage node which is queried by a user with a overlay key, the storage node can easily derive the EPC number (and thus know the user's interest) from the overlay key in off-line dictionary attacks.

A possible solution to this threat is to include a random salt in generating an overlay key. The random salt can be stored in RFID tag so that only the parties which have access to the RFID tag can generate the overlay key and query EPCDS [146, 148]. Instead of using any additional storage to store random salts in RFID tags, we suggest to use existing access password and kill password for the same purpose. With 64 bits access password and kill password, plus certain entropy in 96-bit EPC, it would be difficult for an adversary to derive EPC numbers in off-line dictionary attacks.

Back to the EPCDS models we discussed in the previous chapter, one may use $H(epc, ap, kp)$ to replace *epc* whenever *epc* is used (e.g., in EPCDS data items, user queries, and access control enforcement) so as to achieve anonymity of tag ID in EPCDS, where ap and kp denote access password and kill password for tag *epc*, respectively.

5.2   ANTI-TRACING OF TAG ID IN EPCDS

Unauthorized tracing of RFID tagged objects is one of the most important privacy concerns in RFID applications. Prior research on the prevention of unauthorized tracing at the physical level is presented in Chapter 3. We now consider how to address this privacy concern at the network level.

At the network level, an adversary traces movement of RFID tagged objects by eavesdropping network messages or compromising data center servers. Compared to unauthorized tracing at the physical level, unauthorized tracing at the network level could be even more harmful as the adversary is able to obtain tracing information on a global scale and without physical presence.

It is especially important to address this concern in EPCDS, where all EPCISes register their EPC events. If all registered data are in plaintext, an EPCDS can easily trace EPC events with the same EPC numbers and different time stamps. Even if EPC numbers are replaced with fixed pseudonyms such as EPC hash values as shown in Section 5.1, EPCDS can still trace EPC events with the same pseudonyms. Then, the adversary represented by EPCDS can derive much valuable information such as inventory levels, trading partners, and trading volumes about the EPCISes which register data in EPCDS.

To address this concern, Yan et al. proposed a pseudonym-based discovery service (PBDS for short) which has the following advantages [149].

- *Protection against database reading attack*: PBDS prevents EPCDS from learning any tracing information from event indexing records maintained in its database.

- *Access control for queries*: PBDS enables users to query EPCDS and obtain tag-level tracing information according to certain access control policies defined by data owners.

- *Backward compatibility*: PBDS is backward compatible with existing communication protocols and database schemas of EPCDS.

The basic idea in PBDS is to let each EPCIS I_i choose its own pseudonym key k_i and use it in generating a pseudonym $e = F_{k_i}(epc)$ for epc in event registration, where $F_{k_i}()$ is a pseudo-random function with parameter k_i. It is difficult for EPCDS to trace EPC events since the pseudonyms are different in the event indexing records registered by different EPCISes.

In PBDS, it is assumed that all EPCISes and authorized users are trusted so that they do not disclose pseudonym keys to or collude with the adversary, which is EPCDS. It is also assumed that all message exchanges between EPCISes, users, and EPCDS are carried over authenticated and secure channels.

In the original PBDS design, the time-stamp of event is encrypted using a CPA-secure encryption scheme with key k_i; then, I_i registers an event indexing record with the encrypted time-stamp t instead of *time* (the ciphertext of *time* can be decrypted by an authorized user with k_i when querying EPCDS). The rationale of encrypting the event time is that the disclosure of tracing information from event time-stamps is orthogonal to that from tag identifiers. EPCDS may link multiple event indexing records by grouping and correlating a series of time-stamps regardless of EPC pseudonyms being used or not [149]. While this is true if very few EPC events are registered at each *time*, it does not disclose much tracing information in a practical setting where a large number of EPC events are registered at each *time* with different EPC pseudonyms. In addition, the encryption of event time does not provide much confidentiality anyway since the event time may be inferred by EPCDS according to the time it receives corresponding event registration (usually an EPCIS should register its events in time; otherwise, business processes relying on such event data would be affected or delayed). Therefore, we remove time-stamp encryption in the following discussions.

5.2.1   UNAUTHORIZED TRACING MITIGATION

We use the notation given in Section 4.2. Consider an EPCglobal Network with a single EPCDS D and a set I of EPCISes. Let U be the set of users, where each user is either EPCIS or public who does not represent any EPCIS; that is, $U = I \cup \{public\}$. At EPCIS $I_i \in I$, each event record is a three-tuple $(epc, event, time)$, where epc is an EPC number, $event$ represents an EPC event in which epc is involved, and *time* is the time when $event$ happens.

Each EPCIS I_i chooses a random pseudonym key k_i which is not known by EPCDS. When EPCIS I_i registers its event $(epc, event, time)$ to EPCDS D, it sends an event indexing record $r = (e, time)$ to D, where $r.e = F_{k_i}(epc)$ is a pseudonym for epc. Since different EP-CISes would use different pseudonyms in event registration, PBDS is immune to database read-ing attack, in which EPCDS traces event indexing records maintained in its database. Specifi-cally, given an EPC number epc and two event indexing records r and r', where $r.e = F_{k_i}(epc)$, $r'.e = F_{k_j}(epc')$, $r.time = r'.time$, the probability by which any polynomial time EPCDS can distinguish between r and r' (without knowing k_i and k_j) about which event indexing record relates to epc is no greater than $1/2 + \epsilon$, where ϵ is negligible.

Now consider user queries in PBDS. Assume that a user $u \in U$ would like to know all EPCISes which have registered events about certain EPC number epc. Since all registered events are stored with EPC pseudonyms generated by different EPCISes, user u needs to transform its epc to different pseudonyms for those EPCISes which authorize u to query. After going through certain access control and key management process, which we explain in Section 5.2.2, user u obtains a set of pseudonym keys $K(u) = \{k_i\}$ which represent its privilege to query EPCDS about epc. For all $k_i \in K(u)$, user u transforms epc to a list of pseudonyms $E = \{e_i\}$, where $e_i = F_{k_i}(epc)$. Then, u sends query (E, u) to D, which returns query result $S = \{I_i\}$ to u according to relevant access control policies, where I_i is an EPCIS which has ever registered an event indexing record r with $r.e \in E$. Finally, u may send query $q = (epc, u)$ to some $I_i \in S$ for more detailed event information[1].

We notice that there is a potential attack in the above query process. If EPCDS mon-itors each user's queries, it would know the pseudonyms in E and make a guess that all such pseudonyms relate to the same EPC number. If this is the case, EPCDS can trace its event in-dexing records with pseudonyms in E accordingly. To thwart this attack, u should not query the pseudonyms in E at the same time. Instead, u should mix the pseudonyms of different EPC numbers and send such mixed pseudonyms to EPCDS in each query.

5.2.2 ACCESS CONTROL AND KEY MANAGEMENT

One remaining question in PBDS is how to enforce access control policies for user queries? Since EPCDS cannot trace event indexing records between EPCISes, it is difficult for it to enforce any Chain-BAC or List-BAC with white/black lists for EPC. In PBDS design, List-BAC policies are enforced at user level. For simplicity of presentation, assume that each user u defines a white list $L(u)$ only which is a subset of users in U (it is straightforward to consider black list or both). Such List-BAC policies can be enforced by EPCDS and/or by a separate security manager as explained below.

Solution I   Another remaining question is where and how user u obtains a set of pseudonym keys $K(u)$ before it sends queries to EPCDS? The pseudonym keys cannot be managed by EPCDS for

---

[1]For simplicity, only Directory Service model is considered in PBDS, though it is not difficult to extend it to Query Relay model and ADS model.

anti-tracing purpose. One possible solution suggested in [149] is to introduce an online security manager M for managing all pseudonym keys. This online security manager should be trusted by all EPCISes for managing their pseudonym keys and enforcing their access control policies. Nonetheless, it should not collude with EPCDS, nor be allowed to query EPCDS for anti-tracing purpose.

In this solution, security manager M maintains a database of $(I_i, k_i, L(I_i))$ for all EPCISes I_i, where k_i is I_i's pseudonym key, and $L(I_i) \in 2^U$ is the while list defined by I_i. Before a user u sends any query to EPCDS D, it may send a request to M. Upon authenticating user u, M searches its database for all records $(I_i, k_i, L(I_i))$ such that $u \in L(I_i)$, and returns $K(u) = \{k_i\}$ to u over a secure channel for all k_i in such records.

This solution does not require EPCDS to enforce any access control policies for user queries. It does not specify how to handle user key revocation and hence it is only suitable for EPCglobal Network with static user key assignments. In a dynamic setting where EPCISes may update their access control policies, it is difficult to revoke a pseudonym key which a user has already obtained. Consider a simple case where I_i revokes k_i from user u; it is not sufficient for I_i to simply delete u from its white list $L(I_i)$ in M if user u has already obtained k_i before. One may suggest I_i to update its pseudonym key k_i to a new key k_i' so that u cannot use k_i to access future data. In such case, I_i needs to use the new key k_i' for publishing future event indexing records in EPCDS. Consequently, an authorized user needs both old key and new key for querying the event indexing records published by I_i. Clearly, this is not convenient in a highly dynamic environment.

Solution II To address the problem of pseudonym key revocation, it is suggested to enforce access control policies not only at security manager for distributing pseudonym keys but also at EPCDS for restricting user queries [149]. When EPCIS I_i revokes user u from accessing its event indexing records, I_i deletes u from its white list $L(I_i)$ at both security manager M and at EPCDS D. There is no need of updating the pseudonym key k_i in M because even if user u has already obtained k_i before, u cannot get access to the event indexing records registered by I_i any more due to the policy enforced at EPCDS.

Solution III Both solution I and solution II require the existence of an online security manager to manage pseudonym keys for user queries under access control policies defined by participating EPCISes. The use of an online security manager in EPCglobal Network would increase operational cost and performance overhead. To eliminate the requirement of an online security manager, it is suggested to shift the task of pseudonym key distribution and access control from security manager to EPCDS [149]. Due to anti-tracing requirement, the pseudonym keys are stored in EPCDS in ciphertext. When authorized users request for certain pseudonym keys, EPCDS employs a proxy re-encryption scheme [150] to re-encrypt the ciphertext of requested pseudonym keys for the requesting users so that they can decrypt the pseudonyms keys. In this re-encryption process, EPCDS learns nothing about the underlying plaintext of pseudonym keys.

A proxy re-encryption scheme is a tuple of (possibly probabilistic) polynomial time algorithms (KG, RG, $\mathcal{E}, \mathcal{R}, \mathcal{D}$) [151].

- $(KG, \mathcal{E}, \mathcal{D})$ are standard key generation, encryption, and decryption algorithms for a public key encryption scheme. On input of a security parameter κ, KG outputs a public and private key pair (pk_A, sk_A). On input pk_A and message m, $\mathcal{E}$ outputs a ciphertext $c_A = \mathcal{E}(pk_A, m)$. On input sk_A and ciphertext c_A, $\mathcal{D}$ outputs the original message $m = \mathcal{D}(sk_A, c_A)$.

- On input (pk_A, sk_A, pk_B), the re-encryption key generation algorithm, RG, outputs a re-encryption key $rk_{A \rightarrow B}$ for the proxy.

- On input $rk_{A \rightarrow B}$ and ciphertext c_A, the re-encryption function, $\mathcal{R}$, outputs $\mathcal{R}(rk_{A \rightarrow B}, c_A) = \mathcal{E}(pk_B, m) = c_B$ which can be decrypted using private key sk_B.

In a setting-up phase, each user $u \in U$ chooses a public and private key pair (pk_u, sk_u) under a public key encryption scheme $(KG, \mathcal{E}, \mathcal{D})$. All users' public keys are managed by an offline security manager M, which also has its own public and privacy key pair (pk_M, sk_M) under $(KG, \mathcal{E}, \mathcal{D})$. The offline security manager, on input (pk_M, sk_M, pk_u), generates a re-encryption key $rk_{M \rightarrow u}$ for each user $u \in U$ using algorithm RG. The offline security manager forwards all re-encryption keys $rk_{M \rightarrow u}$ to EPCDS.

All access control policies $L(I_i)$ for $I_i \in I$ are enforced at EPCDS, where each EPCIS I_i is responsible for managing/updating its own policy $L(I_i)$. Each EPCIS $I_i \in I$ encrypts its pseudonym key k_i using the public key of offline security manager M, and publishes the ciphertext $c_i = \mathcal{E}(pk_M, k_i)$ to EPCDS.

In a querying phase (online), a user u may request for all pseudonym keys from EPCDS before sending a query to it. Upon authenticating user u, EPCDS re-encrypts pseudonym key ciphertext as $\mathcal{R}(rk_{M \rightarrow u}, c_i) = \mathcal{E}(pk_u, k_i)$ for all $I_i \in I$ such that $u \in L(I_i)$ holds (which means u is an authorized user according to I_i's policy), and returns the re-encrypted pseudonym keys to the user. The user can decrypt the pseudonym keys using his private key sk_u and then use the pseudonym keys to form his query.

Compared to the solutions requiring an online security manager, this solution replaces the online security manager with an offline security manager, which can stay offline unless any user changes its public key. This solution requires an authenticated distribution of (a) the public key of offline security manager to all EPCISes, (b) the public keys of all users to the offline security manager, and (c) all re-encryption keys from the offline security manager to EPCDS. In most public key cryptosystems, a significant portion of the operational cost is attributed to the management of public keys (e.g., authenticated distribution and revocation of public keys). The management of public keys would be simpler if authenticated and secure channels exist between users, security manager, and EPCDS, which is a pre-requisite even with online security manager.

5.2.3   COMPATIBILITY AND PERFORMANCE ISSUES

The modifications to standard EPCDS [5] are summarized below for adopting the anti-tracing design [149].

- *Query users*: Users are required to acquire pseudonym keys of EPCISes before querying EPCDS. To search for all event indexing records corresponding to a tag identifier, a user provides a set of pseudonyms instead of using the original tag identifier as a query parameter. The pseudonym keys can be obtained from an online security manager or from EPCDS via proxy re-encryption.

- *Networked parties*: Networked parties/EPCISes use pseudonyms instead of tag identifiers for registering event indexing records in EPCDS. If offline security manager is used, EP-CISes also need to encrypt pseudonym keys using the public key of offline security manager and publish the ciphertext of pseudonym keys in EPCDS.

- *EPCDS*: The data structure of event indexing records is the same as before except for one semantic change: the original tag identifier is replaced with a pseudonym. If offline security manager is used, EPCDS needs to store the ciphertext of pseudonym keys for all EPCISes and perform proxy re-encryption on the ciphertext upon users' requests.

- *Security manager*: An online security manager is needed in solutions I and II, and an offline security manager is required in solution III for generating re-encryption keys.

With enhanced privacy protection, the anti-tracing design inevitably impacts the performance of EPCDS as it introduces extra cryptographic operations. This impact is estimated with offline security manager in a demo system [149] based on JHU-MIT Proxy Re-cryptography Library [152]. The demo system is implemented in C++ on Ubuntu Linux. HMAC with SHA-256 is used for pseudonym generation, and bilinear ElGamal proxy re-encryption scheme with 256-bit key [151] is used for proxy re-encryption. The experimental machine consists of a 2.53GHz Intel Core 2 Duo E7200 processor and 4 GB DDR2 800 Hz RAM.

In experiments, on average, it takes 0.30 μs to generate a pseudonym (3.28 M pseudonyms per second). For proxy re-encryption, it takes 3.3 ms to encrypt a pseudonym key, 8.6 ms to re-encrypt the ciphertext of a pseudonym key, and 1.6 ms to decrypt the ciphertext after re-encryption. Although the computation of re-encryption scheme is much slower than HMAC, its performance cost would not become a bottleneck because the result of re-encryption can always be reused as long as the ciphertext of pseudonym keys remain unchanged. Hence, the overall additional cost is not significant for adopting the anti-tracing design.

CHAPTER 6

Summary and Future Directions

Starting from 2002, RFID security and privacy has been one of the fastest developing areas in information security and privacy. Thanks to UCL's Information Security Group in Belgium, headed by Gildas Avoine, most of important research papers in this area are nicely archived in RFID Security & Privacy Lounge [8]. Partially motivated by a widely cited survey by Ari Juels in 2006 [20], we try to provide a systematic overview on this fast-evolving area, which has grown much deeper and wider since its early age.

We interweave the material in this book from two dimensions: (I.1) RFID security and (I.2) privacy at (II.1) physical and (II.2) network levels. At the physical level, RFID devices should be identified with assurance in the presence of attacks (i.e., security) and without disclosure of any valuable information about the devices (i.e., privacy). At the network level, RFID information should be shared with authorized parties only (i.e., security) without disclosure of valuable RFID information to any honest-but-curious server which coordinates information sharing (i.e., privacy). We hope that we have summarized most of important works in each of these categories, and apologize if there is any missing due to limited time and resources in writing this book.

Not only does this book summarize the past, but it also provides new research results, especially at the network level. Due to much on-going work, it would be necessary to update this book significantly in the next few years. In addition, we envision more effort to be made in the following directions so as to advance the research in this area.

- Lightweight RFID authentication protocols: Although much effort has been made in this direction, it is still not clear how lightweight an RFID authentication protocol can be. Formal models should be developed to break the design-attack-revision-attack loop.

- Compared to the privacy notions developed for RFID tag authentication, the development of privacy notions for RFID path authentication is less mature. It is possible to develop new privacy notions for RFID path authentication.

- How does one incorporate practical batch processes in clone tag detection and false event injection detection?

- Practical access control policy enforcement at EPCISes: The current query processes at EP-CISes require EPCISes to query EPCDS for enforcing partner relationship-based policies. It would be more practical to remove EPCDS from such processes.

- Is it possible to enforce partner relationship-based policies at EPCDS if EPCDS is not fully trusted?

- If EPCISes and/or EPCDS are outsourced to be cloud computing services, which is an realistic assumption due to a high volume of RFID data and an emerging trend in the Internet of things, how does one protect data privacy while enabling user queries and enforcing access control policies?

- It is meaningful to promote mature and practical techniques in RFID security and privacy to become part of future RFID standards (e.g., ISO and EPCglobal).

Bibliography

[1] GS1, "EPC Tag Data Standard 1.6, Ratified Standard," Sept 9, 2011. `www.gs1.org/gsmp/kc/epcglobal/tds/tds_1_6-RatifiedStd-20110922.pdf`. 1, 118

[2] EPCglobal, "EPC Radio-Frequency Identity Protocols Class-1 Generation-2 UHF RFID protocol for communications at 860 MHz-960 MHz, version 1.2.0.," 2008. 3, 33

[3] EPCglobal, "The EPCglobal Architecture Framework," `http://www.gs1.org/gsmp/kc/epcglobal/architecture/architecture_1_4-framework-20101215.pdf`, 2010. 3, 100, 101

[4] EPCglobal, "EPC Information Services (EPCIS) Version 1.0 Specification," `http://www.gs1.org/gsmp/kc/epcglobal/epcis/epcis_1_0-standard-20070412.pdf`, 2007. 100, 101

[5] EPCglobal, "Data Discovery (DD JRG) Requirements Document," version 0.0.27, 2009. 100, 123

[6] B. Fabin and O. Günther, "Security challenges of the EPCglobal Network," *Communications of ACM*, vol. 52, no. 7, pp. 121–125, 2009. DOI: 10.1145/1538788.1538816. 100

[7] Wikipedia, "EPCglobal Network," `http://en.wikipedia.org/wiki/EPCglobal_Network`, last updated 7 September 2010, accessed 30 September 2013. 100

[8] Gildas Avoine, "RFID Security and Privacy Lounge," `http://www.avoine.net/rfid/`. 125

[9] Rishab Nithyanand, Gene Tsudik, and Ersin Uzun, "Readers Behaving Badly - Reader Revocation in PKI-Based RFID Systems," *ESORICS*, pp. 19–36, 2010. DOI: 10.1007/978-3-642-15497-3_2. 8

[10] R. Sandhu, "Good-enough security," *IEEE Internet Computing.*, January-February 2003, pp. 66–68, 2003. DOI: 10.1109/MIC.2003.1167341. 5

[11] M. Feldhofer, S. Dominikus, and J. Wolkerstorfer, "Strong authentication for RFID systems using the AES algorithm," *CHES 2004. LNCS,*, vol. 3156, pp. 357–370, 2004. DOI: 10.1007/978-3-540-28632-5_26. 9, 18, 64

[12] M. Feldhofer, "Comparing the Stream Ciphers Trivium and Grain for their Feasibility on RFID tags," *Proceedings of Austrochip,*, 2007. 9

[13] D. Hein, J. Wolkerstorfer, and N. Felber, "ECC is Ready for RFID - A Proof in Silicon," *4th Workshop on RFID Security (RFIDSec)*, 2008. DOI: 10.1007/978-3-642-04159-4_26. 8

[14] M. O'Neill, "Low-Cost SHA-1 Hash Function Architecture for RFID Tags," *4th Workshop on RFID Security (RFIDSec)*, 2008. 9, 18

[15] C. Rolfes, A. Poschmann, and C. Paar, "Security for 1000 Gate Equivalents," *Secure Component and System Identification (SECSI)*, 2008. DOI: 10.1007/978-3-540-85893-5_7. 9, 18

[16] T. Kasper, D. Oswald, and C. Paar, "Side-Channel Analysis of Cryptographic RFIDs with Analog Demodulation," *7th Workshop on RFID Security (RFIDSec)*, pp. 61–77, 2011. DOI: 10.1007/978-3-642-25286-0_5. 7

[17] Tong-Lee Lim, Tieyan Li, and Yingjiu Li, "A Security and Performance Evaluation of Hash-based RFID Protocols," *4th International Conferences on Information Security and Cryptology (Inscrypt)*, pp. 406–424, 2008. DOI: 10.1007/978-3-642-01440-6_30. 9

[18] Yingjiu Li and Xuhua Ding, "Protecting RFID Communications in Supply Chains," *ACM Symposium on InformAtion, Computer, and Communication Security (ASIACCS)*, pp. 234–241, 2007. DOI: 10.1145/1229285.1229318. 16

[19] S. A. Weis, "Radio-Frequency Identification Security and Privacy," *Master's thesis*, M.I.T., June 2003. 18

[20] A. Juels, "RFID Security and Privacy: A Research Survey," *IEEE Journal on Selected Areas in Communication (J-SAC)*, vol. 24, no. 2, pp. 381–395, 2006. DOI: 10.1109/JSAC.2005.861395. 18, 125

[21] A. Bogdanov, G. Leander, C. Paar, A. Poschmann, M. J. Robshaw, Y. Seurin, "Hash Functions and RFID Tags: Mind the Gap," *CHES 2008*, pp. 283–299, 2008. DOI: 10.1007/978-3-540-85053-3_18. 18

[22] P. Peris-Lopez, J. C. Hernandez-Castro, J. M. Estevez-Tapiador, and A. Ribagorda, "LMAP: A Real Lightweight Mutual Authentication Protocol for Low-Cost RFID Tags," *Proc. of 2nd Workshop on RFID Security*, 2006 http://events.iaik.tugraz.at/RFIDSec06/. 18

[23] P. Peris-Lopez, J. C. Hernandez-Castro, J. M. Estevez-Tapiador, and A. Ribagorda, "M²AP: A Minimalist Mutual Authentication Protocol for Low-Cost RFID tags," *Proc. of International Conference on Ubiquitous Intelligence and Computing (UIC'06)*, LNCS 4159, pp. 912–923, 2006. DOI: 10.1007/11833529_93. 18

[24] T. Li and G. Wang, "Security Analysis of Two Ultra-Lightweight RFID Authentication Protocols," IFIP SEC 2007, May 2007. DOI: 10.1007/978-0-387-72367-9_10. 18

[25] Hung-Yu Chien and Chen-Wei Huang, "Security of Ultra-Lightweight RFID Authentication Protocols and Its Improvements," *ACM SIGOPS Operating Systems Review archive*, vol. 41, no. 4, pp. 83–86, 2007. DOI: 10.1145/1278901.1278916. 18

[26] Hung-Yu Chien, "SASI: A New Ultra-Lightweight RFID Authentication Protocol Providing Strong Authentication and Strong Integrity," *IEEE Transactions on Dependable and Secure Computing*, vol. 4, No. 4, pp. 337–340, 2007. DOI: 10.1109/TDSC.2007.70226. 18

[27] Hung-Min Sun, Wei-Chih Ting, and King-Hang Wang, "On the Security of Chien's Ultralightweight RFID Authentication Protocol," *IEEE Transactions on Dependable and Secure Computing*, vol. 8, No. 2, pp. 315–317, 2011. DOI: 10.1109/TDSC.2009.26. 18

[28] G. Avoine, X. Carpent, and B. Martin, "Strong Authentication and Strong Integrity (SASI) Is Not That Strong," *6th Workshop on RFID Security (RFIDSec)*, pp. 50–64, 2010. DOI: 10.1007/978-3-642-16822-2_5. 18

[29] D. M. Konidala, Z. Kim, and K. Kim, "A simple and cost effective RFID tag-reader mutual authentication scheme," *3rd Workshop on RFID Security (RFIDSec)*, 2007. 18, 64

[30] P. Peris-Lopez, J. Hernandez-Castro, J. M. Estevez-Tapiador, and A. Ribagorda, "Practical attacks on a mutual authentication scheme under the EPC Class 1 Generation 2 Standard," *Computer Communications*, vol. 32, 2009. DOI: 10.1016/j.comcom.2009.03.010. 19

[31] Y.-J. Huang, C.-C. Yuan, M.-K. Chen, W.-C. Lin, and H.-C. Teng, "Hardware implementation of RFID mutual authentication protocol," *IEEE Transactions on Industrial Electronics*, vol. 57, no. 5, 2010. DOI: 10.1109/TIE.2009.2037098. 19

[32] Y.-J. Huang, W.-C. Lin, and H.-L.Li, "Efficient implementation of RFID mutual authentication protocol," *IEEE Transactions on Industrial Electronics*, vol. 59, no. 12, pp. 4784–4791, 2012. DOI: 10.1109/TIE.2011.2178215. 19

[33] Seyed Farhad Aghili, Nasour Bagheri, Praveen Gauravaram, Masoumeh Safkhani, and Somitra Kumar Sanadhya, "On the Security of two RFID Mutual Authentication Protocols," *9th Workshop on RFID Security (RFIDSec)*, 2013. DOI: 10.1007/978-3-642-28879-1_7. 19

[34] S. Karthikeyan, and M. Nesterenko, "RFID Security Without Extensive Cryptography," in *3rd ACM Workshop on Security of Ad Hoc and Sensor Networks*, 2005. DOI: 10.1145/1102219.1102229. 64

[35] D. N. Duc, J. Park, H. Lee, and K. Kim, "Enhancing the Security of EPCglobal Gen-2 RFID Tag against Traceability and Cloning," *Symposium on Cryptography and Information Security*, 2006. DOI: 10.1007/978-3-540-71641-9_15.

[36] H. Y. Chien and C. H. Chen, "Mutual Authentication Protocol for RFID Conforming to EPC Class 1 Generation 2 Standards," *Computers Standards & Interfaces*, vol. 29, no. 2, pp 254–259, 2007. DOI: 10.1016/j.csi.2006.04.004.

[37] P. Peris-Lopez, J. C. Hernandez-Castro, J. M. Estevez Tapiador, and A. Ribgorda, "Cryptanalysis of a Novel Authentication Protocol Conforming to EPC-C1G2 Standard," in *Workshop on RFID Security (RFIDSec) '07*, 2007. DOI: 10.1016/j.csi.2008.05.012.

[38] M. Feldhofer, S. Dominikus, and J. Wolkerstorfer, "Strong Authentication for RFID Systems using the AES Algorithm," in *Workshop on Cryptographic Hardware and Embedded Systems (CHES) 2004*, 2004. DOI: 10.1007/978-3-540-28632-5_26.

[39] M. Feldhofer, "Comparing the Stream Ciphers Trivium and Grain for their Feasibility on RFID Tags," in *Proceedings of Austrochip 2007*, 2007.

[40] D. Hein, J. Wolkerstorfer, and N. Felber, "ECC is Ready for RFID - A Proof in Silicon ," in *4th Workshop on RFID Security (RFIDSec) 2008*, 2008. DOI: 10.1007/978-3-642-04159-4_26.

[41] M. O'Neill, "Low-Cost SHA-1 Hash Function Architecture for RFID Tags," in *4th Workshop on RFID Security (RFIDSec) 2008*, 2008.

[42] C. Rolfes, A. Poschmann, and C. Paar, "Security for 1000 Gate Equivalents," in *Secure Component and System Identification (SECSI) 2008*, 2008. DOI: 10.1007/978-3-540-85893-5_7.

[43] Andrey Bogdanov, Lars R. Knudsen, Gregor Leander, Christof Paar, Axel Poschmann, Matthew J. B. Robshaw, Yannick Seurin and C. Vikkelsoe, "PRESENT: An Ultra-Lightweight Block Cipher," *CHES*, pp. 450–466, 2007. DOI: 10.1007/978-3-540-74735-2_31. 64

[44] M. Ohkubo, K. Suzuki, and S. Kinoshita, "Cryptographic Approach to 'Privacy-Friendly' Tags," in *RFID Privacy Workshop, MIT*, 2003. 9

[45] M. Ohkubo, K. Suzuki, and S. Kinoshita, "Efficient Hash-Chain Based RFID Privacy Protection Scheme," *International Conference on Ubiquitous Computing – Ubicomp, Workshop Privacy: Current Status and Future Directions*, 2004. 64

[46] G. Avoine, and P. Oechslin, "A Scalable and Provably Secure Hash Based RFID Protocol," in *Proceedings of the Int'l Workshop on Pervasive Computing and Communication Security (PerSec) 2005*, pp. 110–114, 2005. DOI: 10.1109/PERCOMW.2005.12. 10

[47] T. Dimitriou, "A Lightweight RFID Protocol to Protect against Traceability and Cloning Attacks," in *Proceedings of the IEEE Int'l Conference on Security and Privacy for Emerging Areas in Communications Networks (SecureComm) '05*, 2005. DOI: 10.1109/SECURECOMM.2005.4. 10, 12

[48] G. Tsudik, "YA-TRAP: Yet Another Trivial RFID Authentication Protocol," in *Proceedings of the IEEE Int'l Conference on Pervasive Computing and Communications Workshops (PerComW) 2006*, pp. 640–643, 2006. DOI: 10.1109/PERCOMW.2006.152. 10

[49] C. Chatmon, T. van Le, and M. Burmester, "Secure Anonymous RFID Authentication Protocols," *Technical Report TR-060112*, Florida State University, Computer Science Dept, 2006. 10

[50] T. Dimitriou, "A Secure and Efficient RFID Protocol That Could Make Big Brother (Partially) Obsolete," in *Proceedings of the 1st Int'l Conference on Pervasive Computing and Communications (PerCom) 2006*, pp. 269–275, 2006. 13, 14

[51] D. Molnar, and D. Wagner, "Privacy and Security in Library RFID Issues, Practices and Architectures," in *Proceedings of the ACM Conference on Computer and Communication Security*, 2004. DOI: 10.1145/1030083.1030112. 12, 14

[52] L. Lu, J. S. Han, L. Hu, Y. H. Liu and L. M. Ni, "Dynamic Key-Updating: Privacy-Preserving Authentication for RFID Systems," in *Proceedings of the IEEE Int'l Conference on Pervasive Computing and Communications (PerCom) 2007*, 2007. DOI: 10.1109/PERCOM.2007.13. 13

[53] M. Conti, R. Di Pietro, L. V. Mancini, and A. Spognardi, "RIPP-FS: An RFID Identification, Privacy Preserving Protocol with Forward Secrecy," in *Proceedings of the IEEE Int'l Conference on Pervasive Computing and Communications Workshops (PerComW) 2007*, pp. 229–234, 2007. DOI: 10.1109/PERCOMW.2007.100. 14, 15

[54] D. Henrici, and P. Muller, "Providing Security and Privacy in RFID Systems Using Triggered Hash Chains," in *Proceedings of the IEEE Int'l Conference on Pervasive Computing and Communications (PerCom) 2008*, pp. 50–59, 2008. DOI: 10.1109/PERCOM.2008.67. 15

[55] Tong-Lee Lim, Tieyan Li, and Tao Gu, "Secure RFID Identification and Authentication with Triggered Hash Chain Variants," *Proceedings of the 14th Int'l Conference on Parallel and Distributed Systems (ICPADS) '08*, 2008. DOI: 10.1109/ICPADS.2008.46. 16

[56] N. Hopper and M. Blum, "Secure Human Identification Protocols," *Advances in Cryptography – Asiacrypt 2001*, LNCS 2248, pp. 52–66, 2001. DOI: 10.1007/3-540-45682-1_4. 19

[57] A. Juels and S. Weis, "Authenticating Pervasive Devices with Human Protocols," *Advances in Cryptography – Crypto 2005*, LNCS 3621, pp. 293–308, 2005. DOI: 10.1007/11535218_18. 19

[58] H. Gilbert, H. Sibert, and M. Robshaw, "An active attack against a provably secure lightweight authentication protocol," *Electronics Letters*, vol. 41, no. 21, 2005. DOI: 10.1049/el:20052622. 20

[59] J. Bringer, H. Chabanne and E. Dottax, "HB++: a Lightweight Authentication Protocol Secure against Some Attacks," *Second International Workshop on Security, Privacy and Trust in Pervasive and Ubiquitous Computing (SecPerU 2006)*, pp. 28–33, 2006. 20

[60] J. Munilla and A. Peinado, "HB-MP: A further step in the HB-family of lightweight authentication protocols," *The International Journal of Computer and Telecommunications Networking*, vol. 51, no. 9, pp. 2262–2267, June, 2007. DOI: 10.1016/j.comnet.2007.01.011. 20

[61] D. Duc and K. Kim, "Securing HB+ against GRS main-in-the-middle attack," *2007 Symposium on Cryptography and Information Security (SCIS)*, 2007. 20

[62] X. Leng, K. Mayes, and K. Markantonakis, "HB-MP+ protocol: an improvement on the HB-MP protocol," *2008 IEEE International Conference on RFID*, 2008. DOI: 10.1109/RFID.2008.4519342. 20

[63] J. Bringer and H. Chabanne, "Trusted-HB: a low-cost version of HB secure against man-in-the-middle attacks," `eprint.iacr.org/2008042.pdf`, 2008. DOI: 10.1109/TIT.2008.928290. 20

[64] H. Gilbert, M. Robshaw, and Y. Seurin, "HB$^\#$: Increasing the security and efficiency of HB," *Eurocrypt*, pp. 361–378, 2008. 20

[65] C. Bosley, K. Haralambiev, and A. Nicolosi, "HB^N: An HB-like protocol secure against man-in-the-middle attacks," `eprint.iacr.org/2011/350.pdf`, 2011. 21

[66] K. B. Rasmussen and S. Čapkun, "Realization of RF Distance Bounding," *USENIX Security Symposium*, 2010. 22

[67] S. Brands and D. Chaum, "Distance bounding protocols," *Eurocrypt 1993*, pp. 344–359, 1994. DOI: 10.1007/3-540-48285-7_30. 22

[68] G. P. Hancke and M. G. Kuhn, "An RFID distance bounding protocol," *SecureComm 2005*, pp. 67–73, 2005. DOI: 10.1109/SECURECOMM.2005.56. 22

[69] G. Avoine, M. A. Bingöl, S. Kardaş, C. Lauradoux, and B. Martin, "A framework for analyzing RFID distance bounding protocols," *Journal of Computer Security*, vol. 19, no. 2, pp. 289–317, 2011. DOI: 10.3233/JCS-2010-0408. 21

[70] A. Juels, "Minimalist Cryptography for Low-Cost RFID Tags," *4th International Conference on Security in Communication Networks (SCN)*, 2004. DOI: 10.1007/978-3-540-30598-9_11. 19

[71] D. N. Duc, J. Park, H. Lee and K. Kim, "Enhancing security of EPCglobal Gen2 RFID tag against traceability and cloning," *2006 Symposium on Cryptography and Information Security (SCIS)*, 2006. 19, 64

[72] H.-M. Sun and W.-C. Ting, "A Gen2-Based RFID Authentication Protocol for Security and Privacy," *IEEE Transactions on Mobile Computing*, vol. 8, no. 8, pp. 1052–1062, 2009. DOI: 10.1109/TMC.2008.175. 19

[73] A. Juels, R. Pappu, and B. Parno, "Unidirectional Key Distribution Across Time and Space with Applications to RFID Security," *17th USENIX Security Symposium*, pp. 75–90, 2008. 23, 24, 25, 26, 32, 96

[74] Tieyan Li, Yingjiu Li, and Guilin Wang, "Secure and Practical Key Distribution for RFID-Enabled Supply Chains," *7th International ICST Conference on Security and Privacy in Communication Networks (SecureComm)*, 2011. DOI: 10.1007/978-3-642-31909-9_20. 24, 25, 26, 28, 29, 30

[75] M. Bellare and P. Rogaway, "Robust computational secret sharing and a unified account of classical secret-sharing goals," *Proc. of the 14th conference on Computer and communications security*, pp. 172–184, 2007. DOI: 10.1145/1315245.1315268. 26

[76] R. J. McEliece, and D.V. Sarwate, "On sharing secrets and reed-solomon codes," *Communications of the ACM*, vol. 24, pp. 583–584, 1981. DOI: 10.1145/358746.358762. 27

[77] A. Juels, "Strengthening EPC tags against cloning," *ACM Workshop on Wireless Security – WiSe*, 2005. DOI: 10.1145/1080793.1080805. 31

[78] P. Rogaway, M. Bellare, and J. Black, "OCB: A block-cipher mode of operation for efficient authenticated encryption," *ACM Transactions on Information and System Security (TISSEC)*, vol. 6, no. 3, pp. 365–403, 2003. DOI: 10.1145/937527.937529. 33

[79] A. Juels, "Yoking-proofs for RFID tags," *International workshop on pervasive computing and communication security – PerSec*, pp. 138–143, 2004. DOI: 10.1109/PERCOMW.2004.1276920. 34

[80] Shaoying Cai, Chunhua Su, Yingjiu Li, Robert H. Deng, and Tieyan Li, "Protecting and Restraining the Third Party in RFID-Enabled 3PL Supply Chains," *Sixth International Conference on Information Systems Security (ICISS 2010)*, pp. 246–260, 2010. DOI: 10.1007/978-3-642-17714-9_18. 35

[81] J. Saito and K. Sakurai, "Grouping proof for RFID tags," *19th International Conference on Advanced Information Networking and Applications*, pp. 621–624, 2005. DOI: 10.1109/AINA.2005.197. 34

[82] S. Piramuthu, "On existence proofs for multiple RFID tags," *2006 ACS/IEEE International Conference on Pervasive Services*, pp. 317–320, 2006. DOI: 10.1109/PERSER.2006.1652252. 34

[83] C.-C. Lin, Y.-C. Lai, J. D. Tygar, C.-K. Yang, and C.-L. Chiang, "Coexistence proof using chain of timestamps for multiple RFID tags," *APWeb/WAIM Workshops*, pp. 634–643, 2007. DOI: 10.1007/978-3-540-72909-9_70. 34

[84] M. Burmester, B. de Medeiros, and R. Motta, "Probably secure grouping-proofs for RFID tags," *CARDIS*, pp. 176–190, 2008. 34

[85] ICC Commercial Crime Services, "Counterfeiting intelligence bureau," http://www.icc-ccs.org/home/cib, 2011. 35

[86] E.-O. Blass, K. Elkhiyaoui, and R. Molva, "Tracker: security and privacy for RFID-based supply chains," *NDSS*, pp. 455–472, 2011. 35, 39, 40, 88, 89, 95, 96

[87] E.-O. Blass, K. Elkhiyaoui, and R. Molva, "Tracker: security and privacy for RFID-based supply chains," *Cryptology ePrint Archive*, Report 2010/219, 2010. 89, 90, 91, 95

[88] Erik-Oliver Blass, Kaoutar Elkhiyaoui, and Refik Molva, "CHECKER: on-site checking in RFID-based supply chains," *ACM conference on Security and Privacy in Wireless and Mobile Networks*, pp. 173–184, 2012. DOI: 10.1145/2185448.2185471. 38, 39, 89

[89] S. Cai, Y. Li, and Y. Zhao, "Distributed path authentication for dynamic RFID-enabled supply chains," *IFIP SEC*, 2012. DOI: 10.1007/978-3-642-30436-1_41. 39, 96

[90] H. Wang, Y. Li, Z. Zhang, and Z. Cao, "Two-level path authentication in EPC-global network," *IEEE RFID*, pp. 24-31, 2012. DOI: 10.1109/RFID.2012.6193052. 40

[91] Shaoying Cai, Robert H. Deng, Yingjiu Li, and Yunlei Zhao, "A new framework for privacy of RFID path authentication," *ACNS*, pp. 473–488, 2012. DOI: 10.1007/978-3-642-31284-7_28. 39, 40, 89, 91, 92, 93, 96

[92] G. Noubir, K. Vijayan, and H. J. Nussbaumer, "Singaure-based method for run-time fault detection in communication protocols," *Computer Communications Journal*, vol. 21, no. 5, pp. 405–421, 1998. DOI: 10.1016/S0140-3664(98)00121-2. 36

[93] A. Boldyreva, C. Gentry, A. O'Neill, and D. H. Yum, "Ordered multisignatures and identity-based sequential aggregate signatures with applications to secure routing," *CCS*, pp. 276–285, 2007. DOI: 10.1145/1315245.1315280. 39

[94] D. Zanetti, S. Capkun, and A. Juels, "Tailing RFID tags for clone detection," *NDSS*, 2013. 40, 41, 43, 115

[95] Changshe Ma, Yingjiu Li, Robert H. Deng and Tieyan Li, "RFID privacy: relation between two notions, minimal condition, and efficient construction," *ACM Conference on Computer and Communications Security*, pp. 54–65, 2009. DOI: 10.1145/1653662.1653670. 47, 54, 56, 64, 78

[96] Junzuo Lai, Robert H. Deng, Yingjiu Li, "Revisiting Unpredictability-Based RFID Privacy Models," *8th International Conference on Applied Cryptography and Network Security (ACNS)*, pp. 475–492, 2010. DOI: 10.1007/978-3-642-13708-2_28. 56, 57, 78, 79

[97] Yingjiu Li, Robert H. Deng, Junzuo Lai, and Changshe Ma, "On Two RFID Privacy Notions and Their Relations," *ACM Transactions on Information and System Security (TISSEC)*, vol. 14, no. 4, pp. 30:1–23, ACM, 2011. DOI: 10.1145/2043628.2043631. 47, 56, 57, 59, 60, 61, 62, 64, 78, 79

[98] Ivan Damgård and Michael Østergaard Pedersen, "RFID Security: Tradeoffs between Security and Efficiency," *CT-RSA*, pp. 318–332, 2008. DOI: 10.1007/978-3-540-79263-5_20. 8, 51

[99] Ari Juels and Stephen A. Weis, "Defining Strong Privacy for RFID," *PerCom Workshops*, pp. 342–347, 2007. DOI: 10.1109/PERCOMW.2007.37. 52, 59, 67, 74, 76, 77

[100] Pierangela Samarati and Latanya Sweeney, "Protecting Privacy when Disclosing Information: k-Anonymity and Its Enforcement through Generalization and Suppression," *Technical Report, SRI International*, 1998. 53

[101] JungHoon Ha, Sang-Jae Moon, Jianying Zhou and JaeCheol Ha, "A New Formal Proof Model for RFID Location Privacy," *ESORICS*, pp. 267–281, 2008. DOI: 10.1007/978-3-540-88313-5_18. 53, 78

[102] van Deursen, Ton and Radomirović, Saša, "On a new formal proof model for RFID location privacy," *Inf. Process. Letter*, vol. 110, no. 2, pp. 57–61, 2009. DOI: 10.1016/j.ipl.2009.10.007. 54

[103] Oded Goldreich, Shafi Goldwasser and Silvio Micali, "How to construct random functions," *Journal of ACM*, vol. 33, no. 4, pp. 792–807, 1986. DOI: 10.1145/6490.6503. 64

[104] Hung-Yu Chien and Che-Hao Chen, "Mutual authentication protocol for RFID conforming to EPC Class 1 Generation 2 standards," *Computer Standards & Interfaces*, vol. 29, no. 2, pp. 254–259, 2007. DOI: 10.1016/j.csi.2006.04.004. 64

[105] Pedro Peris-Lopez, Tieyan Li, Tong Lee Lim, Julio Cesar Hernandez-Castro, and Juan M. Estevez-Tapiador, "Vulnerability Analysis of a Mutual Authentication Scheme under the EPC Class-1 Generation-2 Standard," *Workshop on RFID Security – RFIDSec'08*, 2008. 64

[106] T. van Deursen and S. Radomirovic, "Attacks on RFID Protocols," *Cryptology ePrint Archive, Report 2008/310*, 2008. 64

[107] Thomas Eisenbarth, Sandeep Kumar, Christof Paar, Axel Poschmann and Leif Uhsadel, "A Survey of Lightweight-Cryptography Implementations," *IEEE Design & Test of Computers*, vol. 24, no. 6, pp. 522–533, 2007. DOI: 10.1109/MDT.2007.178. 64

[108] Sandeep Kumar and Christof Paar, "Are Standards Compliant Elliptic Curve Cryptosystems feasible on RFID?" *Workshop on RFID Security – RFIDSec'06*, 2006. 64

[109] Pedro Peris-Lopez, Julio César Hernández Castro, Juan M. Estévez-Tapiador and Arturo Ribagorda, "RFID Systems: A Survey on Security Threats and Proposed Solutions," *PWC*, pp. 159–170, 2006. DOI: 10.1007/11872153_14. 64

[110] Robert H. Deng, Yingjiu Li, Moti Yung, Yunlei Zhao, "A New Framework for RFID Privacy," *15th European Symposium on Research in Computer Security (ESORICS)*, pp. 1–18, 2010. DOI: 10.1007/978-3-642-15497-3_1. 8, 65, 66, 87

[111] Robert H. Deng, Yingjiu Li, Moti Yung, Yunlei Zhao, "A Zero-Knowledge Based Framework for RFID Privacy," *Journal of Computer Security (JCS)*, vol. 19, no. 6, pp. 1109–1146, 2011. DOI: 10.3233/JCS-2011-0440. 65, 66, 79, 81, 87

[112] S. Goldwasser, S. Micali and C. Rackoff, "The Knowledge Complexity of Interactive Proof-Systems," *ACM Symposium on Theory of Computing*, pp. 291–304, 1985. 65, 75

[113] O. Goldreich, "The Foundations of Cryptography. volume I, Basic Tools," Cambridge University Press, 2001. 65, 75

[114] O. Goldreich, S. Goldwasser, and S. Micali, "How to construct random functions," *J. ACM*, vol. 33, no. 4, pp. 792–807, 1986. DOI: 10.1145/6490.6503. 65

[115] C. Berbain, O. Billet, J. Etrog and H. Gilbert, "An Efficient Forward Private RFID Protocol," *Conference on Computer and Communications Security – CCS'09*. DOI: 10.1145/1653662.1653669. 67

[116] S. Vaudenay, "On Privacy Models for RFID," *Advances in Cryptology - Asiacrypt 2007*. DOI: 10.1007/978-3-540-76900-2_5. 8, 68, 81, 84, 85

[117] R. L. Paise and S. Vaudenay, "Muthal Authentication in RFID: Security and Privacy," *AsiaCCS*, pp. 292–299, 2008. 81

[118] J. Rompel, "One-Way Functions are Necessary and Sufficient for Digital Signatures," *22nd ACM Symposium on Theory of Computing (STOC'90)*, 1990. DOI: 10.1145/100216.100269. 78

[119] P. Golle, M. Jakobsson, A. Juels, and P. Syverson, "Universal reencryption for mixnets," *Topics in Cryptology–CT-RSA 2004*, LNCS 2964, pp. 163–178, 2004. DOI: 10.1007/978-3-540-24660-2_14. 78

[120] International Standard ISO/IEC 9798 Information technology–Security techniques–Entity authentication–Part 5: Mechanisms using Zero-Knowledge Techniques. 81

[121] C. de Canniere and B. Preneel, "Trivium," In M. Robshaw and O. Billet, editors, *New Stream Cipher Designs: The eSTREAM Finalists*, volume 4986 of LNCS, pp. 244–266, 2008. DOI: 10.1007/978-3-540-68351-3. 81

[122] M. Hell, T. Johansson, and W. Meier, "The Grain Family of Stream Ciphers," In M. Robshaw and O. Billet, editors, *New Stream Cipher Designs: The eSTREAM Finalists*, volume 4986 of LNCS, pp. 179–190, 2008. DOI: 10.1007/978-3-540-68351-3. 81

[123] J.P. Aumasson, L. Henzen, W. Meier and M. Naya-Plasencia, "Quark: A Lightweight Hash," *CHES'10*, pp. 1–15, 2010. DOI: 10.1007/978-3-642-15031-9_1. 81

[124] Daniel Engels, Markku-Juhani O. Saarinen, Peter Schweitzer, and Eric M. Smith, "The Hummingbird-2 Lightweight Authenticated Encryption Algorithm," *Proceedings of the 7th international conference on RFID Security and Privacy (RFIDsec 11)*, pp. 19–31, 2012. DOI: 10.1007/978-3-642-25286-0_2. 81

[125] T.V. Le, M. Burmester and B.D. Medeiros, "Universally Composable and Forward-secure RFID Authentication and Authenticated Key Exchange," *AsiaCCS'07*, pp. 242–252, 2007. DOI: 10.1145/1229285.1229319. 87

[126] M. Burmester, T.V. LE, B.D. Medeiros, and G. Tsudik, "Universally Composable RFID Identification and Authentication Protocols," *ACM Transactions on Information and Systems Security*, vol. 12, no. 4, 2009. DOI: 10.1145/1513601.1513603. 87

[127] Chunhua Su, Yingjiu Li, Tieyan Li, and Robert H. Deng, "RFID mutual authentication protocol with universally composable security," *2011 Workshop on RFID Security (RFIDsec Asia)*, pp. 35–49, 2011. 87

[128] R. Canetti, "Universally Composable Security: A New Paradigm for Cryptographic Protocols," *IEEE Symposium on Foundations of Computer Science*, pp. 136–145, 2001. DOI: 10.1109/SFCS.2001.959888. 87

[129] R. Canetti, Y. Dodis, R. Pass and S. Walfish, "Universal Composable Security with Global Setup," *Theory of Cryptography (TCC) 2007, LNCS 4392*, pp. 61–85, 2007. DOI: 10.1007/978-3-540-70936-7_4. 87

[130] A. C. Yao, F. F. Yao and Y. Zhao, "A Note on the Feasibility of Generalised Universal Composability," *Mathematical Structures in Computer Science*, vol. 19, no. 1, pp. 193–205, 2009. DOI: 10.1017/S0960129508007330. 87

[131] A. C. Yao, F.F.Yao and Y. Zhao, "A Note on Universal Composable Zero-Knowledge in the Common Reference String Model," *Theoretical Computer Science*, vol. 410, no. 11, pp. 1099–1108, 2009. DOI: 10.1016/j.tcs.2008.10.027. 87

[132] B. Song, "RFID tag ownership transfer," *Workshop on RFID Security (RFIDsec)*, 2008. 97

[133] Shaoying Cai, Yingjiu Li, Tieyan Li, Robert H. Deng, "Attacks and improvements to an RFID mutual authentication protocol," *2nd ACM Conference on Wireless Network Security (WiSec)*, pp. 51–58, 2009. DOI: 10.1145/1514274.1514282. 97

[134] A. Fernandez-Mir, R. Trujillo-Rasua, J. Castell-Roca, and J. Domingo-Ferrer, "A scalable RFID authentication protocol supporting ownership transfer and controlled delegation," *RFIDsec*, pp. 147–162, 2011. DOI: 10.1007/978-3-642-25286-0_10. 97

[135] D. Molnar, A. Soppera, and D. Wagner, "A scalable, delegatable pseudonym protocol enabling ownership transfer of RFID tags," *Workshop on Selected Areas in Cryptography (SAC 2005)*, 2006. DOI: 10.1007/11693383_19. 97

[136] C. Y. Ng, W. Susilo, Y. Mu, and R. Safavi-Naini, "Practical RFID Ownership Transfer Scheme," *Journal of Computer Security*, vol. 19, no. 2, pp. 319–341, 2011. DOI: 10.3233/JCS-2010-0409. 97

[137] Su Mon Kywe, Jie Shi, Yingjiu Li, and Raghuwanshi Kailash, "Evaluation of Different Electronic Product Code Discovery Service Models," *Advances in Internet of Things*, vol. 2, pp. 37–46, 2012. DOI: 10.4236/ait.2012.22005. 101, 102, 103

[138] B. Liu and C.-H. Chu, "Security analysis of EPC-enabled RFID network," *IEEE International Conference on RFID Technology and Application*, pp. 239–244, 2010. DOI: 10.1109/RFID-TA.2010.5529931. 100

[139] BRIDGE project, "High level design for discovery services," 2007. 101

[140] J. Müller, J. Oberst, S. Wehrmeyer, J. Witt, A. Zeier and H. Plattner, "An aggregating discovery service for the EPCglobal Network," *43rd Hawaii International Conference on System Sciences*, pp. 1–9, 2010. DOI: 10.1109/HICSS.2010.47. 101

[141] Jie Shi, Darren Sim, Yingjiu Li, and Robert H. Deng, "SecDS: A Secure EPC Discovery Services System in EPCglobal Network," *2nd ACM Conference on Data and Application Security and Privacy (CODASPY)*, pp. 267–274, 2012. DOI: 10.1145/2133601.2133634. 105

[142] E. Grummt and M. Müller, "Fine-grained access control for EPC information services," *IOT*, pp. 35–49, 2008. DOI: 10.1007/978-3-540-78731-0_3. 105

[143] Florian Kerschbaum and Alessandro Sorniotti, "RFID-based supply chain partner authentication and key agreement," *Proceedings of the second ACM conference on Wireless network security (WiSec)*, pp. 41–50, 2009. DOI: 10.1145/1514274.1514281. 100, 111

[144] B. Clifford Neuman and Theodore Ts'o, "Kerberos: An Authentication Service for Computer Networks," *IEEE Communications*, vol. 32, no. 9, pp. 33–8, 1994. DOI: 10.1109/35.312841.

[145] Su Mon Kywe, Yingjiu Li, and Jie Shi, "Attack and Defense Mechanisms of Malicious EPC Event Injection in EPC Discovery Service," *IEEE International Conference on RFID Technologies and Applications (IEEE RFID TA)*, 2013. 111, 112, 113, 114

[146] B. Fabian, T. Ermakova, and C. Müller, "SHARDIS: A Privacy-Enhanced Discovery Service for RFID-Based Product Information," *IEEE Transactions on Industrial Informatics*, vol. 8, no. 3, 707–718, 2012. DOI: 10.1109/TII.2011.2166783. 117, 118

[147] A. Shamir, "How to share a secret," *Communications of the ACM*, vol. 22, no. 11, pp. 612–613, 1979. DOI: 10.1145/359168.359176. 117

[148] B. Fabian and O. Günther, "Distributed ONS and its impact on privacy," *IEEE International Conference on Communications (ICC)*, pp. 1223–1228, 2007. 118

[149] Qiang Yan, Yingjiu Li, and Robert H. Deng, "Anti-Tracking in RFID Discovery Service for Dynamic Supply Chain Systems," *International Journal of RFID Security and Cryptography (IJRFIDSC)*, vol. 1, no. 1/2, pp. 25–35, 2012. 119, 121, 123

[150] M. Blaze, G. Bleumer, and M. Strauss, "Divertible protocols and atomic proxy cryptography," *Proceedings of Eurocrypt'98, LNCS 1403*, pp. 127–144, 1998. 121

[151] G. Ateniese, K. Fu, M. Green, and S. Hohenberger, "Improved proxy re-encryption schemes with applications to secure distributed storage," *Proceedings of the 12th Annual Network and Distributed System Security Symposium (NDSS)*, pp. 29–43, 2005. 122, 123

[152] JHU-MIT Proxy Re-cryptography Library, http://spar.isi.jhu.edu/prl/. 123

Authors' Biographies

YINGJIU LI

Yingjiu Li is currently an Associate Professor in the School of Information Systems at Singapore Management University (SMU). His research interests include RFID Security and Privacy, Applied Cryptography and System Security, Privacy-Preserving Data Analytics, and Data Applications Security. He has published over 100 technical papers in international conferences and journals, including Oakland, CCS, USENIX Security, NDSS, ESORICS, ASIACCS, TISSEC, TDSC, and JCS. He has served in the program committees for over 80 international conferences and workshops, including the most recent ones such as Oakland 2014, CCS 2013, ESORICS 2013, and RFIDSec 2013. He founded the RFID Security Lab in SMU and his research was supported by A*STAR SERC Public Sector Funding (PSF) in Singapore. Yingjiu Li is a senior member of the ACM and a member of the IEEE Computer Society. The URL for his web page is http://www.mysmu.edu/faculty/yjli/

ROBERT H. DENG

Robert H. Deng has been a Professor at the School of Information Systems, Singapore Management University, since 2004. Prior to this, he was Principal Scientist and Manager of Infocomm Security Department, Institute for Infocomm Research, Singapore. His research interests include data security and privacy, multimedia security, network, and system security. He was Associate Editor of the *IEEE Transactions on Information Forensics and Security* from 2009–2012 and Associate Editor of *Security and Communication Networks* from 2007–2013. He is currently Associate Editor of *IEEE Transactions on Dependable and Secure Computing,* and a member of Editorial Board of *Journal of Computer Science and Technology* and *International Journal of Information Security.* He is the chair of the Steering Committee of the ACM Symposium on Information, Computer and Communications Security. He received the University Outstanding Researcher Award from the National University of Singapore in 1999 and the Lee Kuan Yew Fellow for Research Excellence from the Singapore Management University in 2006. He was named Community Service Star and Showcased Senior Information Security Professional by (ISC)² under its Asia-Pacific Information Security Leadership Achievements program in 2010.

ELISA BERTINO

Elisa Bertino is a professor with the Computer Science Department at Purdue University and serves as director of Cyber Center and Research Director of CERIAS. Previously, she was a faculty member in the Department of Computer Science and Communication of the University of Milan. Her main research interests include security, privacy, digital identity management systems, database systems, distributed systems, and multimedia systems. She is a fellow of the IEEE and a fellow of the ACM. She received the 2002 IEEE Computer Society Technical Achievement Award for outstanding contributions to database systems and database security and advanced data management systems and the 2005 IEEE Computer Society Tsutomu Kanai Award for pioneering and innovative research contributions to secure distributed systems.